Also by Kurt Brouwer

KURT BROUWER'S GUIDE TO
MUTUAL FUNDS:
How to Invest with the Pros

MUTUAL FUND MASTERY

MUTUAL FUND MASTERY

Wealth-Building Secrets from America's Investment Pros

KURT BROUWER and STEPHEN JANACHOWSKI

TIMES BUSINESS

RANDOM HOUSE

Copyright © 1997 by Kurt Brouwer and Stephen Janachowski

All rights reserved under International and Pan-American
Copyright Conventions. Published in the United States by
Times Books, a division of Random House, Inc., New York,
and simultaneously in Canada by Random House of
Canada Limited, Toronto.

Library of Congress Cataloging-in-Publication Data is available.

ISBN 0-8129-2720-6

Random House website address: http://www.randomhouse.com/

Printed in the United States of America on acid-free paper

9 8 7 6 5 4 3 2

First Edition

Dedicated to all the hard-working people in America

who want their money to work as hard as they do.

FOREWORD

Growth in the mutual fund industry over the past several years has been very gratifying to me because I have been a strong believer in mutual funds in general, and no-load mutual funds in particular. I believe mutual funds can be a very good investment vehicle for most investors. I use them myself and I recommend them to you.

I have known Kurt Brouwer and Steve Janachowski for a number of years. If you really want to know about mutual funds, this book is a good start.

Investors often ask me about my personal approach to investing. I have followed some very basic investing principles for over thirty-five years (see the interview on page 104 for more on my approach to Investing). While I believe my principles provide a firm foundation for achieving your financial goals, this book provides a lot more. It provides the insights and strategies that will help you make the most of your mutual fund investments. So, if you plan to use mutual funds, reading this book is an essential first step. Best of luck, and happy investing.

Charles R. Schwab

ACKNOWLEDGMENTS

We would like to acknowledge the many people who have helped make this book possible.

Jack Bogle, Shelby Davis, Bill Gross, Richard King, Don Phillips, Mike Price, Jane Bryant Quinn, and Charles Schwab were very generous with their time, despite their demanding schedules.

Betty Nakamoto, our colleague of many years at Brouwer & Janachowski, Inc., made many important contributions on both a practical and a conceptual level. Mike Shatzkin gave us a great deal of advice on the realities of book publishing. Special thanks to Susan Grode, our hard-working attorney at Kaye, Scholer, Fierman, Hays & Handler in Los Angeles. And, thanks to Ed Phillips for timely research.

For letting us pass along their investment histories, we thank James Hutchinson, Gene and Mary Jo Cole, Dr. Stanford Kroopf, Jim Hunter, and Kathy Kueneman.

We would also like to thank our editor, Karl Weber, and his colleagues at Times Books—Don Bender, Mary Beth Roche, and Naomi Osnos.

Finally, we thank both Morningstar, Inc. and Micropal, Ltd., two excellent companies dedicated to providing information and statistics on mutual funds.

K.B.
S.J.

CONTENTS

CONTENTS

INTRODUCTION

The ideas on these pages come from our work in managing an investment advisory firm called Brouwer & Janachowski, Inc. The firm is unusual because we use no-load mutual funds as our sole investment vehicle, and we work strictly on a fee basis.

When we started Brouwer & Janachowski in 1985, we had no clients, no track record, and no one could spell our name. So we figured we had a competitive advantage because we had nothing to lose by trying something new.

We wanted to work with mutual funds because we felt that they were the single best investment vehicle for most investors. We wanted to work on a fee-only basis because it suited our personalities and our ethics.

Since those early days, Brouwer & Janachowski has grown into a firm that manages $500 million in portfolios of no-load mutual funds for private individuals, corporations, and charitable organizations.

Our belief in mutual funds has strengthened over the past 12 years. We have seen first hand that mutual funds are a magnificent innovation suitable for investors with $500 or $500 million. They open up a myriad of possibilities and bring professional management, diversification, safety, and other tangible benefits into the hands of all investors, no matter how much or how little money they have to invest.

If you are like us, you have seen many different newsletters, books, advertisements, and even late-night television infomercials created by self-anointed investment "gurus" who promise guaranteed, "no-risk" ways to achieve wealth—in about an hour. Is it realistic to think someone who had a guaranteed, no-risk way to make money would tell you about it? We do not want to seem cynical, but we think the answer is no. Maybe you've even tried one or two of these schemes, and you know now that they do not work.

Because we are on every mailing list known to the Postal Service, every week we get about 3 or 4 newsletters or junk-mail pieces that try to entice investors with tales of easy money earned without risk—quick schemes to build up wealth without scrimping or saving. Often, the guru is shown next to a Rolls Royce or a private jet and is bragging about owning homes in exotic locales.

Don't get us wrong, though; we do not have anything against making money and living the good life. We thoroughly enjoy the financial success and security we have achieved for our clients, our employees, and ourselves. To us, the critical issue lies not in what you spend your money on, but in whether you have enough money to do what you want—no matter what that is. Achieving that kind of financial freedom does not happen overnight. It takes time, effort, and commitment. That's why we don't get terribly excited about most investment schemes and strategies. They promise far more than they can deliver.

What does get us excited, though, is sharing what we know and seeing people change their lives for the better. We gain tremendous satisfaction from helping our clients achieve their financial goals, and we want to help you also.

We wrote *Mutual Fund Mastery* for you, whether you are a novice or an experienced investor. We want to help you gain every bit of insight and information you need to become a more successful investor, to give you the knowledge and the tools you need to master your financial future, and to help you and your family prosper, not just for a year or two, but for generations. To us, an investment approach that only works for a little while is useless, so we have always searched for timeless ideas—strategies and techniques that will work a hundred years from now as well as they do today. And we acknowledge that many brilliant investment thinkers have gone before us. We are not necessarily creating these ideas just from our fertile imaginations; rather, we are refining and rediscovering ideas from many sources.

In this book, you will learn from great minds such as Charles Mackay, who wrote *Popular Delusions and the Madness of Crowds* in 1841; Benjamin Graham, the father of security analysis and Warren Buffett's mentor; and Warren Buffett himself, the world's richest and most successful investor.

To help you gain perspective, we have interviewed contemporary investment thinkers, commentators, and innovators such as Charles Schwab, John C. Bogle, Jane Bryant Quinn, and Don Phillips.

We will also take you behind the scenes to explore great mutual funds and listen to the brilliant portfolio managers responsible for them. These are people we have worked with and respect—investment pros who have gained valuable experience and are willing to share it with you: Shelby Davis, who heads Selected American Shares and New York Venture Fund; Michael Price, of the Mutual Series fund family; Bill Gross, portfolio manager of PIMCO Total Return and Harbor Bond Fund; and Richard King, portfolio manager of Warburg Pincus International Equity and Warburg Pincus Emerging Markets Funds.

Along the way, we will also introduce you to investors who—just like you—are learning and developing their personal investment skills.

These pages are packed with intelligence, skills, and information. Yet, that is not enough. Many smart, well-informed investors blow it every day—not because they lack knowledge, but because they lack clarity about their investment objectives and goals. We will show you how to uncover these hidden road blocks to your success, and we will give you tips and techniques for developing the mental and emotional toughness you will need if you are to avoid the pitfalls and potholes on the road to investment success and financial security.

We want to help you develop an investment approach that works for many years, one you'll be able to depend on and come back to year after year. You provide the reading time, and we'll lay out in detail our experience as professional investors. Together, we can build your wealth and create the kind of financial future you dream about.

KURT BROUWER
STEVE JANACHOWSKI

Tiburon, California
August 1997

PART ONE

Making Serious Money with Mutual Funds

CHAPTER 1

The Thrill of Victory and the Utter Misery of Defeat

The path to mutual fund mastery begins with you and your goals. You have to learn how mutual funds work, and you need an understanding and appreciation of the financial markets. But that knowledge alone is not enough. The most critical factor in your ultimate success or failure is your personal commitment to a clear and unambiguous goal. So, before we start, let's get 2 vitally important issues on the table.

1. You Must Invest Your Time Before Your Money

If you were planning a long trek in the Himalayas, you *know* you would do serious research before heading out. You'd figure out the proper gear to take, map out your routes for each day, and probably read a few books about the area. You would research such things as the total cost of the trip, the shots you need, and the visa requirements. In short, you would take reasonable steps to make sure the trip is safe and successful.

Have you ever planned a surprise birthday party for a family member, a close friend, or a colleague? You need a great location, a story to cover your tracks, and the unique skills of a CIA agent. You contact everyone on your guest list and swear them to secrecy. You buy presents, organize food and drink, and work out a scheme to get the guest of honor to the party place at an arranged time. All in all, you take on a complicated and time-consuming process.

Or, have you ever trained for a marathon, a golf or tennis tournament, a piano recital, or the role of Puck in your community's production of *A Midsummer Night's Dream?*

All of us, at some point in our lives, have embarked on a project that required many hours of practice and rehearsal, planning, expense, and sacrifice. And we put the time in willingly because the end result was worth it.

If that's what you will do for a vacation, a party, or a sporting or cultural event, what would you be willing to do when it comes to planning your financial future? Making good or bad investment decisions will impact your future much more than a great vacation or a tennis tournament. This seems like simple common sense, yet many people just wing it when it comes to investing. They buy a stock or a mutual fund because it was mentioned in a magazine or because they got a "hot" tip from a friend or stockbroker. Your financial future needs and deserves more care and attention to detail than you give to any vacation, any golf game, or even the plans for your daughter's wedding. But

He Invested His Time, Then His Money

When both of his parents died, James Hutchinson had to grow up fast. Though only 18, he had to make his way in the world, without the guidance his parents would have given. He also had the responsibility of managing an inheritance of $50,000 invested in bank certificates of deposit. At first, it was more like mismanagement. "I can't lie," he said. "I was young, I had no guidance. I went everywhere with a pocketful of money. After I spent about $10,000, I realized I had a TV and a car, but I didn't have much else to show for it, so I decided I had better stop and do something useful with the money."

Fortunately, Jim caught himself. "I finally realized that instead of spending my money, I could use it to make more. But I had no idea how to go about it. I saw that interest rates at the bank were going down, so I decided to try my hand at stocks."

He spotted a company listed in the newspaper's financial pages that was selling at less than $2 per share. Even though he knew absolutely nothing about the company, he bought in. "I was just thinking, if it goes up to $5 or $6, I will make a lot of money," he said. "I didn't call the company, I didn't get a prospectus, I didn't do any homework. I only went in for a little, but it was almost like throwing it away. No matter how big or how small the investment is, you still have to do your homework. Because if you lose, you're still going to be upset and regret the way you went about it."

He knew that he needed a smarter approach, so Jim began to hit the books. He subscribed to *Money* and *Fortune,* and began reading about investors like Peter Lynch and Mario Gabelli. This represented a turnaround in Jim's thinking, "I started getting ideas from guys who are at the top of their field. From there, I took a hard look at mutual funds. I have a long time horizon, and I won't touch this money for years—when I'm ready to enjoy more of life. Mutual funds are great because of the diversification, and I love that. I'm not really into high risk. I'd rather have medium risk with a good return."

BROUWER & JANACHOWSKI'S EVALUATION

Jim, now 28, works as a grocery store clerk for Pak 'N' Save Supermarkets. He is completing a business finance degree at San Jose State University and has been gearing up for his own career as an investment professional. He is already well on his way toward financial success. After some missteps, he learned, at an early age, some of the most important investment fundamentals: Invest your time first, then your money. And learn from the pros. As Jim put it, "After all, they already learned these lessons the hard way. Why should I?"

don't think that planning for investment success has to be drudgery. We'll show you exactly how to get the job done *and* have fun doing it.

2. You Must Hope for the Best While *Planning* for the Worst

No matter how well you prepare and plan, any number of unexpected problems are going to arise. Interest rates and inflation could soar. The stock market could go through a prolonged downward spiral. Deflation could tumble banks and insurance companies that expanded unwisely during the inflationary runup. Natural disasters could strike. Governments could fall.

An exaggeration? All of these happened in Japan recently. An unlikely combination of natural and human disasters ravaged the Japanese stock market and sent it plummeting over 60% from late 1989 through mid-1995. In mid-1997, it looks as though the stage is set for a recovery, but you never know.

If the Japanese stock market seems too far from home, how about our Great Depression in the 1930s? For 10 years, a litany of ills clobbered our economy and our financial markets. Stocks fell. Banks failed. Unemployment hit 25%, and millions of Americans went to sleep hungry each night. We are not predicting another depression, but we are suggesting that unexpected events can and do happen.

Expect the Unexpected

We would be remiss if we did not warn you to expect the unexpected. You need to think positively and hope for the best. But where your life, your future, and your family are concerned, we hope you learn to prepare for the worst too. Hope for the best, but make sure you plan for the worst. If that sounds too negative, call it taking reasonable precautions. If you are having a hundred of your closest friends over for a backyard barbecue, do you count on sunshine or do you plan for the possibility of a downpour?

If the events in Japan or during the Great Depression seem far removed, ask yourself: What if the Federal Reserve goes back to inflationary policies? What if the Fed or a counterpart overseas overreacts and scares the world's financial markets? A recent example was the tumble bonds took in late January 1996, when Newt Gingrich, the Speaker of the House of Representatives, and other Congressional leaders, openly speculated about a U.S. Treasury default. Do political leaders say and do stupid things? Yes; unfortunately, they do. Could a large geopolitical event, coupled with political and fiscal foolishness, wreak havoc with our entire economy? Even though this sequence of events sounds like the plot for a bad movie, oddly enough, it all happened right here, a little over 20 years ago.

In the early 1970s, a very liberal monetary policy allowed inflationary pressures to build up and encouraged the stock market to hit all-time highs even though interest rates also climbed. After Richard Nixon won the 1972 presidential election, the Fed clamped down and triggered even higher interest rates, which led to a drop in stock prices. Then, an unexpected event hit. Arab oil producers decided to embargo oil supplies to the West in retaliation for U.S. support of Israel.

With oil prices moving sharply higher, gasoline prices at the pump shot up and supplies dwindled. Lines formed at gas stations throughout the country, even in Texas, where gasoline is usually plentiful. Higher prices for oil hit everyone hard. Petrochemicals, plastics, home heating oil, electric utility companies—all were victims in a national and worldwide disaster. Interest rates and inflation soared. Stocks plummeted. From late 1972 until late 1974, the Standard & Poor's 500 Stock Index plunged approximately 40%. For those who sold stocks at the low point, this was an unparalleled disaster. For others, of whom Warren Buffett is the most notable, this was the buying opportunity of a lifetime.

Despite this recitation on financial fiascos, we are not alarmists. In fact, we at Brouwer & Janachowski are very optimistic about the U.S. economy. Corporate America has made great strides in learning how to deal with recessions and other normal, but negative, phases of the economic cycle. The United States is the world leader in many industries, most notably, technology and entertainment. Among its assets are personal and political freedom and a relatively young and hard-working labor force. And the unpredictable public servants in Washington have even made a little progress toward real solutions to the twin evils of inflation and deficit spending.

By reminding you of past problems, we hope to create within you a healthy respect for the financial markets. We want you to understand, ahead of time, what can happen. Given that background, you will prepare better before you start investing, and you will handle adversity better if it does come. In Chapter 8, we will show you exactly how to cope with the financial and emotional impact of tough times on Wall Street.

Just as a sailor understands the power and potential of the ocean and the vagaries of winds and tides, so must you understand the awesome power of the financial markets. You need to recognize that, like

I think you have to have some fundamental beliefs to be an investor. You have to be a long-term optimist and focus on the distant horizon, not up close. One that doesn't say the glass is always half empty, but half full, instead. You have to believe in the sweep of American history or the sweep of mankind, that forward progress is made over generations and wealth begets wealth, and that the country grows and the GNP grows and the Federal Reserve banks of the world are there to protect us, not to kill us. . . .

People are lined up to come to this country because it is the land of opportunity. The wave of immigrants waiting to come in here is enormous. Yet, what we are subjected to on TV and by newspapers is constant criticism of this country with all of its flaws, warts, and faults. But, it is the great land of opportunity. And if you approach the world that way, you become an investor in equities and mutual funds because you say, "Hey, this is still a great place where someone can make millions playing basketball or make millions making a movie using animation like Steve Jobs has just done." We have a lot of things that make a country great, especially the freedom to work and create. Maybe we don't like our government so much, but we have freedom, we have relatively low taxes, we have innovation, entrepreneurship, and the ability to have hard work pay off. And someone with an idea can become a winner. I don't care if you're black, white, yellow, or any creed or color—opportunity stories are out there. And, since people make companies, then that must mean there are plenty of opportunities for companies out there, and I think there are.
—SHELBY DAVIS

the ocean, a complex marketplace made up of millions of investors can move in mysterious ways. Financial typhoons, hurricanes, and tidal waves do happen, but if you are forewarned and properly prepared, you can handle anything.

The primary point to remember is: No matter how hard the winds blow, or the rains fall, or the waves crash, all storms eventually blow over. The sun always shines again. As long as your boat remains seaworthy, you can ride anything out. If the storm never materializes, so much the better. But if you survive a financial storm when others are swamped or even sinking, then you will be in a powerful position to prosper when the weather turns balmy.

Our goal is to help you construct a mutual fund portfolio that is like a strong and seaworthy ship. It may be an ocean-going yacht, a snug little sloop, a speedboat, kayak or canoe, . . . but no matter how big (or little) your portfolio is, you can build it well and steer it skillfully, no matter what the weather conditions are like.

A Tale of Two Investors

On Monday, October 19, 1987, the U.S. stock market tumbled 22.5%. Its 508-point plunge set a record for the worst single-day decline in our financial history. Economists, politicians, journalists, investors, and the public, as a whole, were stunned. Many, including some of our clients, predicted a worldwide economic depression.

Prior to the October Crash, our firm had moved into a relatively cautious stance for our clients and, on average, they did very well that day—down 6.7% compared to a 22.5% drop for the S&P 500 Stock Index. We were reasonably happy about taking only a small loss on a day when the stock market experienced such a cataclysm. But no one—not our clients and certainly not our firm—likes to lose money.

After the Crash, we saw that stocks were cheap again, and we decided to buy. We have discretionary control of our clients' portfolios, which means we have the authority to buy and sell mutual funds without consulting clients before each trade. And that's exactly what we did. We bought more stock mutual funds.

That week, many clients called us. Most were concerned; some were in shock. Of all the calls, two really stood out. One man, a physician, was frantic. When told that we were buying more shares of stock mutual funds for his account, he yelled, "Are you crazy? Haven't you read the paper? We're going into a depression. Stocks are going to plummet. Get me out!" So we did, reluctantly.

We also had a call from another client, who saw things very differently. In fact, he grilled us on what and when we were planning to buy. He wanted to be very aggressive because he thought this was the buying opportunity of a lifetime.

These two investors had strategies and philosophies that were worlds apart. The first investor—we'll call him Dr. Doom—lived in fear. He had a modest loss in the Crash, and he felt he had to salvage what he could from the wreckage and protect his assets from a coming catastrophe.

The second investor—we'll call him Mr. Growth—believed the U.S. stock market was inevitably going to go higher. To him, down years, when things would appear to be falling apart, were inevitable. However, he believed that stocks would always come back higher and stronger than ever.

Along with Mr. Growth, we believe in the U.S. (and the world) economy. There will be downturns and tough times, but the future is very bright. We're not saying that buying stock mutual funds is risk-free. We will undoubtedly have to face severe stock market declines periodically in the future. Buying stock funds is a winning strategy most of the time, but not all of the time. And those off-years can really hurt.

No one can accurately forecast when the downturns will come or how long they will last. But we can predict that Mr. Growth, and others like him, will prosper over a period of years because they have found a proven strategy for success. They look at the big picture and invest for the long haul. Mr. Growth's only major problem will be his need to rein in his natural optimism.

Meanwhile, Dr. Doom and his fellow sufferers have a bigger problem. They agonize during good times and bad. During down years, they conjure up countless reasons why things are going to get worse. And they get plenty of encouragement, because things always seem worse than they really are during the bad years. During good times, Doomers often sit on the sidelines, wringing their hands and wondering whether to jump into the game. And when they do jump in, their timing is usually wrong. Dr. Doom's emotions, fears, and fantasies have become a straitjacket that almost ensures poor performance and paltry profits.

Do you see any similarities to your investment history in this narrative? This slice of life extends from our two clients right through to millions of investors. Would you be closer philosophically (and in practice) to Dr. Doom or to Mr. Growth?

We are not suggesting that you try to be like one or the other. Listen to your instincts, because both types can be very successful. But each type can also carry potential problems. Dr. Doom often sees a problem where none exists. And Mr. Growth can fall into the trap of going forward at full speed, despite the fact that there may be a steep drop-off dead ahead. Our goal here is to illustrate two abiding themes in the investment world—and in human nature: greed and fear.

Investors are often asked about their investment objectives. Are they investing for growth or for income? Growth investors seek capital appreciation. They want more, and they are willing to take significant risks in order to get it. Income investors want a little growth too, but their primary goal is to preserve and protect what they have. For them, the fear of loss is more dominant.

Mr. Growth and Dr. Doom are ideal examples of these two themes. Mr. Growth is motivated primarily by growth, aka greed. Fear of loss from a declining stock market is not a big deal for him. Dr. Doom generally seeks primarily income and is driven more by fear of loss than by greed.

In Chapter 8, we will help you understand the personal history and characteristics that drive your investment objectives. Our goal is not necessarily to change them, but to understand and illuminate them. We will also help you develop an investment strategy that is suited to your nature and to the attainment of your personal goals.

Searching for Gold in All the Wrong Places

If you are like the thousands of investors we have met or talked to, you have heard dozens of ideas, tips, rules of thumb, strategies, and techniques for investment success. How to predict short-term stock market movements or interest rate fluctuations. How to find the hot stocks or the hot mutual funds.

The reality? If someone had figured out a way to always win and never lose, he or she would never tell you or anyone else about it. If you found a valley where gold nuggets were just lying around for the taking, would you tell the newspapers and let the whole world muscle in on your claim? Would you sell maps to the spot? We sincerely doubt it.

This is the first thing to remember: There are no gimmicks or sure things from which you can profit without risk. With that said, we would like to introduce you to some concepts that can help you gain an edge in your quest for investment success.

The Laws of Investment Success

There are simple and straightforward laws of investing that have worked for many, many years. We call them the Laws of Investment Success. Investment professionals have known and practiced the techniques associated with these laws during long careers, without necessarily spelling them out.

No one taught us these laws, nor did we invent them. We think of them as signposts set in place by past investors. We utilize them every day to make money for our clients. When we have lost sight of them, it has usually been to our—and our clients'—detriment. We are hoping that you can learn and profit from the mistakes we made and the experiences we have had in the 12 years since we started managing money with no-load mutual funds.

The First Law of Investing: Invest for a Minimum of 20 Years

We know what you are thinking: "I don't have 20 years to wait." The fact is, though, you're probably wrong. Not only do you have an investment horizon of 20 years, but, if you are like most people, your horizon extends well over 50 years. Once you accept the first law, two things will happen:

1. Your investment decisions will improve.

2. You will sleep more soundly.

When we say "Invest for 20 years," people often tell us, "I'll probably be dead by then. I want to get rich now, while I can still enjoy life." First off, who says older people don't enjoy money and life as much as young people? But in any case, investing is not likely to make you rich in the short run, unless you get very lucky. Since that outcome is unlikely, let's talk about what a reasonable investment expectation really means in dollar amounts.

Is it likely that you can take $10,000 and turn it into $100,000 overnight? No. That does not mean it cannot happen; it just does not happen very often. Investors who chase pie-in-the-sky returns generally take huge risks and lose everything. You can, however, have a reasonable chance to turn $10,000 into more than $100,000 if you have 25 years to invest. In your Individual Retirement Account (IRA) or a company 401(k) plan, $10,000 grows to over $108,000 in 25 years if you get a 10% annual return. If you deposit an additional $2,000 into your IRA or 401(k) account each year, the accumulated amount balloons to more than $303,000 during that same period (see Figure 1.1).

If you want to get rich quickly, you need to find a rich aunt or uncle, win a lottery, marry someone with a large inheritance, or strike

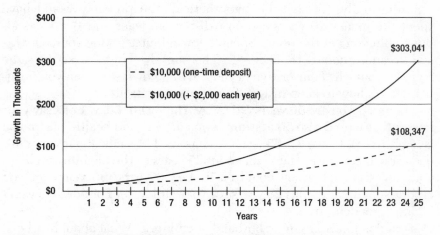

FIGURE 1.1 The Magic of Compounding—Part 1. This chart illustrates the effects of compounding over time for 2 different investors. The first investor makes a one-time investment of $10,000, which compounds for the next 25 years at 10% each year. The second investor makes an initial investment of $10,000 and then adds $2,000 each year for the next 24 years. The second investor's investments compound at 10% each year also. (*Source:* Brouwer & Janachowski, Inc.)

oil in your backyard. If none of those tactics seems likely, a fast fortune may not be in the cards for you.

First, take a few minutes to revile your shortsighted ancestors (parents, grandparents, aunts, and uncles) for not having the foresight to get rich and/or pass along a fortune to you. As Winston Churchill said, *"Saving is a very fine thing. Especially when your parents have done it for you."*[1]

Actually, your forebears might not have needed to be rich; they only needed to have looked ahead and realized that a few dollars put to work for you when you were born would have gone a long way, through the magic of compounding.

If Only

It would have been so easy, too. Let's say you were born in 1950. All your ancestors had to do was put $5,000 into the Mutual Shares Fund or Guardian Fund (now called Neuberger & Berman Guardian Fund) in 1950. If your ancestors added no more money and reinvested the dividends in the fund, you would have between $1,356,802 and $2,235,319 in your account today, assuming you did not have to pay any income taxes. Even after factoring in income taxes (assuming an average 20% federal and state tax rate after reaching the age of majority), you would still have over $1 million (see Figure 1.2).

Admittedly, this is a bit hypothetical. You probably would have spent the money 20 years ago on bell-bottom jeans and Bee Gees albums. But you get the point. Spend a few minutes asking yourself why, and dreaming about "If only . . . . " Then, resolve not to make the same mistake yourself. Four or five decades will go by faster than you imagine. Here's how to keep history from repeating itself.

Let's say you are 50 years old today. Happy birthday. Let's say your husband or wife is also 50. Assuming you are in good health, one of you is likely to live to age 85 (35 years from now). Let's talk about your children. Each generation tacks on about 25 years to the planning cycle, so your investment horizon could easily be 60 years (35 years for you and/or your spouse, plus 25 years for your children). For now, we won't include grandchildren.

You don't have a wife or husband or children? What about brothers, sisters, nieces, or nephews? What about charities you believe in? What about world peace? In other words, almost everyone has a very long investment time horizon. For most people, it is well over 50 years.

---

[1] *And I Quote* (St. Martin's Press).

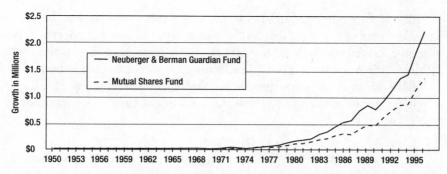

FIGURE 1.2   The Magic of Compounding—Part 2. This chart compares the growth of a $5,000 investment made in 1950 in each of the two funds listed above. Returns include reinvestment of all dividend and capital gain distributions and are net of all fund expenses. (*Source:* Neuberger & Berman Management, Franklin Templeton Group, Micropal, Ltd., Brouwer & Janachowski, Inc.)

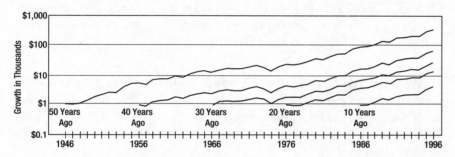

FIGURE 1.3   The Magic of Compounding—Part 3. This chart illustrates the growth of $1,000 invested in the Standard & Poor's Index (S&P 500) beginning at different 10-year intervals. (*Source:* Ibbotson Associates, Micropal, Ltd., Brouwer & Janachowski, Inc.)

But just to mollify the skeptic in you, we will shorten it to 20 years and help you develop a plan that maximizes your investment return for that period of time (see Figure 1.3).

The Second Law of Investing: Place Your Money with the Investment Pros, Don't Bet Against Them

Would you play golf against Tiger Woods for every nickel you have? We doubt it. Would you try to outvolley Steffi Graff in a winner-take-all tennis match? Hopefully not. Would you buy a stock that Peter Lynch or Warren Buffett is selling? Maybe; but chances are you would regret it.

One of our clients, Carl Leonard, made this point better than we can. Carl was retiring (at age 54) as a managing partner of Morrison & Foerster, one of the nation's top 50 law firms. Now, he is a consultant at Hildebrandt Associates, giving law firms all over the country the benefit of his 25 years of experience. He and Kurt were having lunch on a bright, sunny day, and Carl made a stunningly simple, yet profound point. He said:

> Isn't it great? We're sitting here enjoying the sun while all those really bright people on Wall Street are working their tails off for us. Buying, selling, researching and racking their brains to come up with ways to make *us* money, simply because we are using their mutual funds. And it doesn't cost us anything to buy in or to sell out. It's incredible and, even better, it's legal.

As Carl pointed out, by using no-load mutual funds, you can easily and simply profit from the experience, hard work, and professional acumen of the best brains on Wall Street.

Why Do We Use Mutual Funds?   When we started our investment advisory firm in 1985, we had a revelation that no-load mutual funds were the best investment vehicle for most investors. Twelve years later, we still believe they are the best. In fact, that belief is now stronger than ever.

Our overall vision has not changed, but almost everything else has. Mutual funds now hold more assets than are represented by certificates of deposit at commercial banks—a fact that would have been unthinkable in 1985. Today, sophisticated investors want mutual fund portfolios. In 1985, they laughed at the idea.

The enormous popularity of mutual funds means that the world is willing and eager to put resources to work in this industry. Mutual fund companies now routinely offer toll-free telephone lines—twenty-four hours a day, in some cases. You can now trade mutual funds from different fund families through brokerage accounts at Charles Schwab & Co. and other discount brokerage firms. More and more brokerage and mutual fund companies are giving shareholders access to their account information electronically through World Wide Web sites on the Internet. Plus, mutual fund services like Morningstar give you instant access to facts, figures, and performance statistics for thousands of funds. The growing clout of mutual funds gives you an additional edge as you strive to reach your financial goals.

The Third Law of Investing: If You Want Capital Appreciation, Be an Owner Not a Loaner

Over long periods of time, you will make, and keep (after factoring in inflation and taxes), much more money in a stock mutual fund than you will in a bond fund. That does not mean you should never own shares in a bond fund, but you must realize that, over a long time frame, you make more money owning stock funds. Why? Simple economics.

Markets move up or down, but two economic concepts remain constant: dividends and interest. Stocks pay dividends. Bonds pay interest. Dividends tend to increase over time at a rate that equals or exceeds inflation. Not all stocks pay dividends, but those that do, generally increase them periodically, when financial conditions warrant an increase. Conversely, the interest paid on a bond is set when it is issued, and it never changes. A bond's fixed return remains constant until maturity.

So, stock dividends have a built-in advantage. Their dividends grow and keep up with inflation, while bond interest rates remain constant. Since 1982, bonds have done extremely well because interest rates have fallen steadily, as has inflation. We have witnessed the greatest bull market for bonds in history. Yet, over that period, stocks have steadily beaten bonds. Over even longer periods, history suggests that the race will be won by stocks even more decisively (see Figure 1.4).

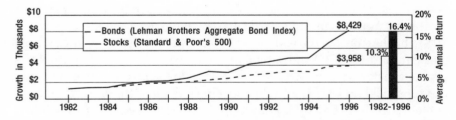

FIGURE 1.4 Stocks Versus Bonds. This chart illustrates the difference in performance between a $1,000 investment in stocks compared to a $1,000 investment in bonds made on December 31, 1982. The lines show how each investment would have grown over the 14 years ending December 31, 1996. Bond returns are based on capital appreciation and reinvested interest income. Stock returns are based on capital appreciation and re-invested dividend income. The bars (far right) show the average annual return that each investment would have earned during that same time period. (*Source:* Micropal, Ltd., Brouwer & Janachowski, Inc.)

The Fourth Law of Investing: You Have to Pay
If You Want to Play

Most of the important lessons we learn come the hard way; it just seems to be our nature. Learning this way is often quite effective, but it is usually pretty expensive, too. We hope that by passing along some of our hard-earned experience, you can reap the benefits without having to foot the bill.

For example, at one point, we invested our portfolios too heavily in so-called "value" mutual funds. Value funds look for stocks with low to moderate price/earnings ratios, strong balance sheets, and other conservative indicators of unrealized value. Growth investors like more aggressive stocks, those that have shown strong growth in sales and earnings. In 1988, value funds beat the stock market averages, and we looked great. But in 1989, when growth stocks soared, those conservative value funds fell far behind.

We also missed out on a huge gain from international stocks in 1985 and 1986, when the dollar plunged and international stocks soared. At that time, we did not invest overseas because we thought our clients were not very comfortable with the concept of exporting their money. With approximately 60% of the world's stock market capitalization on stock exchanges outside our borders, that approach now seems a bit silly.

But in early 1990, we made one of our best decisions—buying Harbor International Fund. At that time, the fund had only about $70 million in assets. Today, it has over $5 billion and is closed to new investors.

Harbor International's portfolio manager, Hakan Castegren, is a unique investor in this era of computers and daily (or even hourly) buy and sell decisions. His database consists of a card file and his very nimble brain. Yet, on an annualized basis, since the fund's inception in 1988, he has outperformed the Morgan Stanley Europe, Australasia and Far East (EAFE) Index by more than 10% per year. The fund has also outperformed the S&P 500 Stock Index—no small feat, because the fund held no U.S. stocks during a period when the U.S. stock market outpaced EAFE by a considerable margin (see Figures 1.5 and 1.6).

Experience Is Just Applied Failure   Generally, making mistakes is not the problem. It's how you handle them that can mess things up. We will spell out more of our successes and failures in later chapters, but the point we are making here is that even pros blow it periodically. We have lots of experience, and we still fail at times. Frankly, the word *experience* is just a euphemism for applied failure. We learn

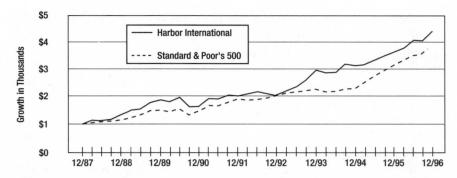

FIGURE 1.5 Harbor International Fund Versus Standard & Poor's 500. This chart illustrates $1,000 invested in the Standard & Poor's 500 versus $1,000 invested in Harbor International Fund on December 31, 1987. (*Source:* Micropal, Ltd., Brouwer & Janachowski, Inc.)

from our successes, but we surely learn much more from our failures, if we pay attention to them.

In our experience, you learn by doing and that means you have to pay in order to play. Everyone makes mistakes; no one is immune. In fact, quite often, mistakes come in bunches. If you make one bad move, it is very easy to make further blunders as you try to "get back to even" or, even worse, to deny that you made an error in the first place.

Never miss an opportunity to learn from your own or other peoples' mistakes. When you blow it, admit it. Then learn from it. Figure

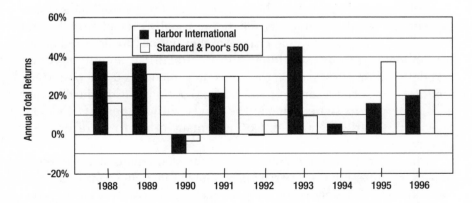

FIGURE 1.6 Harbor International Fund Versus Standard & Poor's 500. This chart illustrates the annual total returns for Harbor International Fund versus the Standard & Poor's 500. (*Source:* Micropal, Ltd., Brouwer & Janachowski, Inc.)

out what you did wrong, and make sure you don't make that mistake again. Not only is intellectual honesty of paramount importance to the care and feeding of your portfolio, it is also good for your soul.

The Fifth Law of Investing?

We saved the fifth law of investing for last because we dislike paying or even talking about income taxes. Actually, that is not quite true. We do not mind paying taxes when there is something to show for the amount levied. Unfortunately, like many other taxpayers, we have gotten pretty cynical about whether our government dollars are working for or against us.

The Fifth Law of Investing: What Counts Is How Much You Keep—After Taxes

> "There is one difference between a tax collector and a taxidermist— the taxidermist leaves the hide."—Mortimer Caplan[2]

What counts is not how much you make, but how much you keep. Unfortunately, you can't do much to avoid paying income taxes. True, you can defer some taxes by investing in qualified retirement plans such as 401(k) plans, IRAs, 403(b) plans (for nonprofit groups and public sector organizations), and Section 457 plans (for government employees). We believe you should maximize your use of tax-deferred retirement plans because they are the easiest and fastest way to build wealth.

Other modest tax-sheltered investments are tax-exempt bonds issued by state and local governments. These are usually exempt from federal and, often, from state income taxes. Another option, tax-deferred annuities, allow you to invest a lump sum in a qualified annuity contract and defer all income taxes on the gains until money is taken out. Many annuities now offer a series of mutual fund options within the contract and allow you to switch among the funds without penalty. Fidelity, Vanguard, Charles Schwab & Co., and many other firms offer these investments.

The most commonly used income tax deductions are for home mortgage interest and property taxes. The actual value to you of these deductions varies, depending on how much you borrow (or pay in property tax). As with other tax advantages, we advise you to determine

---

[2] *And I Quote* (St. Martin's Press).

whether an investment makes sense for you, primarily in light of your investment objectives. Only then should you give any weight or value to the tax savings. For example, buying tax-exempt bonds just because you hate paying income taxes does not make sense unless you really need bonds in your portfolio.

We want to make one final point, before we dig into the world of mutual funds. The Laws of Investment Success seem simple to understand and easy to follow. And they are—kind of. The trouble is, we are all human. If you adopt these laws, circumstances will inevitably challenge your courage and your willingness to stick with the program. Take a look at the laws one more time.

The Laws of Investment Success

1. Invest for a minimum of 20 years.

2. Place your money with the investment pros, don't bet against them.

3. If you want capital appreciation, be an owner not a loaner.

4. You have to pay if you want to play.

5. What counts is how much you keep—after taxes.

Can you make the commitment to live, breathe, and invest by these laws? If you can honestly say yes, we're thrilled. If you still have some doubts, that's fine too. A little skepticism never hurt any investor. Now, let's see what's next on the path to mutual fund mastery.

INTERVIEW

"Everyone Can Be Wealthy"

An Interview with *Shelby M. C. Davis*

Shelby M. C. Davis is a force of nature. An enthusiastic dynamo who loves the investment game, he has compiled one of the best growth records in the business, dating back to 1969, when he began managing Davis New York Venture Fund. His 28-year tenure is almost inconceivable when compared to the average mutual fund manager's mere 3½ years on the job.

Davis and his son, Chris, are also the comanagers of Selected American Shares, one of the country's oldest no-load stock funds.

The Davis philosophy might be called *growth at a good price.* He seeks large, well-managed companies with strong finances and solid records of growth. He likes to know and understand the top managers at each company he owns, and once he buys in, he tends to stick with his portfolio holding. Davis exemplifies the definition of buy and hold because the two funds he comanages have very low portfolio turnover rates.

Davis may have a lot of years on the job, but he exudes energy, enthusiasm, and sheer enjoyment. If there is a fountain of youth for mutual fund portfolio managers, Davis must be a regular visitor.

Mutual Fund Mastery: Let's talk a little about the history of Selected American Shares and how you came to manage that portfolio.

Shelby Davis: Selected American was launched as a mutual fund in 1933, and, as such, is one of the oldest mutual funds in the country.

MFM: When did it go no-load?

SD: It's been no-load all along. We were asked to manage the fund in 1993 and we continue to do so at the discretion of the board of directors. I am a board member and

a comanager with my son, Chris Davis. So far, it's been a wonderful relationship and the Davis family assets now total over 25% of Selected American Shares.

MFM: So you have invested a pretty big chunk of your personal money in Selected American Shares.

SD: Yes, I have, and so has the Davis family through various Davis family charitable trusts and foundations.

MFM: Investing seems to run in the Davis family. Your father was a superb investor, particularly with insurance company stocks, and his record dates back to the late 1940s. Now, you work with your son, Chris, on both Davis New York Venture Fund and Selected American Shares.

SD: That's right. Chris Davis is the comanager of the fund and he is very well thought of. The board likes the idea that we have continuity of management with over two generations and a long-term focus. Some say we have a 60-year-old brain with 30-year-old legs. This fund is unique because Selected American Shares dates back to 1933. The compound rate of return for the past 63 years is well over 12%. That means $1,000 invested then is now worth over $1.5 million now. It blows your mind completely. To me, compounding money is the whole message of mutual funds. Either you get it in 30 seconds or you never get it.

You invest in a fund that is a diversified package of equities in order to compound your money, and the compounding is staggering in equities over a generation, to say nothing over two generations. And Selected

American Shares is over two generations old, and $1,000 is now worth a million-five? Or more? And that's not an extraordinary compound but it's 12%, and 12% beats the heck out of money market funds or CDs or anything else, pretty much. Your other big benefits in mutual funds are diversification, professional management, and the confidence to stay with it, so that time becomes your friend. And if time becomes your friend, then the compound of time will make you rich. It's about that simple. People either get it quickly or they never get it. They are too worried about the market doing this, or the Fed that, or we are going to have a bad election—all these kind of crazy things. But when you step back, you realize that money has to be managed generation after generation, through thick and thin—through wars, depressions, booms, busts. If investors would just get into this regular habit of investing, everyone could become wealthy if they give it enough time.

MFM: If people were willing to do this, particularly at an early age, then I believe it would transform their lives. Not so much that they would be rich, but that people would be in control of their financial future. How would you recommend people start?

SD: Well, the government forces you to be a regular taxpayer—*forces* you by withholding money from your paycheck as soon as you get your first regular job. At the same time, if people had the discipline to start withholding and investing the same way they do to pay their taxes, and get into that withhold and invest habit—they'd be on their way to wealth. It's that simple.

MFM: Once people have saved some money, how should they think about investing? Do you think investors should spend much time worrying about the economy or the balance of trade or the interest rate or the federal deficit or the discount rate or that kind of stuff?

SD: No, I don't. I think you have to have some fundamental beliefs to be an investor. You have to be a long-term optimist and focus on the distant horizon, not up close.

One that doesn't say the glass is always half empty, but half full, instead. You have to believe in the sweep of American history or the sweep of mankind—that forward progress is made over generations and wealth begets wealth, and that the country grows and the GNP grows and the Federal Reserve banks of the world are there to protect us, not to kill us.

MFM: In other words, you believe Federal Reserve Chairman Alan Greenspan and his counterparts around the world are trying to keep our economies on a reasonably steady upward trend.

SD: That's right. It's like a good host and hostess at a party. Their job is to take the punch bowl away when the party's gotten too wild and to restimulate when the economy has a hangover. This doesn't mean they always get it right, because there can always be an accident. But you have to have a belief that, over a 25-year period, you're going to see forward progress in a package of well-managed companies—professionally managed companies—that make up a mutual fund's portfolio.

MFM: You're saying that well-managed companies will continue to do well, despite the ups and down in the economy. Even though there will be dips, or even major downturns in the stock market, the trend will be up. It sounds like you believe a good equity investor must have a belief that our economy is sound and that it will continue to grow. And, presumably, those who do not have that optimism or that faith should not invest in stocks.

SD: Exactly. I guess there are some people who are emotionally not made up to be investors. They are glooming and dooming all the time and worried that the sky is falling. They watch too much television news. Only problems and catastrophes are covered. I've got two sons in the investment business, and they and their optimistic friends aren't worried about the short-term fluctuations in the stock market. They believe they are in the early stages of their careers and they are putting money aside regularly for their retirement, because they are not convinced the government will be there to do it. They are believers, thanks to the Peter Lynches and others who have publicized the potential for equities. The earlier you start, the better off you are. Putting away money regularly in mutual funds is what lots of these people are doing. And the baby boomers have to do it because they may live 25 years after retirement.

MFM: Let me ask you this: For someone just entering the job market, beginning to save, do you think mutual funds are the best investment vehicle for most people?

SD: I think mutual funds are the best investment vehicle for most people simply because they offer instant diversification, professional management, and, therefore, some peace of mind; whereas, if you try to make up a portfolio stock by stock, you can either get too wild or too concentrated in a few stocks. For most people who are trying to bring up a family and manage their own careers, funds are the answer. You know they don't practice law or medicine on themselves. They might as well get a financial professional to manage their long-term financial savings.

MFM: If someone is just entering the job market, what kind of mutual funds do you think they should put their money in? Equity funds?

SD: From my point of view, the general public, especially at a young age, should totally disregard the bond market. Completely disregard it. The bond market has had one terrific period, namely 1982–1995. This is the only time bonds have compounded at a double-digit rate of return over a decade or more. There are many times when equities have done better than a double-digit return.

MFM: Stocks have outperformed bonds in the past, and investors who need or want growth should forget bonds—is that it?

SD: I'm saying, for young persons: (1) they should invest regularly and take advantage of dollar cost averaging, (2) they should forget

bonds, and (3) they should go into equities that have stood the test of time . . . .

MFM: You mean a solid growth fund like Selected American Shares?

SD: A blue chip growth approach, or what we at Selected American call "value growth marriage." Let's call that the main course in your investment diet. We think of Selected American Shares as the main course, the meat and potatoes, or core, of your sustenance.

MFM: So, in the world according to Shelby Davis, you would have blue chip, growing companies at the core of your portfolio?

SD: Large companies that have stood the test of time, that have been through a number of cycles and are being professionally managed. With those companies, you've got staying power, financial power.

MFM: What about aggressive growth funds, technology funds . . . ?

SD: To continue my food analogy, those are for someone who wants an exciting appetizer or dessert for their taste buds. They would be a part of dinner, but not the main course.

MFM: At what point, or under what circumstances, do bonds make sense for investors?

SD: I think they make sense when you think you can yield more than a double-digit return.

MFM: It's more of an opportunistic . . . .

SD: Yes, pure. The studies of bonds show that they offer you single-digit returns, almost always. I think the average return on bonds is 6 to 8%, and I think we're back in that range now. But investors, particularly young investors, should just forget bonds, just forget it!

MFM: What about people who are approaching retirement age—people starting to get concerned about income; how do you think they should deal with that?

SD: Well, that's a little tougher, because the time clock is less in their favor. But the first step is to recognize that the second to die is probably going to live 25 years after retirement—or after they turn 60, anyway. At least one member of a husband-and-wife team is going to live to 85, if they manage to make it to 60. The statistics are out there. Therefore, that still gives you an enormous amount of time. I think you really should function primarily on a total return basis, which means you should still have a very high equity ratio going into retirement and only have as few bonds as possible.

MFM: What would be an allocation between stocks and bonds?

SD: I certainly say you ought to have at least 65% in stocks. I would also have 1 to 3 years in cash in short-term stuff, for emergencies and day-to-day living expenses. Whatever income stream you wanted out of that you should have in cash—3 years of cash, short-term stuff you could dip into, with the rest maybe in bonds, with no more than a 10-year maturity as far as I'm concerned. The rest in equities. The longer your horizon, the more you should have in equities and the more you should believe in the total return theory. Now, maybe you have to spread out the equities to international and various categories of investments. For instance, my son, Andrew, manages a real estate fund, which offers income and growth.

MFM: The reality is, equities are where you want to be—whether domestically or internationally is a different issue.

SD: The way I explain it—and many people just don't want to believe it—a bond is a fixed obligation to get your money back with interest, right? No growth, right? It's just a fixed thing—interest rate fixed, return of principal fixed. Whereas an equity is like investing in a person, because people make up companies, so imagine yourself as a young adult and you watch the earning power of a successful young person develop over 40 years of a working career. That's what successful companies are. They are just like people, whose earning power grows over the years, although maybe not every year. They might have a bad year, or a strike, or become unemployed, or be sick. I guess what it starts with is this: Think of equities not as pieces of paper; equities are fractional ownership shares in companies. So, when you get a basket of equities, you own a group of enterprises that will, hopefully, grow over the decades; whereas bonds are simply a promise to get back your money with interest, but there's no growth.

MFM: Growing people and growing companies. Great analogy.

SD: Yes, and the point is, . . . just envision the company being made up of people and relate it to a child and how a child can grow. And that's where a mutual fund is, hopefully, like gardening. Planting a mix of seedlings or mature plants, selecting them carefully, pruning occasionally, and watching them grow.

MFM: I want to try to get the sweep of history in here, because you're one of the few managers who have gone through such a long period of time, back to 1969, when you started managing Davis New York Venture Fund. We're at a point now where a lot of investors, and many portfolio managers, too, have never seen a real stock market crash. Maybe they've only been investing for 5 or 10 years. Many mutual fund managers have only been around for 5 to 10 years. I'm not concerned about what happens over the next year, but I am concerned with what happens over the next 5 to 10 years. The market's at an all-time high at the time we're having this conversation, and where do you go from here, in terms of looking out over the future?

SD: Well, I've been saying for a while that the 1990s remind me a lot of the 1960s, and I didn't realize how foolish it was to say that to audiences, because when I came into the business in the early '60s, people would talk about the 1920s and it seemed so far back to me, I thought it was irrelevant. I'm sure people today feel that now, when I talk about the '60s. But, the '60s followed a tremendous decade of the '50s, just like the '90s followed the tremendous decade of the 1980s. The

'80s and the '50s were the golden decades for making killings in the market—I mean, you started from such a low base. For the '60s and the '90s, you started from a higher base but, ironically, the public got more interested in equities in the '90s than they did in the '80s and, similarly, in the '60s rather than the '50s. That didn't make them wrong, it just made them a little late. Nobody called the '60s a bad environment for equities; nobody called the corrections in 1962 and 1966 the end of the big bull market. They were just buying opportunities, and I think that's what lies ahead of us. When the stock market corrects, which it is overdue to do anytime, I think it will be looked upon by the vast majority of the public as a buying opportunity. And only after that fails for a few years will people get nervous.

MFM: So that would be like the period from 1969 to 1974 where . . . .

SD: Yes, that's right. Actually, 1969–70 was a down market, and the recovery in 1971 and 1972 was sort of a narrowly based speculative blowoff in what was called the top-tier growth stocks. Xerox, Polaroid, IBM, Avon Products, and a lot of other stocks went to forty to sixty times earnings. But now remember the difference between the late 1960s and the mid-1990s. Thirty years ago, you had a rapid increase in bond yields. Bond yields had been going up gradually since 1949, frankly. But in the mid-1960s, yields started to go up a little bit faster, from 4% to 5%, and then to 6%. The government came out with something called the "magic sixes" and people were so excited to get a 6% yield on a 30-year bond that they lined up around the block at the Federal Reserve Board in New York City. Around the block to buy these bonds because no one had experienced these high yields since the 1920s. And within a year, they yielded 7%—it was a disaster. So bonds from the mid-1960s on were mostly bad news. You know, with intermittent rallies, but most every year, investors had to take tax losses in bonds.

MFM: Social conditions back then were very different as well, with the combination of heavy spending for the Vietnam War and the ambitious social programs President Lyndon Johnson began. How did those things impact the economy?

SD: The government was fighting a war—which came to be called the Vietnam War. Wars are always inflationary. At the same time, you had Lyndon Johnson, who was elected president in 1964, following President John F. Kennedy's assassination in 1963. Johnson's first move as a populist was what he called the "Great Society." The Great Society was a program which, in essence, was a massive expansion of the welfare state and entitlement programs up and down the line. Food stamps, education spending, health spending—every kind of spending you could think of on the entitlement side, he expanded. None of us realized how bad this was at the time for future deficits and inflation. Maybe the old timers did, but I certainly didn't recognize it as much as I should have. And then, toward the end of his term, the war and Johnson's heavy spending cost so much that he had to propose a tax increase, a 10% surtax across the board.

MFM: What happened next?

SD: So, here you had an expansion of welfare spending, you had a war which was an expansion of military spending, and you had a rising budget deficit and then a tax hike and higher interest rates. Boy, what a recipe for the market to collapse, and it finally did in 1970, and then it really spiraled down in 1973–74. Oil prices were going through the moon. Remember, oil was $3 a barrel then and went to $10 and then to $30 in 7 or 8 years. Imagine, that would be like today's oil price of $20 going to $200. To contrast that vicious cycle of higher spending, higher inflation, and unemployment, look where we are today. The debate is about how much we can curtail the growth of welfare spending and the entitlement programs, where we can downsize the defense budget—and we're now at peace. In any event, the Cold War isn't the threat it was when Russia was so strong. And you have some talk of cutting income taxes, and capital gains tax cuts.

Also, you have oil prices sort of on idle, with Iraq oil still mostly out of the market and, therefore, a capping element on prices. You have globalization of trade and you have lots of new sources of raw materials and cheap labor from the former communist or totalitarian places like China, Poland, and Eastern Europe in general. You have, I'd say, quite a benign outlook for inflation. I'm not saying it will get any better; it probably will get a little worse. But it's hard to believe inflation will do anything other than creep up rather than gallop like it was doing back then. With that in mind, you have favorable demographic trends, where people are saving like crazy for their retirement and many more people in the baby boomer generation are doing that. The number of 18- to 30-year-olds is dropping as a percentage of the population and the 40- to 60-year-old group is growing rapidly as a share of the population. So, you've got money flows that logically go into financial assets. So, the money flows are there and the demographics are there to keep it going, and the fundamentals—namely, inflation, interest rates, and the welfare state and entitlement spending—are not as negative as they were, in fact the opposite. So we're sort of in a virtuous cycle. This is not new news, however.

MFM: So, in your opinion, we are moving through a very positive process that could last a long time, right?

SD: My feeling of the sweep of history is we're not at the bottom; who could say that? But these valuation levels are reminiscent of the 1960s. That decade ended badly because everything turned negative in terms of inflation, interest rates, entitlement spending, and taxes. Until you see those things turn bad again, you should just relax and accept these valuation levels. People are lined up to come to this country because it is the land of opportunity. The wave of immigrants waiting to come in here is enormous. Yet, what we are subjected to on TV and by newspapers is constant criticism of this country with all of its flaws, warts, and

faults. But, it is the great land of opportunity. And if you approach the world that way, you become an investor in equities and mutual funds because you say, "Hey, this is still a great place where someone can make millions playing basketball or make millions making a movie using animation like Steve Jobs has just done." We have a lot of things that make a country great, especially the freedom to work and create. Maybe we don't like our government so much, but we have freedom, we have relatively low taxes, we have innovation, entrepreneurship, and the ability to have hard work pay off. And someone with an idea can become a winner. I don't care if you're black, white, yellow, or any creed or color—opportunity stories are out there. And, since people make companies, then that must mean there are plenty of opportunities for companies out there, and I think there are.

MFM: Wow. I feel like buying stock in America. It's a huge growth opportunity. To switch gears a bit, what about the relationship between small, growing companies and companies that are large, but still growing, maybe at a lower rate? Do you think people should look at a small company fund as well as a large company fund such as yours?

SD: Yes, I do. I think the biggest problem with small company investing is that the scoreboard changes so fast. The turnover of small companies that are successful is so rapid that, 2 years later, the companies I liked aren't there any more—they often did not live up to the high expectations.

MFM: The turnover is very high.

SD: Huge. From my point of view, that's not our style. We like to find companies we can believe in, that will be stalwarts in our portfolio. Obviously, things change. I would have a hard time doing research knowing that 60 to 80% of my portfolio needs to be new every year and a half or two years. Don't get me wrong, it's a perfectly legitimate game, but it's not what I do. That's what's so fascinating about Wall Street. There are so many different ways you can make money.

MFM: There's been a lot of publicity about the highly leveraged hedge funds. What do you think is the secret—they've had extraordinary returns in some cases. How does that work?

SD: Oh yes. Well, it works because leverage—borrowing money and then investing it—gives you extraordinary returns if you're clever and you don't get completely blitzed. Leverage works both ways. In the 1920s, you had leverage in equities, you bought on a 5% margin. If it went up 5%, you doubled your money. And with options today, you buy with only 5% or 10% equity. The stock goes up—if IBM goes up 10 points—there are plenty of people who double their money on an option with IBM. But options have time fuses on them, and you have tremendous leverage to being right or wrong. To me, it's not in my repertoire. I'm investing not in pieces of paper, but fractional ownership positions in companies I want to live with for a long period of time.

MFM: I think a lot of people have gotten away from the fact that stocks represent ownership of a company. To them, buying a share of stock is a piece of paper for trading . . . .

SD: Yes, that's the first thing you should get away from. If you're a serious investor, forget trading and other financial maneuvers. It's as though you were buying a house, only the house is called a company. Most people don't trade more than a handful of houses in their lifetime. And the way you're buying a company is as a fractional owner—like you're a condominium owner—a part owner of something. And therefore, I like Warren Buffett's idea, that the way people should really approach investing as opposed to trading, is: Everyone is given a ticket that has only 20 punches in it, and they have only 20 investment punches to use in their lifetime. They could make 20 investment decisions and that was it. They obviously would think long and hard about what they were going to put their money in. I think it would crystallize for them the seriousness of being a long-term investor, and the great wizards who get rich usually are these long-term investors. Whether it was Warren Buffett, the biggest,

or Larry Tisch, or even my father. They were not known as traders. They did careful analysis within a circle of competence, an area they felt comfortable investing in, and it didn't have to be a glamour area. They would buy and hold. They would have done careful work on the characteristics of the company, characteristics of the industry, how the business made its money, what was its staying power—and they would ride it for 10, 20, 30 years. Those are the fundamentals of investing. Investing should not be thought of as trading. Investing is fractional ownership. Sometimes people ask me, "What's your holding period?" I think it averages out to be around 8 years, maybe more. Typically, I tell them: When I buy something, I tend to think of it as a perpetual thing. Until something radical changes, like it gets grossly overpriced, or a big secular thing happens, or I've lost complete confidence in the management which makes up the company.

MFM: What have you learned from working with and studying great investors like your father and Warren Buffett?

SD: What my dad taught me and what Warren Buffett taught me too, is that you must stay within your circle of competence. I've already said mine is not emerging growth markets, or international, or trading, or things like that. Mine is core investing for the long term, and looking for growth at a good price. Just like the supermarket shopper does, or the shoppers today for almost any goods. They want to buy the best brands, but at a discount price. They wait for airline tickets to go on sale, things like that. Then you've got to get to know your investment style and the way you do things. And mine is strictly long-term. Recognize there will be bad quarters. Usually, take advantage of bad quarters to pick up more, rather than dump stocks. Try not to be in too many fad businesses where things change radically. Try to take advantage of the compounding machine, which equities provide.

MFM: Let's say, at some point in the future, someone's reading this book, maybe a year from now, two years from now, and the market has tumbled, interest rates are going up, the economy's in a recession, things don't look so great. What should they do at that point?

SD: Remember that Chinese proverb, "Crisis creates opportunity." Warren Buffett put it this way: If you're a perpetual investor, you should think of yourself like a perpetual human being, that you have to eat; every day you have to buy food, right? So when you go to the supermarket and you see something "on sale," let's say steak, you don't hesitate to buy more steak and put some in the freezer because you know you're going to eat it eventually and it's a bargain today. That's the attitude you should have, rather than panicking when stocks go "on sale." Saying, "Oh my heavens, stocks are 'on sale,' I should sell." When other products in the world go on sale, people want to buy and they are happy. They get excited. Even though they might already have some steaks in their freezer, they buy more at a lower price per pound because they know they're averaging down and they're going to eat those steaks. I think they should have faith in the country for the long term and have faith in their investment choices.

Shelby Davis has been a great investor for many years and one of the best attributes he has is his strong and abiding optimism. He believes this is the land of opportunity, not only for individuals, but also for companies. Another attribute he has is patience. He believes that a portfolio of carefully-selected and well-managed companies will do very well no matter what happens in the short run. There may be temporary setbacks, either for an individual company or for the stock market as a whole, but the portfolio will inevitably become more and more valuable over time.

The next time you are worried about the stock market, interest rates, or investing in general, just come back and spend a little time with Shelby. You'll feel better; and, if you adopt some of his patience and optimism, you'll be a better investor too.

If you do want to become a better investor, just turn the page and we will show you how to make more money with mutual funds.

CHAPTER 2
Make More Money with Mutual Funds

In 1870, a penniless Scotsman boarded a ship bound for the United States. The solitary traveler, Robert Fleming, was a bookkeeper sent over to supervise some American investments for his boss. Fleming got a first-hand glimpse of a new and vibrant country and was so impressed with the growth potential that he went home and organized the Scottish American Trust, an early prototype of what we now know as the mutual fund.

Fleming's Scottish American Trust was formed by a group of investors who wanted to buy American investments. None of these investors could individually afford to travel to America to purchase and supervise a diversified portfolio of investments. But, as a group, they had enough buying power to do all these things. And that was Fleming's stroke of genius.

Fleming had very little personal money, so he was forced to create something new. He realized that, by pooling their investment capital, many smaller investors could develop investment portfolios with professional management and diversification—advantages that had been the exclusive province of very wealthy investors.

Fleming's investment trusts resembled what we now call closed-end funds. Closed-end funds start out by selling a specific number of shares to the public. These shares are traded on a stock exchange. The price of the shares is set, as for any other stock, by supply and demand. Thus, closed-end fund shares can sell at a discount or a premium to the underlying value of the investments they hold.

The legal name for what we now call a mutual fund is an open-end investment company. When mutual fund investors want to buy or sell shares, they do so directly with the fund company at what is called the net asset value. Also, the fund company can sell an unlimited number of shares at that price.

The first modern mutual fund was the Massachusetts Investors Trust, which came along in 1924. But it took years of trial and error and

Net Asset Value (NAV)

At the end of each business day, every mutual fund (and closed-end fund) has to price all of the securities it holds—stocks, bonds, money market instruments, whatever. The value of these assets is divided by the number of shares that are outstanding, to determine what the net asset value (NAV) or share price is for that mutual fund for that day.

For example, on December 29, 1995, the assets in Mutual Shares Fund were valued at $5,224,886,484. There were 60,436,879 shares outstanding on that day. Therefore, the NAV was $86.45:

$$\$5,224,886,484 \text{ divided by } 60,436,879 \text{ shares} = \$86.45$$

---

a lot of misery before the mutual fund industry, as a whole, adopted the structure and safeguards we take for granted today.

The shocking stock market crash of 1929 sparked the Great Depression of the 1930s—10 years of poverty, disillusionment, and despair for many. Yet, out of that disastrous decade came many reforms (such as the Securities Act of 1933, the Glass–Steagal Act of 1933, and the Fair Labor Standards Act) and the creation of many governmental oversight agencies—the Federal Deposit Insurance Corporation (FDIC), the Securities and Exchange Commission (SEC), the National Labor Relations Board (NLRB), and the Federal Communications Commission (FCC), to name a few. For mutual fund investors, the watershed event was the passage by Congress of the Investment Company Act of 1940, which created the mutual fund structure as we know it today.

By way of comparison, let's travel back in time to California in 1959. In case you've forgotten, that was when Jack Kilby and Robert Noyce created the first integrated circuit, a single chip of silicon that replaced thousands of transistors and other electrical components and ushered in an era of unprecedented innovation as computer technology became cheaper and more powerful, year after year. From being the exclusive province of governments and well-funded university research laboratories, computer technology is now so pervasive and so inexpensive that we cannot imagine a world without it.

Just as the integrated circuit (the forebear to what we now call the semiconductor) brought computing power to people everywhere, the creation of the modern mutual fund structure changed the nature of financial services and opened up sophisticated investments to investors of all types. One piece of legislation created a new era for investors by setting up the safeguards and structure that enabled mutual funds to become the dominant investment vehicle they are today. This was a relatively simple innovation that did not receive much notice at the time. Yet, it opened up a myriad of possibilities and brought professional management, diversification, safety, and other tangible benefits into the hands of all investors, no matter how much money or how little money they have.

Today, there are more mutual funds than stocks on the New York Stock Exchange. New funds open daily, offering a dazzling and sometimes intimidating array of choices. The competition for money is so intense that new innovations, marketing approaches, investment styles, and services are being announced daily. The smartest people on Wall Street are eager and willing to work for you, for a nominal annual fee. In all of human history, there has never been a time like this.

Mutual Funds Are the Best Investment Vehicle

Mutual funds offer a package of advantages available nowhere else:

- ◆ Low minimum investment.
- ◆ Immediate diversification.
- ◆ Professional management.
- ◆ Security.
- ◆ Liquidity.
- ◆ Audited track records.

With no-load mutual funds, another advantage is that you save something near and dear to all our hearts—money. When you buy or sell a no-load mutual fund, there is no sales charge, so your total investment goes to work for you. You don't have to pay a stockbroker or financial planner. Our definition of no-load is very simple. A no-load fund is one that does not charge a sales commission either when investors buy in or when they sell out.

Load Versus No-Load

There is quite a bit of confusion over the difference between load and no-load mutual funds. Structurally, there is no difference. All mutual funds have the same structure, and all funds pay their expenses by taking a fee, known as the total expense ratio, which is paid from the mutual fund's assets. This fee, or expense ratio, has nothing to do with sales charges or loads. The funds that charge a load do so to pay brokers, financial planners, and even banks that sell the fund.

We have nothing against stockbrokers or financial planners. After all, we both worked at brokerage firms for several years ourselves. Our concern has to do with the quality of advice and the objectivity of the person delivering it. We do not object to a sales charge if the broker or financial planner gives advice that is objective and suited to the clients' needs. If someone gives clients objective advice and helps them reach their goals, that is a worthwhile endeavor.

The Birth of Mutual Shares

In 1949, a German immigrant named Max Heine formed Mutual Shares Fund (now known as Mutual Series Fund), one of the earliest no-load mutual funds. Heine was a specialist in buying stocks and bonds of bankrupt companies. He pursued his trade in obscurity for many years. But superb performance in the brutal down market of 1973–1974 caught the eye of investors, and the fund slowly gained in size. How well did the fund do in that 2-year period? It broke even. During the same period, the S&P 500 lost nearly 40%.

In 1985, when we were analyzing Mutual Shares for our clients, we asked Max why he did so well in the 1973 downturn. He instantly quipped: "Our stocks were so bad they couldn't go down no more." Because he held undervalued stocks, many of which had gone through hard times, they suffered very little while other stocks were plunging. They literally could not fall any further. It turned out that Heine's emphasis on downtrodden stocks and bonds was pretty astute.

In 1975, Heine made another good move when he brought in a young man named Michael Price to help him analyze stocks. The rest, as they say, is mystery. Mystery? Exactly. How did Heine know that this fast-talking kid with an undergraduate degree from Oklahoma State University would turn into an excellent portfolio manager (see our interview with Michael Price)?

Shortly after Mutual Shares was formed, another visionary started the Guardian Fund (now Neuberger & Berman Guardian Fund). Just like Heine, Roy Neuberger wanted to create an investment vehicle that eliminated the fat fees so prevalent on Wall Street at that time. As the cofounder of Neuberger & Berman, a successful Wall Street brokerage and investment advisory firm, Neuberger could have just as easily kept on working only for wealthy clients. But he was also an art collector, a philanthropist, and a sincere humanitarian who wanted to level the playing field for all investors.

From being an idea in the minds of men like Heine and Neuberger, the no-load industry expanded quietly over the decades to the point that it now has over 3,000 funds and more than $1.5 trillion in assets.

Roy Neuberger and Sales Loads

Several years ago, Kurt interviewed Roy Neuberger for *Kurt Brouwer's Guide to Mutual Funds* (Wiley). Here is what Neuberger said about why he started his first no-load mutual fund in 1950.

I believed it was a sensible method for a person to invest and I disliked the 8.5% sales load most mutual funds charged, because I thought it was excessive. I still do. With a load fund, when you put $10,000 in a fund, after commissions you are down to $9,150. The only essential difference between a load and a no-load fund is the commission. The management may be the same people in many cases.

One of the big misconceptions about mutual funds in general is that they are vehicles only for investing in stocks. In fact, stock mutual funds control less than 45% of all mutual fund assets. Bond and money market funds share the rest.

The term "mutual fund" simply refers to a type of company formed for investment. Mutual funds come in many flavors, including stocks, bonds, money market instruments, and more exotic varieties such as gold, natural resources, and real estate. One way to begin looking at mutual funds is to break them into categories that denote their level of risk. The aggressive growth category is generally the riskiest, although certain funds in other categories such as international and specialty are also high-risk funds. On the opposite end of the risk spectrum are money market funds and short-term bond funds.

One stumbling block to understanding mutual funds is that some terms, such as *growth,* mean more than one thing. Growth can refer to a fund's investment objective, that is, growing or increasing your capital investment. Or, it can mean that the fund invests primarily in so-called growth stocks, which are a particular category of companies that are experiencing rapid growth.

Mutual Fund Structure: How the Funds Really Work

The word "mutual" is derived from the fact that a mutual fund is owned by its shareholders. One occasional point of confusion is that the company that manages the mutual fund—for example, Fidelity Management & Research, Davis Selected Advisors, or Harris Associates—can be privately owned. A mutual fund company can manage multiple funds. But each mutual fund is run by a board of trustees and is owned and run by and for its shareholders. The Vanguard Group is the only large fund group that is owned and operated by its shareholders without a privately owned management company running the day-to-day operations.

The Investment Company Act of 1940 requires that a mutual fund maintain a specific structure. The necessary components are:

♦ **Board of Trustees (or directors).** This is the governing body of the mutual fund. It has the authority to hire (or fire) the portfolio manager and other service providers for the fund. It acts much like the board of directors of a corporation and, like a corporation, its trustees are elected by shareholders.

♦ **Custodian.** The custodian is usually a bank or trust company that physically holds all the mutual fund's stocks, bonds or other securities, and cash. By law, it must be independent and separate from the fund's portfolio management group. This is an essential part of the checks and balances set up to protect mutual fund investors.

♦ **Transfer Agent.** The transfer agent keeps track of the shareholders and the shares they buy and sell. It also pays dividends and capital gains distributions, and it issues shareholder account statements and purchase and sale confirmations.

♦ **Investment Adviser.** The adviser is an individual or a company that acts as the fund's portfolio manager or investment adviser. The adviser is paid a portion of the fund's assets (on average, 0.50%) to manage investments for the fund.

By law, mutual funds must distribute their net income each year (interest, dividends, realized gains/losses). This income is paid out as either a cash dividend or a share dividend (the cash dividend is reinvested in more shares of the fund). No matter how you choose to take your dividends, they are taxable except in the case of certain tax-exempt bond and money market funds, or shares that are held by retirement accounts. Income taxes are also deferred for dividends paid in tax-deferred annuities.

The following eight mutual fund categories are, by definition, simply convenient ways of sorting out the thousands of mutual funds, but not all funds fit neatly into a category. For example, many Growth and Income funds are relatively conservative, but some are really "closet" growth funds. Use these categories as a rough guide, but do not rely on

Eight Types of Mutual Funds

them exclusively. Morningstar uses many more categories, based on a given fund's investment objectives.

1. Money Market Funds: Safety First

USES:

♦ As a home for your "rainy day" money (a stash of cash), which you need to keep safe, secure, and liquid, in case you have a financial emergency. Your rainy day stash should be equal to your living expenses for a minimum of 3 months.

♦ As a parking place for money you know you will be spending in the next 12 months or so. Could cover a down payment on a home, the price of a new car, an income tax payment, a vacation, and so on.

♦ As a temporary cache when you are accumulating cash for a specific investment you plan to make in the future, or when you are making periodic investments.

ABUSES:

♦ Using a money market fund as a long-term investment vehicle for a substantial portion of your assets. Many people leave cash in a money market fund or bank account for years, simply because they cannot decide what to do. If you have money that you are not going to use for 2 years or more, the money market fund is probably not the best place to store it. You could get a higher return with reasonable safety in a short-term bond fund.

Investment Objective   Money market funds are designed to provide safety, liquidity, and a reasonable rate of return. Portfolio holdings generally have a maturity of one year or less, and the average maturity for all portfolio holdings is usually under 90 days. Treasury bills, certificates of deposit, and commercial paper are the main investments used. Some funds invest only in Treasury bills and other short-term government obligations. The government-only money funds are considered the safest.

Often, investors shop for the highest yielding (yield is the amount of interest the fund pays) money market fund, thinking that the highest yield makes it the best. Not true. They are forgetting the first rule of money market funds: *Safety first.* In trying to eke out an extra half-percent yield, a fund has to increase its risk quite a bit. Much of the controversy over the use of derivatives has been stirred by questionable or even improper tactics by portfolio managers who are trying in vain to pump up the yield on their money market fund. Why do they do this? Because they know that is what investors shop for.

Under Investment Objective, we listed a reasonable rate of return as the third goal of a money market fund. Look first to the safety and liquidity of your money market fund, and just make sure the yield is *reasonable.* Use this fund as a parking place for cash that is awaiting investment or as a secure place to put rainy day money or other money you may need in the next couple of years. As long as your money market fund has a competitive yield, don't fret about it or jump ship for a higher yielding fund (see Figure 2.1).

If you want higher returns than money market funds can give, consider the next category.

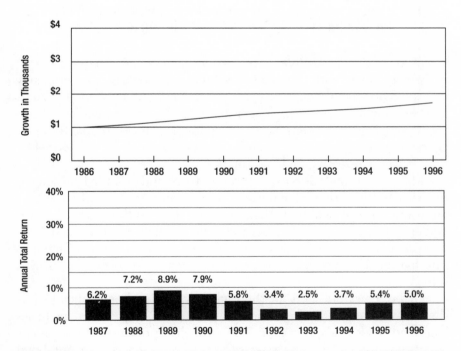

FIGURE 2.1 Money Market Funds. The top chart illustrates the growth of $1,000 invested in money market funds beginning December 31, 1986. The bottom chart illustrates the annual total returns for money market funds from 1987 through 1996. (*Source:* Micropal, Ltd., Brouwer & Janachowski, Inc.)

2. Bond Funds: Think Total Return

USES:

♦ As a long-term investment vehicle that adds the stability of income-producing assets to your portfolio.

♦ As a parking place for money you plan to spend 2 or 3 years from now. Generally, for this purpose, you should stick to short-term bond funds with an average maturity of 3 years or less.

ABUSES:

♦ Buying the highest yielding bond fund without understanding the level of interest rate risk it incurs.

♦ Using a bond fund simply because you do not understand stock funds.

♦ Putting all your retirement assets in a bond fund.

♦ Putting money with a 10-year (or longer) time horizon (such as a young child's college money) in a bond fund.

Investment Objective To provide income and a moderate rate of return along with reasonable safety and liquidity. Like money market funds, bond funds invest in government and corporate fixed-income securities, only with longer maturities. This is a very broad category ranging from conservative, short-term bond funds to more aggressive long-term funds. It also includes some very aggressive selections, such as zero coupon bond funds.

Many bond funds also use futures, options, and other hybrid securities that fall into that "demonized" area known as derivatives. These are useful professional tools that, when used carefully, enhance shareholder value. When used incorrectly or deceptively, they can have painful consequences for investors. If you are buying a bond fund as a safe harbor for a portion of your assets, then make sure it is, in fact, safe.

Often, investors shop for the highest yields on bond funds just as they do with money market funds. Big mistake. Using yield alone to select bond funds leads to trouble. The term *yield* presumes that capital is not at risk and that the sole issue is the yield or rate of return. Yet, bond funds all carry some capital risk, which increases with longer maturities and lower-quality bonds. If you buy the highest yielding bond fund, you should realize that the one you select will probably be a long-term bond fund, and that means it could be one of the riskiest bond funds.

Bond funds, unlike money market funds, should be analyzed only in terms of total return (interest income plus capital gains and losses).

Like money market fund portfolio managers, bond fund managers can get into trouble when they try to squeeze out a slightly higher yield. To get more yield, they have to significantly increase their interest rate risk or buy lower-quality bonds. The fund's yield should be a relatively minor consideration in your purchase decision. Focus on total return when you make a selection (see Figure 2.2).

Use bond funds when you need income from your portfolio. They can also provide stability to a portfolio when financial storms are raging. If you want higher returns, you may be ready for the next step up the risk-and-reward ladder.

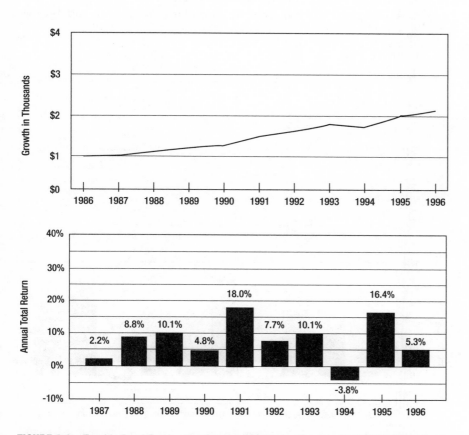

FIGURE 2.2 Taxable Bond Funds. The top chart illustrates the growth of $1,000 invested in taxable bond mutual funds beginning December 31, 1986. The bottom chart illustrates the annual total returns for taxable bond mutual funds from 1987 through 1996. (*Source:* Micropal, Ltd., Brouwer & Janachowski, Inc.)

3. Growth and Income Funds: Balancing Greed and Fear

USES:

♦ As a complete investment vehicle for those who need capital appreciation with a moderate amount of risk.

ABUSES:

♦ Putting short-term money in a Growth & Income fund.

Investment Objective Growth and Income (G&I) funds cover a rather broad spectrum between bond funds and growth funds. Funds in this category range from conservative balanced funds such as Vanguard Wellington and Neuberger & Berman Guardian to much more

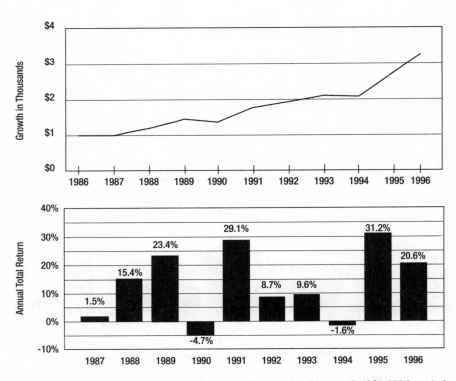

FIGURE 2.3 Growth & Income Funds. The top chart illustrates the growth of $1,000 invested in growth and income mutual funds beginning December 31, 1986. The bottom chart illustrates the annual total returns for growth and income mutual funds from 1987 through 1996. (*Source:* Micropal, Ltd., Brouwer & Janachowski, Inc.)

Fad Funds

Wall Street and its sometimes sneaky denizens have your number—at least they think they do. Whether your hot button is a social or an environmental cause, or you're a sports nut or even a couch potato, the Street's marketing mavens have a "fad fund" they hope you will buy.

Don't fall for the sales pitch. If you love sports, then go for it. Play basketball, golf, or tennis. Buy a ticket to your favorite spectator sport. If you're an environmentalist, help clean up your local wetlands, or do your part to save the whales. Put your energy into whatever works for you.

But when you want to invest, put your money in great mutual funds with broad diversification. Just say no to the sales gimmicks. We think you'll have more money and fewer headaches. It's bad enough to watch your sports heroes take a fall. How much worse would it be if your financial future took the plunge with them?

growth-oriented funds such as 20th Century Balanced Investors or Selected American Shares.

G&I funds generally invest a majority of their assets in stocks, often with a bias toward larger, more conservative companies. Many also have some of their assets in bonds. The philosophy is to earn solid returns from stocks and to use bonds to reduce the volatility of an all-stock portfolio (see Figure 2.3).

4. Growth Funds: Fasten Your Seat Belt

USES:

♦ As a source of capital appreciation for assets you can afford to invest for at least 5 years.

♦ As an investment vehicle for assets in a retirement plan, such as an IRA, a 401(k) or 403(b) plan, a SEP-IRA, or a Keogh plan.

♦ As a vehicle for a college fund for children younger than 10 years old. Because of the volatility of these funds, as your children get closer to college age, you should gradually move into more conservative funds.

ABUSES:

♦ Using Growth funds for assets you might need in 5 years or less.

Investment Objective Growth funds *go for it.* They seek big gains. Unfortunately, the term *growth* is a bit confusing, because it has two meanings in the context of investing. Growth stock is a term first used by great investors such as T. Rowe Price (founder of the fund family that bears his name) and Phillip Fisher. It refers to a company that has certain characteristics—a great business franchise or concept, high rates of growth in revenues and unit sales, strong management, and excellent finances.

When used to categorize a mutual fund, the term *growth* means something different. It is a general term that refers to a fund that seeks capital appreciation in its stock selection. Generating income is not normally an objective. Some growth funds such as Harbor Capital Appreciation specialize in "growth" stocks, but other growth funds buy anything they believe is undervalued (see Figure 2.4).

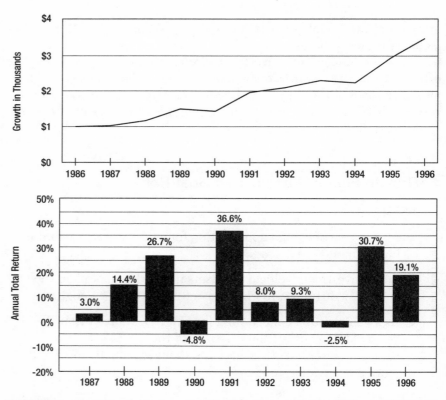

FIGURE 2.4 Growth Funds. The top chart illustrates the growth of $1,000 invested in growth mutual funds beginning December 31, 1986. The bottom chart illustrates the annual total returns for growth mutual funds from 1987 through 1996. (*Source:* Micropal, Ltd., Brouwer & Janachowski, Inc.)

If you thought Growth funds weren't quite exciting enough, then Aggressive Growth funds should fit the bill.

5. Aggressive Growth Funds: Putting the Pedal to the Metal

USES:

♦ As a source of capital appreciation for long-term assets you can afford to invest for no less than 10 years.

♦ As an investment vehicle for assets in a retirement plan, such as an IRA, a 401(k) or 403(b) plan, a SEP-IRA, or a Keogh plan, if you have 10 or more working years ahead of you.

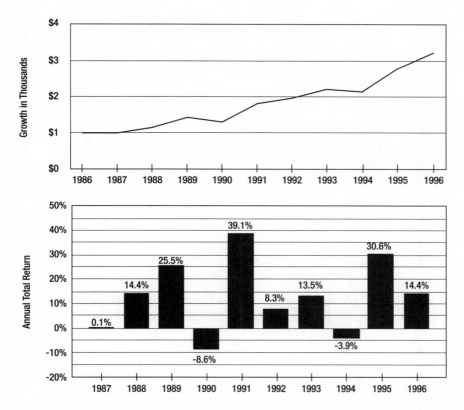

FIGURE 2.5 Aggressive Growth Funds. The top chart illustrates the growth of $1,000 invested in aggressive mutual funds beginning December 31, 1986. The bottom chart illustrates the annual total returns for aggressive growth mutual funds from 1987 through 1996. (*Source:* Micropal, Ltd., Brouwer & Janachowski, Inc.)

♦ As a vehicle for a college fund for children younger than 5 years old. Because of the volatility of these funds, as children get closer to college age, you should gradually move into more conservative funds.

ABUSES:

♦ Using Aggressive Growth funds for assets you might need to spend in 10 years or less.

Investment Objective Aggressive Growth funds do not mess around. They go flat out, and their goal is to win the race at all costs. Because of their commitment to making big gains, Aggressive Growth funds periodically crash. They can have brutal years when the overall stock market falls, but they can also tumble in more benign years just because the portfolio managers guessed wrong. The good news is that these funds can turn in really big numbers when they're hot. Like Growth funds, they invest in stocks with no concern for income. In addition, Aggressive Growth funds often invest in stocks of small, rapidly growing companies, which are generally more volatile than larger companies (see Figure 2.5).

6. International/Global Stock Funds: The World Is Your Oyster

USES:

♦ As a method of diversifying assets outside of the U.S. stock markets.

♦ As a way to gain higher returns from more rapidly growing economies overseas.

♦ As a strategy for smoothing out the overall volatility of your portfolio by adding another asset class.

ABUSES:

♦ Investing without understanding the risk and volatility of international investing.

Investment Objective This very broad category covers stock funds that invest exclusively in foreign countries (international funds) and stock funds that invest in both foreign countries and the United States (global funds). The distinction relates to geography (where the funds invest) rather than style of investment. When people speak of international funds, they usually are referring to stock funds. International stock funds come in all varieties, just as domestic stock funds do. Some specialize in large, blue chip companies. Others buy small company stocks. Some diversify around the world. Others focus on a specific region or an individual country.

Having an international stock fund in your portfolio makes sense both intellectually and instinctively. Over 60% of the world's stock market value can be found outside the United States, so it is a good idea to have some money overseas. For instance, in 1993, the S&P 500 earned a solid 10%, but Harbor International soared to over 45%. The flip side also shows up. In 1995, the S&P sizzled to a 37.5% return while Harbor International turned in a respectable, but much lower, 16.1% return (see Figure 2.6).

International funds are often more volatile than their domestic counterparts because of currency transactions and because foreign stock markets are often more volatile than the U.S. domestic stock markets. These funds use local currencies to buy stocks in foreign markets. When the stocks gain or lose, those gains or losses have to be translated back into the U.S. dollar (see Figure 2.7).

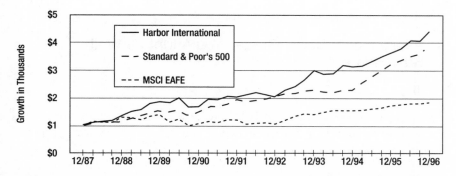

FIGURE 2.6 Harbor International Fund, Standard & Poor's 500, and MSCI EAFE. This chart illustrates $1,000 invested in the Standard & Poor's 500, $1,000 invested in the Morgan Stanley Europe, Australasia & Far East (MSCI EAFE) Index and $1,000 invested in Harbor International Fund on December 31, 1987. (*Source:* Micropal, Ltd., Brouwer & Janachowski, Inc.)

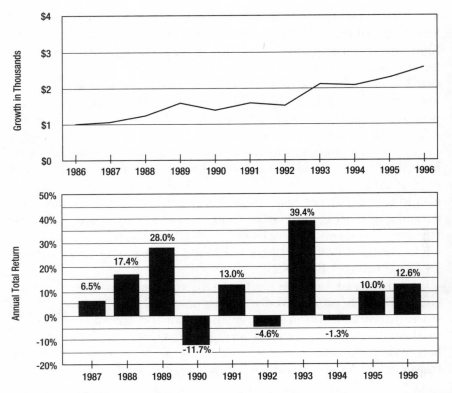

FIGURE 2.7 International Equity Funds. The top chart illustrates the growth of $1,000 invested in international equity mutual funds beginning December 31, 1986. The bottom chart illustrates the annual total returns for international equity mutual funds from 1987 through 1996. (*Source:* Micropal, Ltd., Brouwer & Janachowski, Inc.)

7. International Bond Funds: You Might as Well Stay Home

USES:

♦ As a target of opportunity when foreign interest rates are much higher than U.S. rates *and* when you believe those foreign rates are due to fall.

ABUSES:

♦ Using international bond funds as an alternative to earning low rates in bank accounts and money market funds. Investors have learned that higher yields on overseas bonds carry higher risk too.

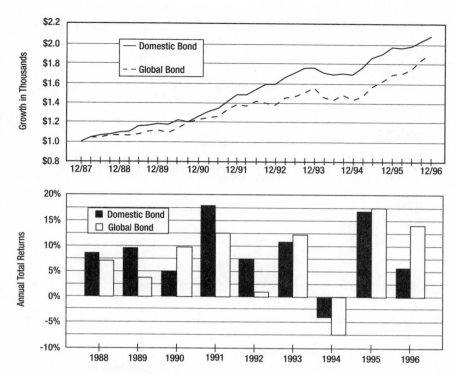

FIGURE 2.8 Domestic Bond Funds Versus Global Bond Funds. The top chart illustrates $1,000 invested in global bond funds versus $1,000 invested in domestic bond funds on December 31, 1987. The bottom chart illustrates the annual total returns for the domestic bond funds and global bond funds. (*Source:* Micropal, Ltd., Brouwer & Janachowski, Inc.)

Investment Objective   International and global bond funds have a mixed record. Much of what we said about international stock funds in the preceding section applies to international bond funds. They come in a range of types, from quite conservative to very aggressive. Some invest in conservative bonds from foreign governments; others buy risky securities from emerging markets countries.

We include this category because it exists, but we do not recommend a permanent allocation to foreign bond mutual funds. These funds usually only make sense when foreign bonds are very attractive (see Figure 2.8).

8. Specialty Funds: Not So Special After All

USES:

♦ Gold funds: a way to ease concern about the outbreak of high inflation.

- Real estate funds: a way to invest in real estate without all the hard work.

- Asset allocation funds: a way to diversify investments among stocks, bonds, and money market funds without having to decide on specific selections for the portfolio.

ABUSES:

- Putting any more than 5% of your assets in a gold fund. If you believe in gold as a hedge against inflation, you should view it as an insurance policy.

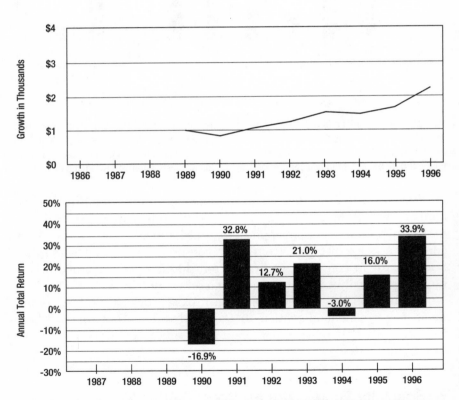

FIGURE 2.9 Real Estate Funds. The top chart illustrates the growth of $1,000 invested in real estate mutual funds beginning December 31, 1989. The bottom chart illustrates the annual total returns for real estate mutual funds from 1990 through 1996. (*Source:* Micropal, Ltd., Brouwer & Janachowski, Inc.)

♦ Putting a large portion of your assets in a fund that allocates your assets for you. We believe that you should make the asset allocation decision for your money. We will cover this in more detail later on.

Investment Objective   This is a catch-all category for a very diverse group of funds. Precious metals, real estate, social/environmental, asset allocation, life cycle, fund of funds, and other categories are included. Each type of fund appeals to a different type of investor (see Figures 2.9, 2.10, and 2.11).

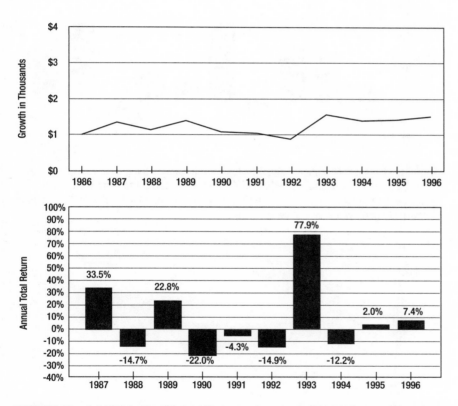

FIGURE 2.10   Gold Funds. The top chart illustrates the growth of $1,000 invested in gold mutual funds beginning December 31, 1986. The bottom chart illustrates the annual total returns for gold mutual funds from 1987 through 1996. (*Source:* Micropal, Ltd.)

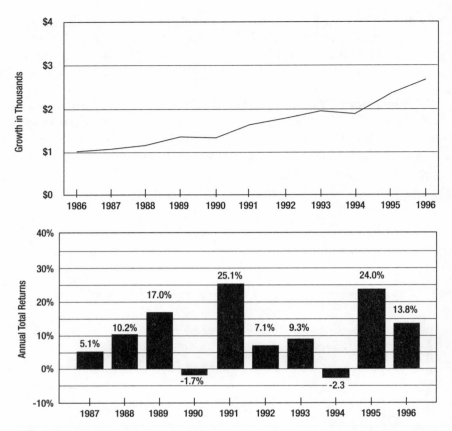

FIGURE 2.11 Asset Allocation Funds. The top chart illustrates the growth of $1,000 invested in asset allocation mutual funds beginning December 31, 1986. The bottom chart illustrates the annual total returns for asset allocation mutual funds from 1987 through 1996. (*Source:* Micropal, Ltd., Brouwer & Janachowski, Inc.)

Are Your Funds Clean?

Environmental funds are staging a bit of a comeback. In addition to the normal investment research, these funds add an extra element—environmental screening. And they come in two types:

1. "Clean" funds. These funds look for stocks with upside potential, provided the company also has a good record of dealing with the environment. The stocks may be in almost any industry.

2. "Pollution control" funds. These funds simply buy stocks in companies whose business is in some way related to the environment—waste management, garbage dumps, pollution control.

If you wish to invest in "clean" companies, make sure you pick one of the "clean" funds. But there is a catch. Neither of the two types of environmental funds has done very well. One problem is that the focus of both types tends to be quite narrow, and narrow specialization almost always hurts performance in the long run. Narrowly focused funds often have a couple of years of stellar performance followed by several years of abysmal numbers. One alternative to these types of funds is to invest in normal diversified funds and donate a portion of your gains to your favorite environmental cause (see figure below).

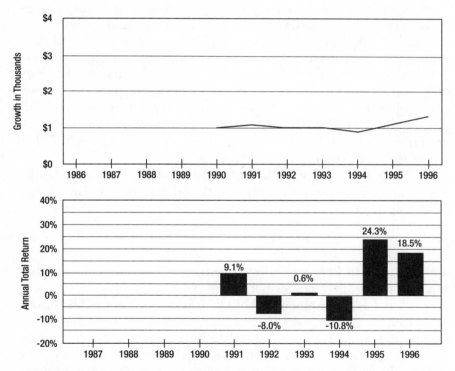

Environmental Funds   The top chart illustrates the growth of $1,000 invested in environmental mutual funds beginning December 31, 1990. The bottom chart illustrates the annual total returns for environmental mutual funds from 1991 through 1996. (*Source:* Micropal, Ltd., Brouwer & Janachowski, Inc.)

A Few Knocks Against Mutual Funds

We would be remiss if we did not point out some disadvantages to using mutual funds. Even though we believe mutual funds are the best investment vehicle for most investors, we know they are not perfect.

In our opinion, one of the disadvantages to using mutual funds is in the area of income taxes. If you own individual stocks, you can control the timing of any sales of shares and the realization of capital gains or losses. With mutual funds, the fund manager decides when to buy or sell individual securities, so you cannot directly control the tax consequences of portfolio transactions within a given tax year. By law, mutual funds must distribute all of the income they receive and all of the capital gains realized during the year.

A negative feature for some bond investors is the fact that mutual funds do not have a specific maturity date. If you buy a 10-year bond, you know that—barring default—you will get your money back in 10 years. An intermediate-term bond fund may own similar bonds, but because the fund owns a portfolio of bonds with varying maturity dates, there is never a specific date of maturity for the fund as a whole.

Another disadvantage is in the area of money flowing in and flowing out. You have no control over other investors. When a fund you own gets hot, money can flow in so fast that the portfolio manager has trouble investing it. This is more of a factor for small company stock funds, which often buy shares in companies whose stock does not trade very much on a given day. During a stock market downturn, panicky investors could dump the fund, forcing the portfolio manager to sell good stocks in order to fund those redemptions.

We believe the benefits far outweigh these disadvantages, but we want you to be aware of the entire picture before you buy any mutual fund shares.

In the News Today, it is hard to avoid seeing or hearing information about mutual funds. It is carried in newspapers, magazines, and junk mail; on television and radio; and even on billboards. If you go to your public library (something we recommend highly), you will most likely see *Morningstar* and other resources (see Part Two, *The Toolbox,* for a more complete listing of mutual fund resources). Among mutual fund investors, the most popular resources are generally local newspapers, followed by national financial magazines. We read the following publications regularly and, in our opinion, they do a good job of providing mutual fund and investment information:

- *The Wall Street Journal*
- *The New York Times*
- *Money*
- *Forbes*
- *Business Week*
- *Newsweek*
- *Fortune*
- *Kiplinger's Personal Finance Magazine*
- *Barron's*
- *Investor's Business Daily*
- *USA Today*
- *Smart Money*
- *U.S. News & World Report*
- *Worth*
- *The San Francisco Chronicle*
- *The San Jose Mercury News*
- *The Los Angeles Times*

The resource we recommend most for mutual fund investors is *Morningstar Mutual Funds* and *Morningstar Principia.* For a complete description of Morningstar resources and how to use them, see Part Two, *The Toolbox.*

Congratulations—You just made it through a tough chapter that is full of facts and figures. You need this information, but the going was a little heavy at times. In Chapter 3, we're going to change the pace a bit. We'll talk about what it takes to make a mutual fund a top performer.

INTERVIEW

"Investing Begins with a Great Education"

An Interview with *John C. "Jack" Bogle*

If there is one individual who is most closely associated with the rise of no-load mutual funds, it is Jack Bogle. As chairman and founder of The Vanguard Group, he has been at the helm of one of the industry's most dynamic success stories. Vanguard is the second largest fund group in the world, and it is the largest exclusively no-load group.

Jack has been obsessed with mutual funds since his college days. In fact, way back in 1951, he wrote his senior thesis at Princeton on the benefits of mutual fund investing. In one of the world's greatest turnarounds, he founded Vanguard in 1974, shortly after being fired by Wellington Management Company. His decision to create Vanguard as a shareholder-owned company has had enormous implications not only for Vanguard investors, but also for the industry as a whole, because Vanguard has become the industry's low-cost provider of mutual fund services and, in many ways, its conscience. In addition, by changing Vanguard from a load fund group to a no-load in 1977, Bogle provided tremendous momentum for the movement away from load funds.

Jack also has a well-earned reputation as an original thinker on investment themes. He has written many articles for professional journals, and his recent book, *Bogle on Mutual Funds: New Perspectives for the Intelligent Investor* (Irwin), has been a best-seller since it came out in 1993.

Jack has the kind of useful obsession that has driven innovators since time began. He sees things a certain way, and he will move heaven and earth to get the world to swing around to his point of view. Why? Because it's the right point of view, of course.

Yet, even though he is very determined, he is also intellectually rigorous. If you can make an excellent argument, he will consider it thoughtfully, and, if you're right, he will change his opinion. But make sure you have thought your opinion through very carefully before you open your mouth, because Jack does not suffer fools gladly.

Alongside his many accomplishments, one of the things that has always struck us about Jack Bogle is that he is—plain and simple—a great guy and a quintessential American success story. This "boy next door" has made good. He is warm and funny, impressively well-informed, and interested in everyone and everything. He is not shy, particularly when he gets onto his favorite topic—mutual funds; but then why should he be? An intellectual, a man of action, and a person who has great concern and compassion for people, Jack Bogle is the guy we call Mr. Mutual Fund.

Mutual Fund Mastery: Why do you think mutual funds have had such explosive growth in the past 10 years?

Jack Bogle: The awareness and understanding of mutual funds grew because they offer fundamentally sound principles such as diversification and professional management. Even in an index fund, there has to be a competent professional manager who is sorting things out and organizing and trying to meet the fund's objectives. Another factor favoring mutual funds is simple convenience. It is easier to buy and use mutual funds than just about any other financial instrument there is. In the past 10 years, the education on those points and the knowledge of the fund industry have grown by quantum leaps. You can talk about mutual funds to many, many people today who, 10 years ago, wouldn't have known anything about them.

MFM: What about retirement investing, starting with IRAs in the 1980s and then with 401(k) plans in the 1990s?

JB: A huge force for mutual fund growth has been tax-advantaged investing such as IRAs, 401(k) plans, 403(b) plans, and self-employment plans such as Keoghs. The mutual fund happens to be a perfect solution to investing through those kinds of plans, so a lot of what happens in the next 10 years will first depend on the extent to which the regular investor in these tax-advantaged plans stays the course.

MFM: How will investors react to bear markets?

JB: My own view is that people will react quite badly to bear markets. I don't think this industry has done a very good job of informing investors about risk. When the market goes up for 15 years in a row, you can talk about risk a lot, but risk is something you almost have to experience to recognize. Warnings, while that's all we can do, are not enough.

MFM: Do you agree or disagree with the statement, "Mutual funds are the single best investment vehicle for most investors"?

JB: Of course they are. I can't think of a statement you could make that is more valid.

MFM: Are you invested in mutual funds?

JB: That's all I'm invested in.

MFM: Which ones do you use?

JB: I must say that my circumstances are different from someone else's. Even though I'm not going to retire, I'm still getting closer to the end of the football game. When I started investing in 1951, I used only Wellington Fund. That was the basis of my early investment program. When we brought Windsor Fund out in 1958, there was a great argument about whether the successful mutual fund company would have one fund or two. We'd had only one fund—Wellington, a balanced fund—from 1929 through 1958, and we thought it was time to bring out a fund that would be all equities. I immediately added Windsor.

MFM: When did Vanguard actually begin operations?

JB: We incorporated in 1974 and started operations on May 1, 1975. It seemed a little foolish to be the low-cost provider on the fee, or fund expenses, side, and to charge big fat commissions. So, we went no-load in 1977.

MFM: You and your small original staff had all come out of Wellington Management Company, right?

JB: Yes. Actually, I was fired by Wellington. If I hadn't gotten fired, Vanguard wouldn't have happened.

MFM: So, your getting fired was the best thing that ever happened to the industry.

JB: No, our competitors probably think that it is the worst thing that ever happened to the industry. But I think it is the best thing that happened to the shareholder.

MFM: Why did you get fired?

JB: Oh, I guess I was then what I am today: opinionated, self-confident, determined to do things my way—not necessarily admirable characteristics, but, I would say, necessary characteristics for an innovator.

MFM: There is a saying that reasonable people adapt themselves to the rules of society and try to live within them. The unreasonable person tries to adapt society to fit his or her own rules, and, therefore, all progress depends on the unreasonable person.

JB: I think that that is fair. I'm not sure that you could find one of our competitors that would call our unique "at-cost" structure *progress*, but I think you could find one heck of a lot of shareholders, in and out of Vanguard, who would.

MFM: In a roundabout way, your story must be encouraging to people who've recently lost their jobs. If someone like you prospered after having been fired, then the loss of a job may not be the end of the world. That person may be on the verge of a whole new opportunity, just like you were in 1975.

JB: Whatever it was and however it happened, I don't think anybody would disagree that we made the most of it, starting from picking the name.

MFM: It's a great name. At first, Vanguard was a load fund group. A couple of years later, you changed that, but it was not a sure thing, was it?

JB: We made the vote to go no-load by a very narrow margin. It was a tight vote by our board of directors: 8 to 5 in favor.

MFM: You were on the majority side and probably brought some people with you, and that was the start of no-load history for Vanguard.

JB: And it was, in a sense, a watershed event for no-load funds in general, because Vanguard immediately became the second largest no-load company (behind T. Rowe Price). I like to think that we contributed a lot to the momentum for no-load acceptance. Some say that we just rode the wave, but I think that we helped create the wave.

MFM: Another area you pioneered was index funds.

JB: Let me say on the subject of index funds, one of America's best kept secrets, that I'm a big booster.

MFM: Since you have the biggest index operation and the lowest-cost funds, somehow we're not surprised that you're a booster. Do you use index funds for personal investing?

JB: Earlier, I mentioned that no one should just do what I do, because my circumstances might be very different. I am the founder of approximately 85% of the funds we have, and, since I write every shareholders' letter, I own shares of every fund we have. As I said, the emphasis began with Wellington and Windsor. Then I picked up the index funds—initially, just the Vanguard Index Trust 500, the first index mutual fund and Vanguard's first independent fund, which we began in 1976. I put some money in PRIMECAP Fund when it began, and that has become a significant investment. Now, as I grow older, I am using more and more of what I call *defined asset class* mutual funds,

such as our short-term and intermediate-term municipal bond funds.

MFM: If you had to put all of your money in one single fund and leave it there for at least 5 years, which one would it be?

JB: For someone in my age and circumstances, I wouldn't wait one second in making a pick. What I would pick—and it happens to be a Vanguard fund—is the Vanguard Tax-Managed Fund—Balanced Portfolio. First, it is 50% invested in intermediate-term municipal bonds, which means you are going to improve on short-term bond returns, under most circumstances, but have a reduced exposure to the fluctuations you would experience in long-term bond funds. The other 50% of it is a stock index fund, which is modeled on the Russell 1000 Index, but with a growth bias. It has a very low dividend yield because of the growth bias—and a pretty good interest yield, which is all tax-free. It really fits me in a very, very precise way that directly meets my needs. When you come right down to it, I really wouldn't need anything else. I could put in every penny I had (leaving out my retirement plans, because they are not impacted by taxes) in that one fund and it would not be ridiculous.

MFM: Let's say you're talking to someone who was just entering the job market, starting to save a little bit of money and invest. What advice would you give?

JB: Well, what I'd start with is 100% equities. I'm assuming that he or she is starting to invest at the rate of $100 a month, and if the market goes down 50% at the start, that's still a long way from bankruptcy. It's much easier when you've got all the time in the world—a working lifetime in front of you—and a modest amount of money to invest as you grow and learn what you're doing.

MFM: What about someone who is investing for a child's education fund?

JB: Well, that's very much the same kind of thing. If the child has just been born, I would certainly start off investing 100% in equities. We all know roughly what an education is going to cost 20 years from now, and I think that the only way of keeping up with or reaching that goal is with stock funds. Now, if the child has 10 years before college, I'd say 50% stock funds, 50% intermediate-term bond funds.

MFM: Why the combination of stock funds and bond funds?

JB: There is one simple, very simple answer—balance. In fact, the wonderful Vanguard Balanced Index Fund is grossly underused by investors. And by Balanced, I do not mean an asset allocation fund that can go from cattle futures to cash overnight, but one that holds relatively stable proportions of stocks and bonds.

MFM: You would not be referring to Fidelity Asset Manager Fund, would you?

JB: I suppose I had it in mind, but there are many other "market timing" funds that follow similar strategies. I don't think that most investors should fuss with them.

MFM: With all the good and sometimes great mutual funds, why do so many investors still get poor returns?

JB: About half of your investment return over time is determined by the portfolio you have selected. The other half is determined by your character and by the decisions you make. It's not just numbers and classes of financial assets, but who you are. The fact is, I could identify people who should never own anything but a bank certificate of deposit or a U.S. Treasury money market fund. Some people can't stomach short-term risk. And in volatile financial markets, fear and greed usually dictate counterproductive decisions.

MFM: How should you invest?

JB: I think investing begins with a process of great education, much more than we have today. Forewarned is forearmed. Being strongly aware that the stock market goes down as well as up. I fear that there are many investors who would regard a 20% stock market decline as inconceivable, even though it can and does happen. If you can get them to acknowledge the downside ahead of time, I think you can get them to act in a more intelligent manner when it happens.

MFM: How can you help educate investors?

JB: It is not easy, even though we try very hard. I do not think that most mutual fund companies do enough to educate their shareholders. There is also a problem because, since 1982, we have had two of the greatest bull markets in history, one in stocks and one in bonds. So, mutual fund companies and investors should not confuse genius with the luck of being in bull markets. And there is the matter of perception. After a great year like 1995, what can you say? This is not going to happen again in my lifetime? It probably won't, but who knows?

MFM: What can you learn from a year like 1995?

JB: You want to be able to learn from a bull market just as well as you learn from a bear market, and about one in every thousand investors does.

MFM: So, what should we learn from this bull market?

JB: Enjoy the ride. But don't expect it to go on forever. Despite evidence to the contrary, the law of gravity has not been repealed. Or, to put it in more conversational terms, what goes up must go down, and what goes down must go up.

MFM: When investors think of Vanguard, they first think of bond funds, then money market funds and index funds. Not stock funds. Why is that, and are you doing something about it?

JB: In the first place, I think it is a fair statement of the public perception. But I don't agree with it.

MFM: You have good, solid funds, but you don't have the kind of funds that catch the public attention—the kind of funds that have chart-busting performance.

JB: Yes, that is correct.

MFM: There is Windsor because of its track record and its longevity, and, of course, PRIMECAP, but Windsor is closed to new investors. You don't really have the most outstanding stock funds.

JB: Well, if you define them as those with the highest returns and the highest risks, that's right. I think it is largely because most of our funds are in the more conservative groups that are not attention-getting. But if you look at our stock funds, you will see that they compare very favorably to similar funds. Even in these periods that are regarded as somewhat difficult for us, we are in the top quartile, on average. Or, looking at it another way, with 100% being the best, we are in the 75% range, on average, outpacing three quarters of the other funds in each category over most recent periods. I think that's very good. And when you add the last year or so, we look quite outstanding. For example, Wellington Fund was ninth out of 306 balanced funds for the past 3 years.

MFM: Are the new Vanguard Horizon funds an effort to create funds that are more aggressive, more high-flying?

JB: Our purpose in forming them is for people who want a much more aggressive fund, on the theory that, in the long run, it will pay off. We want to give them an opportunity to do it. I hope these funds do not grow too quickly. That's why we have engaged in very little marketing of them. We have also done one of the great no-no's of this business: If you want to be successful in the marketplace, don't charge an exit fee. But we decided anyway to have a redemption fee. You have to pay 1% of your market value if you sell your shares within the first 5 years. It goes directly to the other shareholders of the fund.

MFM: I'm assuming your purpose for the redemption fee is to keep out short-term investors and market timers?

JB: Yes. A lot of people, even my own staff, said, "5 years is too long." But we went ahead

after some heated internal discussions. The point of the Horizon Funds for Vanguard is that we want to be competitive pretty much across the board in this business, not with 27 growth and aggressive growth funds such as one of our competitors has, but a half dozen or so. And we think it is in our interest if we can do it right and get the right portfolio managers. Only time will tell how good a job we did. We have Horizon Fund Global Asset Allocation Portfolio because we think that, in Michael Duffy and Strategic Investment Management, we've found one of the really good investment managers in that type of high-risk investing. We think that if anybody can do global asset allocation successfully, they can.

MFM: Of the Horizon funds, it seems the Capital Opportunity Portfolio is the wildest and the most uncharacteristic Vanguard fund.

JB: Capital Opportunity is certainly the riskiest of the group. It is run by Frank Husic, a San Francisco investment adviser. We have used him successfully in managing about 10% of the Morgan Growth Fund. We knew he was aggressive, we knew he was risk-oriented. When it comes to Capital Opportunity, it is very aggressive, almost unlimited in its investment charter. The fund can't do exotic derivatives and that kind of thing, but it can sell short up to 10% of the fund's assets. Short selling is not a risky behavior on the face of it—anymore than owning a derivative is risky on the face of it—but it involves the kinds of risks that our people are not accustomed to taking. So, the Horizon funds are really a statement that we are interested in allowing our shareholders to have an opportunity to be more aggressive, if that is what they want.

MFM: Plus, you have a big cost advantage with this fund over most aggressive growth funds.

JB: The Horizon funds will have annual expense ratios that are at least 1% less than other aggressive growth and global funds, and, of course, have no sales loads. These are important, if not critical, cost advantages to the investor.

MFM: What's coming up for Vanguard?

JB: We are trying to be represented in each investment objective category that makes sense. Let's call it, for the purposes of simplification, each Morningstar fund category. We haven't had a fund in global asset allocation, and we think it is a legitimate category, so we want to be represented there. But we are not going to have a second global asset allocation fund, and we are also, very importantly in terms of our firm's philosophy, skeptical of many of the new categories that get created in this lunatic business.

MFM: All the so-called new products?

JB: We don't allow the use of the word "product" in the office because a mutual fund is not a product. Beer, toothpaste, dog food, yes. But not mutual funds. When I see it called a new product, I'm even more apprehensive, and when I see it called a "hot new product," I just about faint. We don't want hot new products.

MFM: So it's a service rather than a product.

JB: Yes, a service, or a mutual fund, or an investment portfolio, or a trust account. When I read about "packaged products," it almost makes me actively ill.

MFM: Don't even say that, Jack. We don't want you ill, whether it's active or not. Let's switch gears a bit. How do you find new mutual fund portfolio managers?

JB: First, we look at the people. Are they people we want to be in business with? We look at character, integrity, and experience—things like that. Then we look at their firm's investment philosophy, which is a very important thing, a critical thing in our hiring. Then, what we like to do is really carefully evaluate their portfolio to see if it is consistent with their stated philosophy. And finally, we look at their performance. People don't believe this, but it's true. We look at that last. No matter who the people are, they are going to have years

of good performance and years of bad performance, but what we want to do is see if their performance is consistent with their philosophy and their portfolios. And I have to say quickly, lest that looks too heroic a statement, once they have been retained, we look at performance first. They are measured against some mutually agreed-upon set of objectives that we can track pretty easily. We use three: (1) an appropriate unmanaged market index; (2) the average fund in its objective group; and (3) a 6-fund competitive group, a peer group, 6 funds that we think are most similar to the fund involved.

MFM: And these would be funds across all mutual fund families?

JB: Well, we place a heavy emphasis on no-load funds, just because that is the marketplace. We'll pick the S&P 500 as the market index, and growth and income funds as the broad objective group for, say, Windsor Fund. Then, we will have no hesitancy in saying "Here's what we intend to do in terms of performance." And the shareholder gets it candidly, and doesn't have to worry about being misled. Parenthetically, he's going to know what is happening anyway. We expect our advisers to outperform the competition in a fair battle.

MFM: In other words, the portfolio manager has to beat his or her peers before costs are factored in. Just because Vanguard has a cost advantage, it does not mean the manager did a great job.

JB: Exactly.

MFM: Let's say that you have a portfolio manager that you selected, who is just not living up to your expectations. How long do you wait before you pull the plug?

JB: Well, there is not really a firm rule on that, but you could say being in the bottom quartile of an objective group, with any frequency, over a period of 3 years, would be a very big negative. Being in the bottom half for 5 years, would be something that would cause considerable examination. Five years is somewhat arbitrary, but that kind of a time frame is about right.

MFM: Your book, *Bogle on Mutual Funds* (Irwin), was a big, big seller for a mutual fund book, probably the biggest. How many copies have sold so far?

JB: Around 250,000.

MFM: In the book, you talked about mutual fund shareholders becoming more active and more skeptical. Are you saying that until shareholders speak out, many of the mutual fund industry's problems won't be addressed?

JB: I am saying exactly that. If shareholders don't demand candor in annual reports, for example, they are not going to get it. Ultimately, shareholders should sell shares and, in effect, vote with their feet when it comes to subpar performance or fee increases, which are still quite frequent in this business.

MFM: And even as assets have grown significantly, expense ratios have, in some cases, gone up.

JB: Not at Vanguard. In 1996, we announced 18 fund advisory fee reductions. In 1993, we had 16 fund fee reductions. We have reduced fees because we believe the shareholders who create all of these economies of scale deserve to participate in them.

MFM: Are you saying that most funds don't have an incentive to address costs and fees because no one has really forced them to? As we know, industries very seldom get competitive out of goodwill. They get competitive only

when they have to. Whether it is cars, steel, anything else. And it may be that, in the next 10 years, fees become much more of an issue.

JB: Right. One important factor we have not discussed is the independent directors or trustees. Each fund has them, but they have become a sort of lost breed. I think directors have to be much tougher in their evaluation of fees because they have an obligation to protect the shareholders, a huge obligation. I would even say a legal obligation to put the shareholders' interests first—ahead of the interests of the fund's adviser—and they simply are not doing it.

MFM: Why aren't the independent directors doing it? Why aren't they more on the side of the shareholders?

JB: I think it's inertia and the selection process. They don't know where to start; that's where the inertia is, and that's where I think even the Securities and Exchange Commission has been much too generous in its appraisal of directors, infinitely too generous. A big part of the problem lies in the view a director takes toward this responsibility. Is he or she really there to put the shareholders first or there as a crony of the fund's investment adviser? Directors should be asking tough questions. Does a $50 billion fund complex really need another company to run it? Surely, $50 billion ought to be able to get its own advisers, its own administrators, its own distributors, and save the shareholders a fortune. The structure of the industry is sort of like the appendix, a vestige of a past so long forgotten, that we don't know how it got there in the first place.

CHAPTER 3

We're Looking for a Few Good Funds

It is very easy to look at a financial publication and pick out winning mutual funds of the past. Just tally up the returns and pick the ones that outperformed all others in their category. The hard part comes when you look ahead. Even though the future seems misty and uncertain and the past is comfortingly clear, you have to select mutual funds for the future, not the past.

For example, if you like to buy a mutual fund and hold on to it for many years, you may be comfortable with a high flier that occasionally takes a big fall. Since you are taking a very long-term outlook, the fact that the fund takes a hit one year may not bother you at all provided it generally has excellent returns. In fact, if you have faith in the portfolio manager, you may be thrilled to buy the fund precisely because it has just gone through a dry spell.

To get an idea of what we mean, look at CGM Capital Development Fund. The fund has a remarkable record dating back to 1977 when Ken Heebner began running it. The fund is closed to new investors so we include it by way of example only. As the chart below shows, Heebner's long-term track record has been nothing short of spectacular. For the past 20 years ending April 1997, CGM Capital's average annual total return was nearly 22% versus 15.4% for the Standard & Poor's 500. Long-term investors who could tolerate the volatility were well rewarded.

In a volatile fund such as CGM Capital, investors can have their patience tested. For example, during the 3 years from October 1987 through September 1990 the fund lost 18.9% while the S&P 500 earned a positive 5.8%. Due to the emphasis on quarterly comparisons versus the S&P 500, many investors have a hard time staying with an underperforming fund for that long. By the end of 1990, assets in CGM Capital had dropped to $140 million. Those who stayed with the fund looked pretty smart the next year as Heebner and the fund turned in a gain of nearly 100% in 1991 (see Figure 3.1).

The Winners of the Past

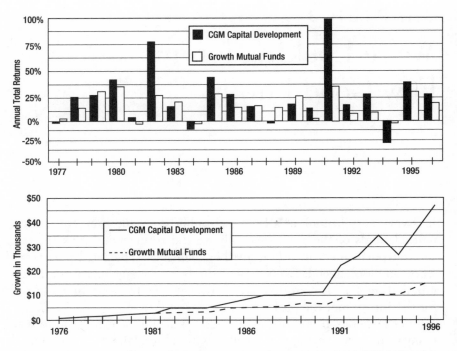

FIGURE 3.1 CGM Capital Development Versus Growth Mutual Funds. The top chart illustrates the annual total returns for CGM Capital Development Fund versus the Micropal Growth Mutual Fund Index. Notice the dramatically higher volatility of annual returns for the CGM fund versus the growth index. The short-term volatility of the CGM fund might take your breath away, but over longer time periods, the fund has really shone (see bottom chart). The bottom chart illustrates the growth of $1,000 invested in CGM Capital Development Fund and $1,000 invested in the Micropal Growth Mutual Fund Index on December 31, 1976. Higher short-term volatility makes the CGM fund a bit racey for the timid (see the chart at the top of the page) but has rewarded patient long-term investors. (*Source:* Micropal, Ltd., Brouwer & Janachowski, Inc.)

Before we go further, we want to let you know what we mean by good mutual funds. The assumptions, values, principles, and prejudices we bring to the table will influence our selection of funds. To be on our list of good funds, a mutual fund must have 5 essential qualities:

1. A record of adding value over an appropriate index for at least 5 years.
2. An understandable and disciplined investment strategy.
3. An understandable and disciplined strategy for managing risk.
4. Stable portfolio management.
5. A no-load cost structure (no sales charge) and a competitive expense ratio.

1. A Record of Adding Value over an Appropriate Index for at Least 5 Years

To be interesting to us, an actively-managed mutual fund has to out-perform an appropriate index over the long haul. One misconception about fund performance is that good funds should beat their index every year. That is clearly not the case. As we illustrated with Ken Heebner's CGM Capital Development Fund, even good funds suffer through periods of underperformance, lasting as long as 3 years. Yet, they still came through with superior results, **provided investors stayed with them**. We know first-hand how difficult it is to stay with a fund that is lagging, but if you truly believe you picked an excellent mutual fund and portfolio manager, then you should stay with the fund as long as nothing fundamental changes.

Looking at the Trees, Not the Forest

We recently had a meeting with the investment committee for one of our firm's pension plan clients. The last time we had met (3 months earlier), all of their mutual funds were beating their representative index. This time, several had underperformed for the quarter because stocks of very large companies were soaring while everything else stalled. This time, committee members expressed a lot of concern and asked what should be done? Our reply: Nothing. Last quarter, the funds outperformed. This time they lagged. Variable short-term performance is simply a normal function of the financial markets. We showed them that their portfolio's long-term performance was significantly ahead of their benchmark index. Then we pointed out that it is dangerous to look at short-term results too much because you might start making frequent and ill-advised changes.

Having said all this, we know that the question will pop up again, not only with that committee, but with investors everywhere because they look at investment returns in much the same way they review bank balances or even gas gauges. What do these things have in common? Bank balances and gas gauges only become an issue when they are low. In other words, if you have plenty of money in the bank or lots of gas in the tank, you don't give it a thought. It's only when the bank balance is low or the gas gauge is on empty, that you give it much thought. Unfortunately, investors often view short-term performance as something to be looked into *only* when it falls short of expectations, that is, when it underperforms versus an index.

The net result is that investors put all their energy into tracking short-term performance. In order to become a better investor, we believe you must ignore most of the short-term, day-to-day market movements. Instead, spend your time thinking about long-term results and the big picture. There is an old saying, "They cannot see the forest for the trees." Many investors lose sight of the big picture (the forest) because they spend all their time fretting about what might happen tomorrow (the trees).

Short-term performance, good or bad, is largely meaningless. If you grasp that single essential fact, you will immediately become a better investor. Short-term results only mean something in a context. For example, if growth funds are booming and your growth funds are falling behind, then you may have reason for concern. But if all growth funds are lagging the S&P 500 because only cyclical stocks are hot, there is nothing to be concerned about.

2. An Understandable and Disciplined Investment Strategy

To know if a fund suits your investment objectives, you have to understand what it does. This does not mean you have to understand precisely why the fund bought a particular stock or bond, but you must have a solid understanding of how the portfolio manager invests.

For example, the large portfolio management team led by Foster Friess at Brandywine Fund has an excellent long-term record of buying growth stocks. Their investment approach is such that the team members do not spend much time worrying about the economy. Nor do they worry about interest rates. They just look for great stocks to buy. And they usually have a very large proportion of the portfolio in fast-growing technology stocks. In a given year, this means the fund will be relatively volatile because growth stocks tend to bounce around a lot.

Nonetheless, performance has been both consistent and superb (from its inception in 1986 through April, 1997, Brandywine returned over 18.3%, beating the S&P 500 by nearly 2.3% per year). Another aspect of the fund's investment style is rapid portfolio turnover. The folks at Brandywine continually review current holdings and compare them to prospective stock purchases. If the new ideas have a more compelling investment story, the Brandywine team sells out the old and buys in the new. This rapid buying and selling gives the fund a high rate of portfolio turnover. Higher turnover results in higher expenses and can also mean higher taxes (see "Mutual Funds, Income Taxes and You" in Part Two: The Toolbox).

One good way to get to know a portfolio manager's style is to read as much as you can about the fund. You can call the mutual fund family and ask for all the material they have on the fund, including articles about the portfolio manager. See if you can get annual reports from prior years to develop an understanding of how the fund works in different market environments. Also, dig up articles about the fund and the portfolio manager at your public library or through an online service such as Dow Jones, America OnLine, or CompuServe.

You can also read all the Morningstar pages going back to when they began covering the fund, that is, if Morningstar has coverage on it. And certainly the prospectus will give you some information too although after reading it, you may have doubts about your command of English.

As you can guess by now, we like to own funds whose approach we understand. Also, we like funds that stick to what they know best. If you have determined what type of approach you want to take, it is critical that you understand which funds fit your strategy and leave all others aside. Funds that get our vote are those that have an understandable strategy that is carried out in a consistent and disciplined manner.

3. An Understandable and Disciplined Strategy for Managing Risk

We like mutual funds that have a well thought-out and disciplined approach to managing risk. Let's figure out what risk is before we look at how funds can manage it. Investors face three types of risk—default risk, sector risk, and market risk. As an investor in mutual funds, you generally don't have to worry about the first two types of risk—unless you are investing in a nondiversified mutual fund such as a sector fund—because most mutual funds are so well diversified. The three major types of investment risk are:

♦ **Default risk.** If you put all your money in a stock or bond of a single company, you stand to take a big hit if that company folds. And companies both large and small can go under. That is why diversification in a mutual fund is so critical.

♦ **Sector risk.** If you put all your money in one narrow sector of the stock market (such as electric utility stocks or semiconductor stocks) or the real estate market or any other kind of market, you are subject to sector risk. Again, it pays to diversify broadly across many different sectors of whatever market you are in— and most mutual funds accomplish this goal.

- ♦ **Market risk.** Unfortunately, you can't get rid of market risk by diversifying. Whether you own 10 stocks or 100 stocks, you still have all the risks of being in the stock market. If you own stocks or stock mutual funds, they will generally fluctuate in relationship to the stock market. Maybe a bit more or less, but they will still move somewhat in line with the overall stock market. On the plus side, though, by diversifying your portfolio broadly (U.S. stocks, international stocks, small stocks, large stocks, value stocks, growth stocks, etc.), you may be able to smooth out some of the volatility of market risk—all sectors don't usually move in the same direction at the same time (we will go into this in more detail in Chapter 6). Diversification can be comforting in a theoretical sense, but when the stock market tumbles, your stock funds will usually fall right along with everything else. For example, during the stock market crash in 1987, most stock markets around the world fell sharply and diversification really didn't help in the short run. During severe bear markets, there is no escaping market risk.

There is one final caveat about assessing a fund's market risk potential. If a fund has a relatively short track record and has not gone through a bear market (most funds as of this writing are relatively new and haven't faced a real down market), then assessing market risk can be rather difficult. For example, an aggressive growth fund may have done extremely well, but if the period in question was generally positive for stocks, you may not be getting a clear picture of the volatility or turbulence you may encounter with that fund when stocks fall.

Here's a cautionary tale about investors who were lulled into complacency by a bond fund that did too well—for a while.

Bond Funds—Shopping for Yield Can Be Dangerous

The Piper Jaffray Institutional Government Income Portfolio was a top-rated short-term government bond fund that had received Morningstar's coveted 5 Star rating. During its glory years, it averaged 14.7% versus 11.0% for the Lehman Brothers Government Bond Index. That kind of return for a short-term government bond sounded too good to be true—and it was. In 1994, the fund lost 28.3% compared to a loss of 3.4% for the index. This huge loss stunned investors who reacted angrily and complained that they had not been informed of the risks. Many sued the firm. This sad tale illuminates an aspect of investing that many bond fund investors overlook—it's called RISK.

In the absence of a track record during a prolonged down market, you may not be able to get a hard number on a specific fund's risk. However, we can say this as a rule of thumb: If you are analyzing a stock fund or a bond fund, you should assume that its risk level has a strong relationship to the total returns the fund has generated. It is also reasonable to assume that a stock fund that went up by 43% in a given year has the potential to fall that much in a severe stock market decline. Similarly, if a bond fund had capital appreciation of 14% one year (not including the interest income), you can assume that fund could also depreciate by that much.

4. Stable Portfolio Management

This is relatively easy to determine. Just call the fund up and ask how long the portfolio manager has been there. Or, you can look it up in Morningstar. But, if a fund has multiple managers, Morningstar uses a weighted average tenure that may understate the original portfolio manager's tenure at the fund.

Whether it is a fast-track growth fund or an S&P 500 index fund, the principle is the same—both types of funds need management that can deliver superior results in line with the fund's objectives. With many actively managed funds, the portfolio manager is so critical that a management changeover throws significant doubt on the continued validity of the fund's track record. Some funds are managed by teams or have a style that is readily transferable, but in many cases, if the portfolio manager moves on, we do, too.

Magellan's Management Turnover Troubles

In July 1992, Jeff Vinik took over the management of Fidelity Magellan Fund from Morris Smith, who had succeeded Peter Lynch. Magellan's phenomenal track record was built by Lynch (and Smith) using a strategy of being as fully invested as possible. This meant the fund took its lumps in down markets, but it also meant that it was ready to go when the stock market soared. When Jeff Vinik took over, he said he was making changes and that he would let cash build up if he thought the stock market was about to tumble.

On May 23, 1996, Jeff Vinik announced his departure. Fidelity chose Robert Stansky as the next victim, that is, portfolio manager, of the world's biggest fund. Vinik had taken Magellan away from its classic style and had made the decision to sell some stocks and buy bonds. The new strategy did not work well in the short run and Vinik fell into disfavor. Prior to Vinik, Magellan had remained fully invested in stocks (with a couple of exceptions) for many years. Under Vinik, Magellan underperformed the S&P 500 by over 13 points for the twelve months ending June 30, 1996—performance neither the shareholders nor Fidelity was accustomed to for this fund.

Bob Stansky compiled a very successful record running Fidelity Growth Company Fund beginning in April 1987. He seems to be a very good choice to run Magellan and to return it to its strategy of investing solely in stocks selected for their potential for capital appreciation.

As a sidenote to the well-publicized elevation of Bob Stansky, we had an interesting dilemma: We were using the fund Bob Stansky was managing before he took over Magellan. We had been very happy with him as the portfolio manager and we felt he was a good choice to run Magellan, but when he accepted the Magellan job, we reluctantly moved on to a different non-Fidelity growth fund.

5. A No-Load Cost Structure (No Sales Charge) and a Competitive Expense Ratio

Another factor to consider is expenses. If you were to buy a new car, you would probably consider performance, durability, and accessories. More than likely, you would also look at the cost of operating the vehicle—mileage per gallon, maintenance costs, insurance premiums, etc. With mutual funds, we look at what it costs to own that fund for a year. That is shown in its expense ratio—the percentage of net assets that it costs to run the fund each year. The more that comes off the top, the less you get. Yet there is not necessarily a direct correlation between lower expenses and higher returns. Many funds with

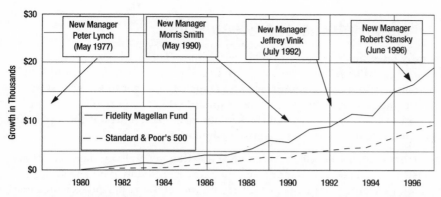

FIGURE 3.2 Fidelity Magellan Fund Versus Standard & Poor's 500. Despite several managerial changes, the Fidelity Magellan Fund has had extraordinary growth: $1,000 invested in December 1980 would have been worth over $19,400 by December 1996, while $1,000 invested in the Standard & Poor's 500 would have grown to about $9,700 during the same time period. (*Source:* Morningstar, Inc., Micropal, Ltd., Brouwer & Janachowski, Inc.)

high expenses still can generate excellent returns. For example, the Kaufman Fund has very high expenses and very good performance, too. Take a look at expenses, but do not let them become the critical factor in your decision.

Even though a number of mutual funds do well in spite of their high expenses, we look very hard at this number and we are reluctant to use a fund with above-average expenses. We would only select such a fund if it were head and shoulders above similar funds. If you are analyzing 2 funds with track records and investment objectives that are very similar, you should consider choosing the one with lower expenses. But make sure they really are comparable funds.

In Chapter 5, we will give you our list of good funds you can use. Or, you can also use Morningstar to create your own list. If you have Morningstar, start looking for good funds based on your needs and your investment objectives. There are many mutual funds that exemplify the 5 qualities we covered in this chapter: excellent records, understandable investment and risk management strategies, stable management, and moderate expenses. So why not limit your search to funds with those qualities. By doing so, you narrow the field to a very select group and that will make your selection process much easier.

High Returns at a Steep Price

The Kaufmann Fund generally buys small, rapidly growing companies. The fund buys most of its holdings as initial public offerings (IPOs). These positions are usually quite small, and as the Kaufmann Fund's two portfolio managers—Lawrence Auriana and Hans Utsch—get to know a company, they will either dump it or buy more. Once a stock becomes established in the portfolio, they will hold on to it for years, as long as the company stays on track. They will hold on even if the stock falls because of an earnings disappointment or a temporary change in market conditions.

The fund has had a great run ever since 1987 (it plummeted 37.1% that year). Even including that disastrous year, the fund has still averaged 17.4% per year since its inception in 1986 through May 1997, compared to the S&P 500's average annual return of 15.9% for the same period. Auriana and Utsch have deliberately built a reputation of being tough, hard-nosed risk takers, yet their investment practices are very disciplined. They buy small companies that have the potential to get big. They hold on as long as the company performs, and they maintain a diversified portfolio. In addition, they work very hard and they are smart. All in all, they have a very good formula for success.

Many mutual fund analysts (ourselves included) balk at the Kaufmann Fund's very high expense ratio (more than 2%), its size (almost $5 billion and growing), and its potential for volatility. Despite these impediments, the fund has really delivered.

But When Is It Time to Sell a Mutual Fund?

So far we have talked about selecting good funds, but what about selling? Our philosophy on selling is that we do so reluctantly. We spend so much time selecting a mutual fund, that we do not like to sell unless it is absolutely necessary. In general, we are very confident in our selection process because we understand the fund's investment approach and we place great confidence in the portfolio manager we selected. Given this methodology, it should come as no surprise that our most critical concerns are changes in these areas. There are any number of other events that can cause us to put a fund under review, but the following 2 situations are often precipitating factors for a sale. We usually sell a fund when:

1. **The lead portfolio manager leaves.** Portfolio managers have a big impact on a fund's results and we buy a fund in large part because we believe it has a superior portfolio manager. We look for managers who are intelligent, disciplined, experienced, hard-working and very passionate about their work. When they move on, we usually do too.

2. **The investment strategy changes significantly.** A fund's track record and its investment strategy are irrevocably linked. If a fund did well as a small company stock fund, we do not know what it will do if it switches to large company stocks. Perhaps the superior performance will continue, but we simply cannot take that for granted.

Other factors that may cause us to sell are:

♦ **The fund company is sold.** If the acquiring company takes a hands-off attitude, the change in ownership may be a non-event. However, in many cases, key people leave, administrative duties increase, and the portfolio managers can be distracted by all the activity.

♦ **The lead portfolio manager starts managing the business rather than the portfolio.** When a fund management group grows, the portfolio manager can get caught up with administrative details. If this happens, there is less time to spend picking stocks or bonds. It is not always easy to determine this, but if the fund company adds a number of new funds to be managed by this manager, he or she will inevitably get caught up in administrative details.

♦ **Fund performance versus similar funds deteriorates for 2 years or more.** Although we do not panic when a fund falls into a slump, we get concerned if the fund is falling apart while similar funds are doing fine. If you have a growth fund that is falling way behind other growth funds, then that is cause for concern. Conversely, if all growth funds are down, then it is probably not an issue.

Gabelli Asset Fund

Mario Gabelli is one of the mutual fund industry's better known managers, and, in our opinion, he is an excellent stockpicker. We used Gabelli Asset Fund for 2 years and it was a decent, albeit unspectacular performer during that time. We sold the fund because we lost confidence, not in Gabelli's stockpicking expertise, but in his time management. Mario Gabelli is still running as fast as ever but, Gabelli Asset Fund's record since we left has not been very exciting. (See Figure 3.3.)

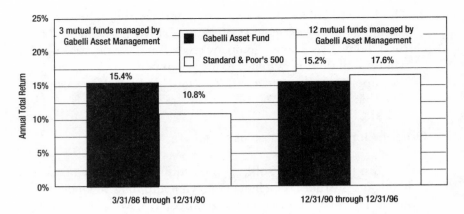

FIGURE 3.3 Gabelli Asset Fund Versus Standard & Poor's 500. Mario Gabelli's flagship mutual fund, Gabelli Asset Fund, began operations in March 1986. Results for the first 4¾ years, beginning March 31, 1986, were exceptional, outstripping the S&P 500 by 4.6% each year. During this period, Gabelli Asset Management managed 3 mutual funds. In the next 6 years, Gabelli Asset Management added 9 new mutual funds to its operations. Does the slide in performance illustrated above reflect the distraction of additional management responsibility? (*Source:* Morningstar, Inc., Micropal, Ltd., Brouwer & Janachowski, Inc.)

Coming up next, we are going to take you through an in-depth analysis of 4 mutual funds—2 very good ones and 2 mediocre ones. All will be revealed when we put them under the microscope. Plus, we will show you how to analyze, probe and dissect funds using resources that are readily available to you.

INTERVIEW

"Find Stocks to Buy from the Bottom Up"

An Interview with *Michael Price*

Michael Price manages the top-performing Mutual Series Fund which has a number of different portfolios: Mutual Shares, Mutual Qualified, Mutual Beacon, Mutual Discovery, and Mutual European. As you will see in the interview, Price has a unique investment philosophy he developed working alongside the fund's founder, Max Heine.

The first fund in the group, Mutual Shares, has an illustrious history dating back nearly 50 years. It was one of the first no-load funds. The fund's no-load status ended in 1996 when Price merged his management company with the Franklin Templeton Group, a very large mutual fund family that sells its shares primarily through brokerage firms and financial planners.

Despite the change, we are confident Price will continue to invest the way he always has. He looks for value in all the "wrong" places: bankruptcies, turn-arounds, and takeovers. And he keeps finding it.

Mutual Fund Mastery: How would you define the basic investment approach that you use for all the funds in your Mutual Series portfolios?

Michael Price: Well, you know, we're value investors. We work on analyzing companies and finding stocks to buy from the bottom up. And we work on 3 kinds of situations:

1. *Plain old common stocks* that are cheap, based on their basic value, that is, on what we think smart investors would pay for the company. This is probably 60% of what we do.

2. Then there are companies involved in *mergers, takeovers, and buyouts.* We do a fair bit of this when that area is busy, like now, and less of it when there are fewer

deals, obviously. In the late 1980s, there was a lot of this activity too.

3. The third area we work on is *bankruptcy.* We analyze companies that are involved in the bankruptcy process. That could mean going into bankruptcy, or coming out of bankruptcy. Often, we end up buying their bank loans or other debt, to set up some new equity and recapitalize the company so it can move forward again.

MFM: Could you explain how the process works in a typical bankruptcy situation and how it happens that bankrupt companies can sometimes be excellent investments?

MP: Well, companies often go into Chapter 11 (which is the most common category of corporate bankruptcies) because they have too much debt. And they can't pay the debt when it comes due. They also go into bankruptcy because of claims against them other than debt, like litigation judgments. Or environmental liabilities. And whatever the liability that cannot be funded is, the company has to devise a plan to come up with the money to fund it.

MFM: Or to get rid of the obligation somehow.

MP: And, basically what you have is a swap of debt into the ownership or the equity of the company on terms that get the creditors—that is, the people owning the debt—to accept it as a settlement. The more senior debt gets more money, and the more junior debt gets less money. And if there is anything left over after paying the creditors, it goes to the common stockholders.

MFM: In other words, the creditors, the people who loaned money to the corporation, have first call on any assets, and there is a pecking order among them. They must all agree to a settlement, and only then do the common stockholders get considered. The stockholders are last in line.

MP: Absolutely last in line. Before the common stock comes the preferred stock. Then the junior debt, then the senior debt, and first in line is the government, for tax claims, and the lawyers for administrative claims. So, what happens is, we are able to work on this situation with more disclosure because instead of quarterly filings with the Securities and Exchange Commission, you often have daily, weekly, and monthly filings in bankruptcy court. We often have consultants' and appraisers' reports that are available through the bankruptcy court, and there are also committees set up, of the different classes of creditors. They have bankers and lawyers working on protecting their claims. By looking at all this information, you can find ways to come in that make good, sound investment sense. Once we own some of the securities, we can then try and influence the process. And the word *influence* could mean hold up the process. It could mean push the process forward. It could mean change the process positively, to get more value for our shareholders.

MFM: People talk about bonds selling for 50 cents on the dollar, 10 cents on the dollar. Essentially, this means these bonds have been discounted well below their initial or par value, so you could come in and buy that debt at a big discount. Once you own it, you could then influence the outcome of the bankruptcy process.

MP: Yes. The bankruptcy law says that, for a plan to be accepted, two-thirds of the value and half the number of the claimants in a class, such as senior bondholders, have to approve a plan. So, if two-thirds of the number of claims in a class have to approve a claim, that means that one-third of that amount can block it.

MFM: One-third plus one.

MP: One-third plus one. And, the word *block* could not only mean destroy, but it could also mean, get leverage to make it better for you.

MFM: So, it's a battle. You're not just buying IBM or Citicorp stock and hoping it goes up. You're operating in an arena in which knowledge is power. It is a more inefficient market than the normal stock market because far fewer people are active in it. You can influence events much more than you could otherwise.

MP: You can influence events and, by working harder, you can do better research; and, often, you can buy things cheaper. Once a company is bankrupt, people think it's worthless and people will sell securities for less than what they're worth because they just want to get out.

MFM: And some institutions can't hold issues that are bankrupt because their organizational rules may prohibit it. In that case, they would be forced to dump something, once bankruptcy is imminent.

MP: That's right.

MFM: So, how do you determine that a bankruptcy situation is attractive? What are you specifically looking for?

MP: It begins by noticing companies that have too much debt and other claims against them. And then you do a similar type of analysis that you do on normal stocks. You start to look at the annual and quarterly reports and the balance sheet, and you start to value the assets of the business. And then, instead of focusing on where the common stock is trading, as you do with a normal company, you start focusing on where the debt is trading. And you try and get the debt at a discount to what it would be worth if the company were liquidated. Liquidation of a company is the worst-case scenario in which you don't get much for the value of the business itself. You have to just sell off the assets. Now, those types of pure liquidation deals are extremely hard to find. So, often you have to estimate a certain amount of value for the business itself. You assume the business is worth 10 or 20 cents on each dollar of revenue. Which seems cheap, depending on the industry.

MFM: So, in effect, you're saying the company is in trouble now, but the core business would be worth something once the crushing burden of debt is eased. And when you buy the debt, even if it's at a big discount, you become the owners of the company.

MP: Right.

MFM: How do you know what the business is worth and what the assets are worth?

MP: There are always comparables. Remember, we've got thousands of companies here that trade publicly. So, whether it is a disk drive manufacturer or a real estate developer or a cement company, there are comparables. And you look at recent prices paid, you look at where other stocks trade, you get multiples of earnings and cash flow, and you say, yes, this will be worth $300 million. If the assets are worth $300 million and the whole capitalization of the company is trading for $150 million, it's going to be pretty attractive.

MFM: How does your investment philosophy with its three facets—cheap stocks, takeovers, and bankruptcies—differ from other value investors, like Mario Gabelli or the Sequoia Fund?

MP: Sequoia Fund has much fewer issues than we do and they buy quality companies that are cheap. We buy some of those, but we're much more special-situation-oriented. We get involved in deals, proxy fights, and bankruptcies. They don't. Gabelli does a little bit of what we do; he does some of the arbitrage deals, he does not do any of the bankruptcies.

MFM: Changing the subject again, you've generally held pretty significant cash positions in your funds. Is that so that you will have cash available for opportunities? What is the thinking behind that?

MP: It's really not a top-down decision. I don't sit down and decide I want to have 20% in cash. Often, it is a function of new money from investors coming into the fund. That causes cash to go up. Other times, we get paid on takeovers or stock sales, and the proceeds from what we've sold causes cash to build up.

MFM: There has been a lot of news about tobacco stocks and how people are shying away from that industry. Is there a point at which you think they're attractive because of the fact that other people are shying away from them?

MP: Yes. We own RJR Nabisco, which has Marlboro and other tobacco brands. We own Reynolds because we believe the real value of the company is $50 a share and the stock is selling at $30. We own it also because 2 smart guys are bothering them. And trying to push and bust them up.

MFM: You think at some point the value is going to be realized when they break up the company?

MP: Yes.

MFM: What about the other big tobacco companies that you don't have?

MP: We don't own them because they don't have enough people bothering them. They may be cheap, but without someone pushing them, they could stay cheap for years.

MFM: Why is it that so-called value stocks and value mutual funds slow down when the stock market is roaring ahead?

MP: Because we do not own the hot stocks—technology or telecommunications or something. We owned no tech stocks in 1995. We owned none of the stocks with high price-to-earnings ratios, which are better performers in bull markets.

MFM: Now that Mutual Series Fund is part of the Franklin Templeton Group, are you going to remain as the head portfolio manager?

MP: Yes. Unquestionably. I do not anticipate going anywhere, but we have 16 analysts on our staff. Within that group are 5 senior people who are terrific. For example, Ray Garea was largely responsible for the Chase Manhattan deal we did last year. He is a bank analyst. He also works on healthcare stocks. Rob Friedman works on insurance and drug stocks, and he has also been largely responsible for a lot of our success in Europe. He is based in London now. Peter Langerman, who is a bankruptcy lawyer, works on a lot of our bankruptcy deals. Jeff Altman works with him, and Larry Sondike works on some of the conglomerates and spin-off situations and mergers here. And those people have all been here for 5 years or more, and they are very, very competent. Plus, the other 11 analysts are terrific.

MFM: Would one of them be the portfolio manager, or how would that work?

MP: A little bit of a collective or team approach.

MFM: What is it that sets you apart from other portfolio managers? There have certainly been other people who tried to do some of the things you do, and yet not all of them have been so successful. What is it that makes you different?

MP: I don't know. I don't know.

MFM: OK, let me ask that question in a different way. You mentioned 5 of your analysts who really stand out. You've had a lot of people over the years. Why are they the ones whom you have faith in?

MP: First, we have had very little turnover during the past 20 years. However, at this point in time, those 5 have shown me that they are independent thinkers, they are very smart, they know how to do the work, they believe in the value approach we use, and they are disciplined people. They have a really good work ethic.

MFM: Yet, there are a lot of people like that. What else? There has to be something else that makes those 5 stand out. What is it that makes them different?

MP: They are smart. They work hard and analyze things very intelligently. The final intangible is that they know when to pull the trigger and when to pull back. Pull the trigger—that is a big part.

MFM: So, they have to be able to research and analyze, but at some point they have to say, yes, this is the one. Of all the people you've worked with over a period of time, you feel the most comfortable with these 5?

MP: That's right.

MFM: If you had to put all your money in 1 single mutual fund and had to leave it there for at least 5 years, which one would it be?

MP: Mutual Shares.

MFM: So, it would be Mutual Shares rather than Mutual Beacon?

MP: Oh, it doesn't matter. They are so similar.

MFM: Why is it, out of all the possible investment styles, you picked this style and you stuck with it? What is it about this particular style of investing that makes you such a believer?

MP: Well, in my first years with Max Heine, I saw how it worked, particularly in 1974. That year, the stock market was crashing and we went up a bit. I saw how the bankruptcies worked when Penn Central Railroad went bankrupt.

MFM: So what happened in that period?

MP: We were buying bonds at huge discounts with just no risk at all. And we had really good returns. I saw how the arbitrage deals worked. And I saw how cheap stocks work. I'm a real believer in coupling all three of these styles in a portfolio. And I've also seen how growth stock investing doesn't work when there's a problem. The risk in a growth stock is much higher than the risk you take in a value stock.

MFM: You're saying that growth stocks may have more up side, but they have a lot more risk. When the stock market is low, as in the early 1980s, I can see how you would have a lot to buy. But what about when the stock market is very high, as in the 1990s. Isn't it hard to find good buys?

MP: We are finding things all the time. There is always a busted stock or a beaten up group. Between here, Canada, and Europe, where we are primarily involved, we find enough opportunities.

MFM: In some cases, like the Sunbeam–Oster deal, make an opportunity. How did that actually come about?

MP: You know, it actually goes way back to the 1970s. We owned some of the companies that were taken over by Sunbeam, which was then bought by Allegheny International. We never owned Allegheny International. We never liked the guy running it, nor did we like the valuation of its common stock. We owned some of its preferred stock and bonds, which we got out of. After we got out of them, they ran into trouble in the mid-1980s. After the company filed for Chapter 11 bankruptcy reorganization in 1988, we started to watch it. Eight different groups bid for its assets. And it turns out that the man who used to run one of the subsidiaries became the interim chairman of Allegheny—Ollie Travers, from Baltimore. So we knew the management, we were familiar with some of the businesses. The securities had traded way down. And then we got hooked up with Michael Steinhardt and Paul Kazarian. Among the three of us, we combined forces and bought out public bonds through a tender, bought bank loans

and private deals, and then wrote our own reorganization plan and pushed it through in the bankruptcy court.

MFM: You dropped Allegheny International and went back to the name Sunbeam–Oster.

MP: It is a wonderful brand name.

MFM: What is your personal benchmark for performance with the funds? When do you say, hey, we're on track, we're not on track?

MP: We're not in a *relative* performance game versus the S&P 500. We're in an *absolute* performance game. I look at what people can earn risk-free on short-term cash. I want to earn an increment above that, without a lot of risk. An increment could be 4 or 5 points. When interest rates are 12%, I want to earn in the upper teens. I do not care about how we do versus the market. The whole key is not losing money. We don't care about how well we do during bull markets, because everybody makes money. We really want to earn decent returns in sideways and bear markets.

Mike Price has found something that works for him and his investors. Bull markets take care of themselves. His goal is to make decent returns even in the tough markets. That, alone, is a great lesson. But he also does his homework. Before he makes an investment, he puts a stock under the microscope and checks it out.

In the next chapter, we are going to show you how to analyze mutual funds by putting them under the microscope.

CHAPTER 4

Mutual Funds Under the Microscope

Welcome to the mutual funds laboratory. Now, you're going to learn how to put mutual funds under the microscope. In Chapter 3, we reviewed the factors that we look for in good funds. In this chapter, we are going to show you how to analyze mutual funds.

It's time to roll up your sleeves, turn off the radio or television, and banish the dog, the kids, and any other distractions. Fortunately, this won't take long. There will be quite a bit of analysis, but we will keep it as brief as possible. We are taking you through this process to illustrate precisely what makes a mutual fund good or bad. To distinguish good funds, we have to take you on a tour of not-so-good funds, too. Our inspection tour includes 2 good funds and two mediocre ones. Ironically, in each case, the mediocre fund has more assets than the good fund.

We will not spend much time on mediocre funds because it does not matter why poor performers are the way they are. Their record tells the story and not much has to be said about them other than asking plaintively, "Why does anyone stay in them?" (See page 77.)

Next, we are going to compare two growth funds, Mairs & Power Growth Fund and Fidelity Trend Fund. Then we'll compare two bond funds, Harbor Bond Fund and T. Rowe Price New Income Fund. The Mairs & Power Growth Fund and Harbor Bond Fund meet our 5 criteria (see Chapter 3) that qualify them as good funds.

Because we have access to powerful computers, expensive databases, and specialized analytical software, we can perform some very intricate analyses. You are probably not going to hock your life savings to duplicate our setup, so we have developed a simplified version of our analysis that you can perform yourself.

To begin, you will need access to Morningstar Mutual Funds. This subscription service is available at most public libraries, and it is relatively inexpensive if you want to subscribe at home. Morningstar has other mutual fund services available. Refer to Part Two, The Toolbox, for descriptions of all the Morningstar services.

The "Deadman Funds" Live

That the Steadman Funds still exist is one of the world's bizarre unexplained phenomena—like the mystery of the Great Sphinx. This family of 4 mutual funds has had performance that is so bad it can hardly be fathomed (see figure below).

Expenses are so high that they eat up almost 9% on average per year, yet some investors remain in the funds. There are reports that a significant percentage of the remaining shareholders are actually dead (no joke), and that is why they have remained on the books. For years, people in the industry have jokingly referred to these as the "Deadman Funds" (a play on the name Steadman and their abysmal performance). Maybe that name has more relevance than we thought.

On 2 separate occasions, the company itself has come back from the dead, settling disputes with the Securities and Exchange Commission that could have resulted in closure. This woeful tale has 3 important lessons for you to learn from:

1. The portfolio manager and the fund's management team. In Steadman, bad management has taken a once strong fund family and relegated it to a sideshow of the mutual fund industry.

2. Diversification. These funds often have only a few stocks (an average of 13 stocks in each of the 4 funds in June 1996), and it shows.

3. The need for vigilance on the part of shareholders. If Steadman Fund shareholders had paid attention, they would not have put up with such a sad situation.

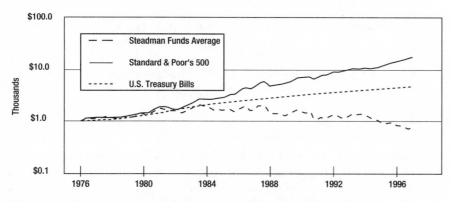

Steadman Funds Continue Sinking This chart illustrates $1,000 invested in each of the following: the S&P 500, 30-day U.S. Treasury Bills, and a basket of the four Steadman mutual funds weighted equally (Steadman American Industry Fund, the Steadman Associated Fund, the Steadman Investment Fund, and the Steadman Technology Growth Fund). (*Source:* Morningstar Inc., Micropal, Ltd., Brouwer & Janachowski, Inc.)

Morningstar is the single best source of mutual fund information. It qualifies as one of the great all-time values in investment research. The statistical information given on the typical Morningstar page is very useful, and the editorial comments can help you gain more insight into a given fund's investment strategies. The star ratings are of limited value in picking funds (for more on this issue, see our interview with Don Phillips of Morningstar following Chapter 8). So let's dive in.

For each of the funds we analyze, we'll show you the latest full Morningstar page. As we work through each fund, we'll show you exactly where on the Morningstar page to find the reference. (In the comparisons below, the numbers in parentheses are keyed to a reference on the applicable fund's Morningstar page.)

Mairs & Power Growth Fund

Mairs & Power Growth Fund is one of the best-kept secrets in the growth mutual fund category (see Figure 4.1). The fund gets impressive marks in all five categories that we covered in Chapter 3. As a refresher, our criteria for good funds are:

- ♦ A record of adding value over an appropriate index for at least 5 years.
- ♦ An understandable and disciplined investment strategy.
- ♦ An understandable and disciplined strategy for managing risk.
- ♦ Stable portfolio management.
- ♦ A no-load cost structure (no sales charge) and a competitive expense ratio.

Morningstar classifies the fund as having a mid-cap blend ⑤Ⓐ investment style. Actually the fund tends to focus its portfolio in both mid-sized stocks ④Ⓐ (usually $1 billion to $5 billion in company market capitalization) and large company stocks (above $5 billion in market capitalization). The portfolio is neither a pure growth fund nor a pure value fund, but rather it is a combination of the two. Morningstar calls it a blend fund. Growth funds of this type are often referred to as funds that seek growth at a good price.

The fund has been managed continuously by George Mairs since January 1980 ⑦Ⓐ with a distinct investment style ①Ⓐ and ⑮Ⓐ. During his tenure, Mairs has assembled an impressive track record. For the past 12 years, the fund has had a good performance record when compared with other growth funds. It has spent the majority of the past 12 years in the first (top) and second quartiles ⑥Ⓐ. This means that the fund

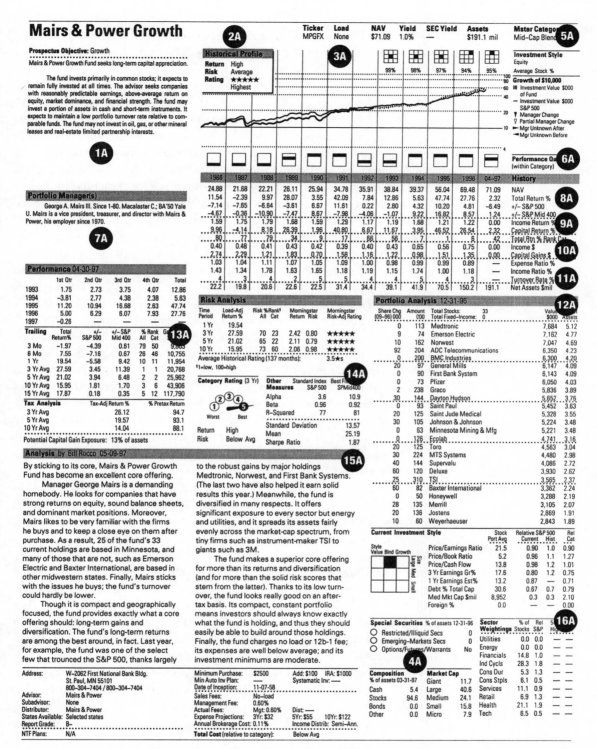

FIGURE 4.1 Mairs & Power Growth's Morningstar Page. (*Source: Morningstar*, Volume 30, Issue 4, May 23, 1997. ©1997 Morningstar, Inc. All rights reserved. 225 W. Wacker Dr. Chicago, IL. 50606, 312-696-6000. Although Data are gathered from reliable sources, Morningstar cannot guarantee correctness and accuracy.)

outperformed 50% to 75% or more of comparable growth mutual funds for a majority of the past 12 years. The fund has also done very well compared to an appropriate index.

Since this is a mid-cap fund, we will compare it to the S&P 400 (mid-cap index) and also, we will use the standard equity benchmark index, the S&P 500 Ⓐ. As we mentioned in Chapter 3, short-term performance is meaningless. In fact short-term performance can be quite deceiving. For example the fund has an erratic record on a year-by-year basis. Some years are bountiful with significant outperformance, while others are index lagging years ⑨Ⓐ. Long-term performance is the key to investment success, and as you can see from the columns "+/− S&P 500" and "+/− S&P Mid 400" ⑬Ⓐ, the fund has significantly outperformed its indexes and peers. For example, the fund has beaten the S&P 500 by 3.45% per year for the past 3 years, 3.94% per year for the past 5 years, and 1.81% for the past 10 years. It has also outperformed most of its peers during these same periods. The "% Rank Category" column ⑬Ⓐ shows that the fund has outperformed 99%, 98%, and 94% of all comparable funds during the past 3, 5, and 10 years.

Morningstar rates the fund's risk as "average" ②Ⓐ. Our experience is that this fund is somewhat more volatile than the S&P 500. This is not reflected in its beta of .96% ⑭Ⓐ. A beta of 1.00 means that a fund is as volatile as its comparative index, in this case, the S&P 500. A beta of .96% indicates that the fund is slightly less volatile than the S&P 500. In other words, if the S&P 500 rose 1%, you would expect this fund to rise .96%, and vice versa. Because the fund outperforms or underperforms the S&P 500 by a significant margin ⑨Ⓐ, we suspect that beta may understate its true volatility. In a market correction, we would expect this fund to be down somewhat more than the S&P 500. Nonetheless, it has been a very consistent earner. It had only 1 negative year in the previous 12 years ⑧Ⓐ. Even though the fund owns only 33 stocks ⑫Ⓐ, it is well diversified within different industry groups ⑯Ⓐ.

Performance really is the bottom line because it includes all management fees and other administrative expenses the fund bears. But if performance were equal between 2 funds, we would always pick the fund with the lower expense ratio. The expense ratio is like an anchor around a fund's neck. It's harder for a fund to turn in consistently great performance with a high expense ratio. Mairs & Power is very reasonable because its expense ratio has been running consistently under 1% for the past several years ⑩Ⓐ. The average stock fund has an expense ratio of over 1.5%, so Mairs & Power is a thrifty choice. The fund is no-load ③Ⓐ and so costs nothing to join. An added bonus for tax-paying investors is that the fund has very low portfolio turnover—typically 5% or less each year ⑪Ⓐ.

To summarize, the fund has stable management, a consistent investment style, excellent performance, a diversified portfolio to reduce risk, and very competitive expenses.

___

Fidelity Trend Fund

For comparison, we will now review a similar fund with a less distinguished track record (see Figure 4.2). This is a growth fund that is similar in style to the Mairs & Power Growth Fund. Both funds are categorized by Morningstar as having a "mid-cap blend" investment style ③B.

If you read Chapter 3, you will notice an immediate problem with this fund. It lists 4 different portfolio managers since 1987 ④B. As you can see, this fund has a revolving door for portfolio managers—4 different managers during the past 11 years. Track records and othe historical information are snapshots of what has happened in the past. They are reflections of what a portfolio manager has accomplished.

This fund's rapid portfolio manager turnover does not make it easy to analyze its track record. It really doesn't have 1 cohesive track record. Instead it has loosely strung together bits and pieces of performance data from various portfolio managers with different investment styles. To get a true reading on the new manager, Arieh Coll, we would need to review his past performance while managing other similar funds. But even this would not necessarily be much help, because his prior experience is in managing narrowly defined sector funds. Anyone investing in Fidelity Trend now would be guessing and betting on future performance. And with so many great portfolio managers with identifiable track records, such as George Mairs with the Mairs & Power Growth Fund, we would not consider Fidelity Trend Fund further.

However, many investors have chosen this fund and will stay with it despite its poor past results. So, for educational purposes, let's dissect this fund further to illustrate the dramatic differences between its results and those of funds with superior records.

The fund has had a poor performance record when compared with other growth funds. It has spent the majority of the past 12 years in the third and fourth (bottom) quartiles ⑤B. This means that 50% to 75% (or) more of mutual funds in this category outperformed this fund for a majority of the past 12 years.

Like Mairs & Power, this fund has had a consistent investment style of buying mostly mid-sized company stocks ②B. Since it is a mid-cap fund, we will compare it to the S&P 400 (mid-cap index) and also, we will use the standard equity benchmark index, the S&P 500 ⑩B. As you

Fidelity Trend

	Ticker	Load	NAV	Yield	SEC Yield	Assets	Mstar Category
	FTRNX	None	$51.04	0.8%	—	$1,163.3 mil	Mid–Cap Blend

Prospectus Objective: Growth

Fidelity Trend Fund seeks growth of capital.

The fund invests in securities of well-known and established companies, as well as smaller, less well-known companies. It considers all factors that influence security prices and studies the momentum of earnings trends and security prices of individual companies, industries, and the market in general. The fund may invest in any type of foreign or domestic security. It is designed to be extremely responsive to companies' changes and market reactions, and it may invest substantially in cyclical or defensive industries.

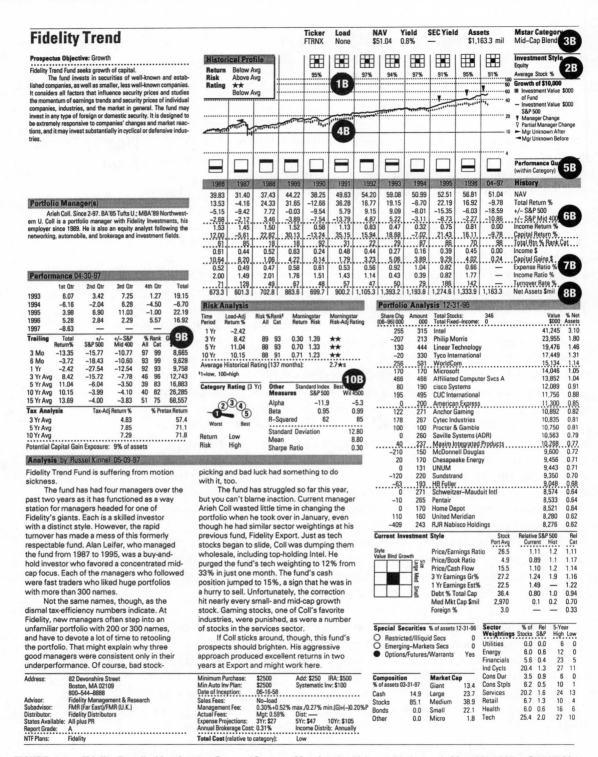

Historical Profile

Return	Below Avg
Risk	Above Avg
Rating	★★ Below Avg

95% · 97% · 94% · 97% · 91% · 95% · 91%

Investment Style Equity — Average Stock %

Growth of $10,000
- Investment Value $000 of Fund
- Investment Value $000 S&P 500
- ▼ Manager Change
- ▽ Partial Manager Change
- ◄ Mgr Unknown After
- ◄ Mgr Unknown Before

Performance Quartile (within Category)

History

	1986	1987	1988	1989	1990	1991	1992	1993	1994	1995	1996	04-97	
	39.83	31.40	37.43	44.22	38.25	49.63	54.20	59.08	50.99	52.51	56.81	51.04	NAV
	13.53	-4.16	24.33	31.65	-12.66	36.28	16.77	19.15	-6.70	22.19	16.92	-9.78	Total Return %
	-5.15	-9.42	7.72	-0.03	-9.54	5.79	9.15	9.09	-8.01	-15.35	-6.03	-18.59	+/– S&P 500
	-2.66	-2.12	3.46	-3.89	-7.54	-13.79	4.87	5.22	-3.11	-8.73	-2.27	-10.86	+/– S&P Mid 400
	1.53	1.45	1.50	1.52	0.58	1.13	0.83	0.47	0.32	0.75	0.81	0.00	Income Return %
	12.00	-5.61	22.82	30.13	-13.24	35.15	15.94	18.69	-7.02	21.43	16.11	-9.78	Capital Return %
	.61	.85	.18	.18	.92	.31	.22	.29	.87	.86	.70	.98	Total Rtn % Rank Cat
	0.61	0.44	0.52	0.63	0.24	0.48	0.44	0.27	0.16	0.39	0.45	0.00	Income $
	10.64	6.20	1.06	4.22	0.14	1.79	3.23	5.06	3.89	9.29	4.02	0.24	Capital Gains $
	0.52	0.49	0.47	0.58	0.51	0.53	0.56	0.92	1.04	0.82	0.66	—	Expense Ratio %
	2.00	1.49	2.01	1.76	1.51	1.43	1.14	0.43	0.39	0.82	1.77	—	Income Ratio %
	.71	.129	.49	.67	.48	.57	.47	.50	.29	.186	.142	—	Turnover Rate %
	673.3	601.3	702.8	883.6	699.7	900.2	1,105.3	1,393.2	1,193.8	1,274.6	1,333.9	1,163.3	Net Assets $mil

Portfolio Manager(s)

Arieh Coll. Since 2-97. BA '85 Tufts U.; MBA '89 Northwestern U. Coll is a portfolio manager with Fidelity Investments, his employer since 1989. He is also an equity analyst following the networking, automobile, and brokerage and investment fields.

Performance 04-30-97

	1st Qtr	2nd Qtr	3rd Qtr	4th Qtr	Total
1993	6.07	3.42	7.25	1.27	19.15
1994	-6.16	-2.04	6.28	-4.50	-6.70
1995	3.98	6.90	11.03	-1.00	22.19
1996	5.28	2.84	2.29	5.57	16.92
1997	-8.63	—	—	—	—

Trailing	Total Return%	+/– S&P 500	+/– S&P Mid 400	% Rank All Cat	Growth $
3 Mo	-13.35	-15.77	-10.77	97 99	8,665
6 Mo	-3.72	-18.43	-10.60	93 99	9,628
1 Yr	-2.42	-27.54	-12.54	92 93	9,758
3 Yr Avg	8.42	-15.72	-7.78	46 96	12,743
5 Yr Avg	11.04	-6.04	-3.50	39 83	16,883
10 Yr Avg	10.15	-3.99	-4.10	40 82	26,285
15 Yr Avg	13.69	-4.00	-3.83	51 75	68,557

Tax Analysis	Tax-Adj Return %	% Pretax Return
3 Yr Avg	4.83	57.4
5 Yr Avg	7.85	71.1
10 Yr Avg	7.29	71.8

Potential Capital Gain Exposure: 9% of assets

Risk Analysis

Time Period	Load-Adj Return %	Risk %Rank[1] All Cat	Morningstar Return Risk	Morningstar Risk-Adj Rating
1 Yr	-2.42			
3 Yr	8.42	89 93	0.30 1.39	★★
5 Yr	11.04	88 93	0.70 1.33	★★
10 Yr	10.15	88 91	0.71 1.23	★★

Average Historical Rating (137 months): 2.7★s

[1]=low, 100=high

Category Rating (3 Yr) ① ② ③ ④ ⑤ — Worst / Best

Return Low
Risk High

Other Measures	Standard Index S&P 500	Best Fit Wil 4500
Alpha	-11.9	-5.3
Beta	0.95	0.99
R-Squared	62	85
Standard Deviation	12.80	
Mean	8.80	
Sharpe Ratio	0.30	

Portfolio Analysis 12-31-95

Share Chg (06–96) 000	Amount 000	Total Stocks: 346 Total Fixed-Income: 0	Value $000	% Net Assets
255	315	Intel	41,245	3.10
-207	213	Philip Morris	23,955	1.80
130	444	Linear Technology	19,476	1.46
-20	330	Tyco International	17,449	1.31
256	531	WorldCom	15,134	1.14
170	170	Microsoft	14,046	1.05
466	466	Affiliated Computer Svcs A	13,852	1.04
80	190	cisco Systems	12,089	0.91
195	495	CUC International	11,756	0.88
0	200	American Express	11,300	0.85
122	271	Anchor Gaming	10,892	0.82
178	267	Cytec Industries	10,835	0.81
100	100	Procter & Gamble	10,750	0.81
0	260	Saville Systems (ADR)	10,563	0.79
40	237	Maxim Integrated Products	10,268	0.77
-210	150	McDonnell Douglas	9,600	0.72
20	170	Chesapeake Energy	9,456	0.71
0	131	UNUM	9,443	0.71
-120	220	Sundstrand	9,350	0.70
-63	193	HB Fuller	9,048	0.68
0	271	Schweitzer–Mauduit Intl	8,574	0.64
-10	265	Pentair	8,533	0.64
0	170	Home Depot	8,521	0.64
110	160	United Meridian	8,280	0.62
-409	243	RJR Nabisco Holdings	8,276	0.62

Current Investment Style

Style: Value / Blend / Growth — Size: Large / Med / Small

	Stock Port Avg	Relative S&P 500 Current Hist	Rel Cat
Price/Earnings Ratio	26.5	1.11 1.2	1.11
Price/Book Ratio	4.9	0.89 1.1	1.17
Price/Cash Flow	15.5	1.10 1.2	1.14
3 Yr Earnings Gr%	27.2	1.24 1.9	1.16
1 Yr Earnings Est%	22.5	1.49 —	1.22
Debt % Total Cap	36.4	0.80 1.0	0.94
Med Mkt Cap $mil	2,970	0.1 0.2	0.70
Foreign %	3.0		0.33

Special Securities % of assets 12-31-96

○ Restricted/Illiquid Secs	0
○ Emerging–Markets Secs	0
● Options/Futures/Warrants	Yes

Composition % of assets 03-31-97

Cash	14.9
Stocks	85.1
Bonds	0.0
Other	0.0

Market Cap

Giant	13.4
Large	23.7
Medium	38.9
Small	22.1
Micro	1.8

Sector Weightings

	% of Stocks	Rel S&P	5-Year High Low
Utilities	0.0	0.0	6 0
Energy	6.0	0.6	12 0
Financials	5.6	0.4	23 5
Ind Cycls	20.4	1.3	27 11
Cons Dur	3.5	0.9	6 0
Cons Stpls	6.2	0.5	10 1
Services	20.2	1.6	24 13
Retail	6.7	1.3	10 4
Health	6.0	0.6	16 6
Tech	25.4	2.0	27 10

Analysis by Russel Kinnel 05-09-97

Fidelity Trend Fund is suffering from motion sickness.

The fund has had four managers over the past two years as it has functioned as a way station for managers headed for one of Fidelity's giants. Each is a skilled investor with a distinct style. However, the rapid turnover has made a mess of this formerly respectable fund. Alan Leifer, who managed the fund from 1987 to 1995, was a buy-and-hold investor who favored a concentrated mid-cap focus. Each of the managers who followed were fast traders who liked huge portfolios with more than 300 names.

Not the same names, though, as the dismal tax-efficiency numbers indicate. At Fidelity, new managers often step into an unfamiliar portfolio with 200 or 300 names, and have to devote a lot of time to retooling the portfolio. That might explain why three good managers were consistent only in their underperformance. Of course, bad stock-picking and bad luck had something to do with it, too.

The fund has struggled so far this year, but you can't blame inaction. Current manager Arieh Coll wasted little time in changing the portfolio when he took over in January, even though he had similar sector weightings at his previous fund, Fidelity Export. Just as tech stocks began to slide, Coll was dumping them wholesale, including top-holding Intel. He purged the fund's tech weighting to 12% from 33% in just one month. The fund's cash position jumped to 15%, a sign that he was in a hurry to sell. Unfortunately, the correction hit nearly every small- and mid-cap growth stock. Gaming stocks, one of Coll's favorite industries, were punished, as were a number of stocks in the services sector.

If Coll sticks around, though, this fund's prospects should brighten. His aggressive approach produced excellent returns in two years at Export and might work here.

Address:	82 Devonshire Street Boston, MA 02109 800–544–8888
Advisor:	Fidelity Management & Research
Subadvisor:	FMR (Far East)/FMR (U.K.)
Distributor:	Fidelity Distributors
States Available:	All plus PR
Report Grade:	A
NTF Plans:	Fidelity

Minimum Purchase:	$2500	Add: $250	IRA: $500
Min Auto Inv Plan:	$2500		Systematic Inv: $100
Date of Inception:	06-16-58		
Sales Fees:	No-load		
Management Fee:	0.30%+0.52% max./0.27% min.(G)+(-)0.20%P		
Actual Fees:	Mgt: 0.59%	Dist: —	
Expense Projections:	3Yr: $27	5Yr: $47	10Yr: $105
Annual Brokerage Cost: 0.31%		Income Distrib: Annually	
Total Cost (relative to category):	Low		

FIGURE 4.2 Fidelity Trend's Morningstar Page. (*Source: Morningstar,* Volume 30, Issue 4, May 23, 1997. ©1997 Morningstar, Inc. All rights reserved. 225 W. Wacker Dr. Chicago, IL. 50606, 312-696-6000. Although Data are gathered from reliable sources, Morningstar cannot guarantee correctness and accuracy.)

can see, the fund has lagged each index for most years ⑥ⓑ. As we mentioned in Chapter 3, however, short-term performance is not usually meaningful, so let's take a look at its long-term performance to see how it stacks up. As you can see, the fund has lagged its indexes over all extended time periods ⑨ⓑ. For the past 3 years, it underperformed the S&P 500 by 15.72% each year; for the past 5 years, it underperformed by 6.04% each year; and for the past 10 years, it underperformed by 3.99% each year. And by referring to the "% Rank Category" column ⑨ⓑ, you can see that over these respective time periods 96%, 83%, and 82% of funds in the same category out-performed this fund.

Many times the reason that a fund has low returns is because it is also taking less risk than its benchmark index. In this case, however, Fidelity Trend not only underperformed the S&P 500 but also took on *more* risk. Fidelity Trend's beta of .95% is misleading ⑩ⓑ. This indicates that the fund is slightly less volatile than the S&P 500. A better way of reviewing a fund's risk is to see how it did relative to the S&P 500 during down periods. The last negative year for the S&P 500 was 1990, where the index had a return of −3.12%. Fidelity Trend had a return of −12.66% for that year. This year alone indicates to us that the fund's 6% beta probably understates its true volatility.

From a cost standpoint, the fund is no-load ①ⓑ and expenses are very competitive. While the average equity fund has an expense ratio of approximately 1.5% of assets, Fidelity Trend's expenses are under 1% of assets for most years ⑦ⓑ. Curiously, however, expenses have climbed over the past several years even as net assets (total assets in the fund) ⑧ⓑ have grown substantially.

To summarize, even though this fund has a competitive cost structure, it is no bargain. It fails on our other 4 criteria. It lacks consistent management and a consistent investment style. It took on more risk than its representative benchmark indexes while underperforming each significantly.

Let's change our focus and look now at 2 bond funds.

Harbor Bond Fund

Harbor Bond is managed by our favorite fixed-income manager, Bill Gross (see Figure 4.3). Gross has dazzled bond investors since 1971, when he joined Pacific Investment Management Company ③ⓒ. The fund invests in an eclectic blend of government securities, mortgage- and asset-backed securities, and corporate debt ②ⓒ. Morningstar classifies this fund as Intermediate-Term Bond ①ⓒ, but we consider it a

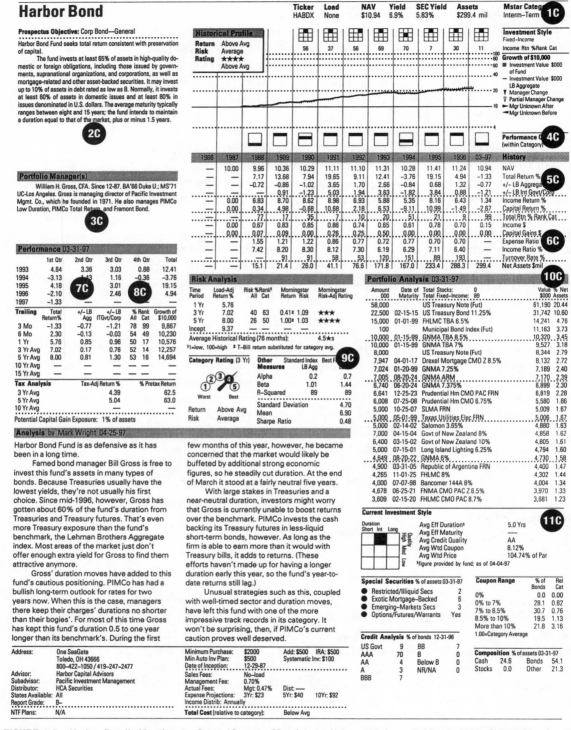

FIGURE 4.3 Harbor Bond's Morningstar Page. (*Source: Morningstar,* Volume 30, Issue 3, May 9, 1997. ©1997 Morningstar, Inc. All rights reserved. 225 W. Wacker Dr. Chicago, IL. 50606, 312-696-6000. Although Data are gathered from reliable sources, Morningstar cannot guarantee correctness and accuracy.)

high-quality (AA average credit quality) ⑪ⓒ, diversified (portfolio of 89 securities) ⑩ⓒ, intermediate-term ⑪ⓒ bond fund. It has generally placed in the first (top) quartile versus its peers ④ⓒ. This means that it has tended to outperform 75% or more of comparable bond funds.

The fund has an average duration of 5.0 years ⑪ⓒ. Duration is a measure of a bond fund's interest rate sensitivity. It is a comprehensive measure of how long it takes to recoup your entire bond investment, which consists of the payback of principal when the bond matures and the interest payments that are collected along the way. In essence, duration is the bond's maturity shortened by the weighted interest payments that are received during the life of the bond. Short-term bond funds have durations less than 3 years; intermediate-term bond funds have durations between 3 and 6 years, and long-term bond funds have durations over 6 years. The average credit quality is AA ⑪ⓒ. The most comparable index to Harbor Bond is the Lehman Brother's Aggregate Bond Index ⑨ⓒ, an index of government and corporate bonds, and mortgage- and asset-backed securities. Compared to stock funds, bond funds have an even tougher job of adding value over an unmanaged index. This is due, in part, to the efficiency of the bond markets, which are more streamlined than the stock markets. Despite the difficulties, Harbor Bond has added about 0.81% per year over the performance of its Lehman Brothers benchmark index for the past 5-year period ⑦ⓒ and outperformed 84% of comparable funds for this period (% rank category) ⑧ⓒ. The fund has consistently performed near its index for most individual years ⑤ⓒ.

Consistency counts. A fund can appear to have a very good record, but closer scrutiny might reveal that it really had just 1 or 2 hot years. Without those years, an apparently mediocre or good performer is then revealed as a poor performer. And you never know how long you will be invested with a fund. That's why Harbor Bond's record is so exceptional. Its long-term returns beat the index returns, yet are very consistent.

Bond fund expense ratios tend to be lower than those of stock funds, and the average bond fund expense ratio is slightly more than 1.0%. Harbor Bond's current 0.7% expense ratio ⑥ⓒ makes it a bargain.

Morningstar categorizes this fund as Intermediate-Term Bond ①ⅅ (see Figure 4.4), the same as Harbor Bond. We consider this a good quality (AA average credit quality) ⑧ⅅ, diversified ⑦ⅅ, intermediate-term ⑧ⅅ bond fund.

T. Rowe Price New Income Fund

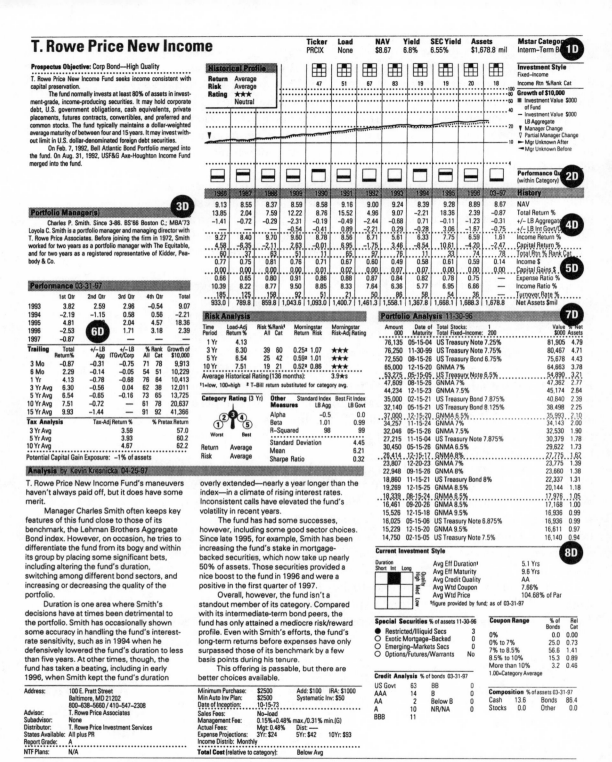

FIGURE 4.4 T. Rowe Price New Income's Morningstar Page. (*Source: Morningstar*, Volume 30, Issue 3, May 9, 1997. ©1997 Morningstar, Inc. All rights reserved. 225 W. Wacker Dr. Chicago, IL. 50606, 312-696-6000. Although Data are gathered from reliable sources, Morningstar cannot guarantee correctness and accuracy.)

We always look first at the portfolio manager's tenure. Charles Smith has managed this fund for 13 years, since 1986 ③D. Scanning Smith's record, we see that the fund has had a less consistent record than Harbor Bond in terms of both outperforming its peer group ②D and beating its comparative index ④D and ⑥D. The fund has had volatile swings from the top to the bottom quartile since 1986 ②D.

In summary, T. Rowe Price New Income Fund has a reasonable expense ratio of .75% ⑤D, and the manager has turned in a reasonable but less than stellar long-term track record ⑥D. Considering that an index fund would match the Lehman Brothers Aggregate Bond Index minus .2% or so of expenses, Smith is not too far off the mark. Nonetheless, we would not use this fund because there are funds (such as Harbor Bond) that are superior to it.

That's it for this chapter. You've hung in there well, through a very technical section. Now, you can ease up a bit as we show you our list of good mutual funds. The funds we profile in the next chapter are the best and the brightest Wall Street has to offer.

INTERVIEW

"Either Know What You're Doing or Find Someone Who Does"

An Interview with *Bill Gross*

Bill Gross joined Pacific Investment Management Company (PIMCO) as a fixed-income analyst in 1971. The timing couldn't have been better, for him or for PIMCO. Back then, PIMCO was a small investment management subsidiary of Pacific Mutual Life Insurance Company, based in Newport Beach, California. PIMCO managed only separate accounts and had no mutual funds. Today, assets in PIMCO's fixed-income mutual funds alone total almost $20 billion. And the PIMCO family name now extends to many equity mutual funds as well.

In the investment industry, Gross is very well known and highly regarded for the track record he and the PIMCO portfolio managers have achieved. PIMCO Total Return, the firm's flagship bond fund, has earned an annual total return of 10% since inception, handily outpacing the Lehman Brothers Aggregate Bond Index, which returned 9.2%. He is also famous—or infamous, according to some—for his monthly essays, which cover everything from popular culture and politics to the latest forecasts from PIMCO. He has also written a book—his second—entitled *Everything You've Heard About Investing Is Wrong!* (Times Books, 1997).

Despite all the glitz and the glamour of being an author and a frequent guest on television financial programs, Bill Gross hasn't changed all that much. He still comes to work every morning at 6 A.M., and his single, overriding goal is to beat the bond market. It's a pretty good bet that he'll succeed; he has done so every year since the fund began in 1988.

Mutual Fund Mastery: Tell us exactly how you start looking at the bond market.

Bill Gross: One important effort we make is to develop a long-term secular outlook on the economies around the globe, as well as the U.S. economy. We also develop a long-term outlook (3 to 4 years out) about the financial markets. Taking a long-term point of view tends to focus you on the fundamentals and the primary influences on the bond market. A long-term perspective also helps you avoid selling at the bottoms and buying at the tops, which is a tendency not only for individual investors but, believe it or not, for professional investors as well. We focus on longer-term, strategic policies, such as the outlook for the dollar, the outlook for global trade, changes in demographics. Is the budget going to be balanced, or is it moving into increasing deficits? Those types of things tell us if we're in a disinflationary or an inflationary environment. Of course, having an opinion about whether we are moving toward lower inflation or higher inflation has enormous implications for your outlook on interest rates and the direction of bond prices.

MFM: Let's talk about PIMCO Total Return Fund and the similar funds you manage, Harbor Bond Fund and Fremont Bond Fund. Those are intermediate-term bond portfolios that have the flexibility to go from government bonds to corporates to mortgage-backed and even some foreign government bonds. What is the advantage of having that kind of investment flexibility?

BG: When PIMCO was in its infancy, in the early 1970s, we decided to utilize as many sectors of the bond market as possible. A bond manager who is limited to one type of bond is limited in that all types of bonds—Treasuries, corporates, etc.—move in and out of favor with investors. A lot of that has to do with whether we're in a strong economic recovery or a recession. For example, if investors believe a recession is coming, they often sell corporate bonds and move into government bonds. We look at those situations for opportunities, much like it pays for a stock investor to move from growth stocks to cyclicals to utilities. We wanted that flexibility and we've been able to use it throughout the years, not only to take advantage of the highest yields available at the moment, but to take advantage of those bonds we feel have the most attractive price appreciation potential at a given point in time.

MFM: Who should invest in a bond fund like PIMCO Total Return or Harbor Bond or Fremont Bond?

BG: The purpose of those funds is really for total return, and that's a rather confusing issue with many individual bond investors. Individual investors tend to focus on yield. Yield is only part of the equation in terms of bonds, and only part of the total equation in terms of the stock market as well. Bonds go up and down in price, and it is that capital gain or loss added to yield that provides what I call total return. So, an investor in PIMCO or Harbor or Fremont should focus on the total return. That includes yield and price appreciation because that's truly what the bottom line is at the end of the day, or the end of the year, or whatever your investment objective is in terms of time frame.

MFM: What is the relationship between returns for PIMCO and for the bond market in general?

BG: PIMCO tends to mirror the bond market in its intermediate-term focus. The bond market has an average maturity of about 8 years, and these funds will move around that specific maturity, either longer or shorter, but not too far away from it. So, when investors buy PIMCO or Harbor or Fremont, they are really buying the bond market with a view toward longer-term secular

trends and with a view toward preserving and building the total dollar worth of the fund at the end of the day.

MFM: What about interest rates? From the early 1980s through 1995, we saw a relatively steady interest rate decline. Since then, rates have bounced around a bit. Where do we go from here? What is the long-term outlook for rates, and how should people view bond funds over the next 10 years or so?

BG: We had a very long bull market that started in 1981, when long-term Treasury bonds peaked with a yield of more than 15%. Recently, long-term Treasury yields got down as low as 5.8%. So there's no doubt we're in the home stretch for this bull market. With bonds, you know there's a certain level beyond which yields cannot go. I don't know where the bottom is, but when you talk about 6% interest rates, or 5%, you know you're inching closer to that end point. But having said that, I think we have to remember it doesn't necessarily mean we reverse course and have interest rates start running in the other direction. It's my view that, over the next several years, interest rates for long-term Treasury bonds will fluctuate within a 5% to 7% range. When you think about it, that is still quite an attractive scenario for bonds, if inflation is running around 2% or a little more. Bonds will not provide the double-digit returns we've seen during the past, but I still think we're in for a few more years of 6% to 8% of total return numbers, and that's attractive in a low-inflation environment.

MFM: What about average maturity? Should investors lean toward an intermediate maturity on average, or possibly even a shorter maturity?

BG: It depends on your outlook for interest rates. I think for the next 7 to 8 years, we're in an environment without much interest rate risk. Intermediate bond funds offer an opportunity to earn high yields without a high degree of risk. For those who want less risk, short-term funds are very attractive.

MFM: What about the PIMCO Low Duration Fund, with its average maturity of under 3½ years? Unlike the PIMCO Total Return strategy, which is available at a low minimum investment through Harbor Bond Fund and Fremont Bond Fund, there is no way for average investors to access PIMCO Low Duration's strategy. Are there any plans for that?

BG: It's a good question, but there isn't a good answer other than: No fund distribution companies such as Harbor or Fremont have asked. There aren't any current plans, but it certainly would be a logical alternative. A short-term bond fund fits into the investment schemes of a lot of investors. It's longer than money market but close to the volatility of a money market fund, and yet I think that would be an attractive idea. PIMCO Total Return and PIMCO Low Duration are great no-load funds, but they are at minimums most people cannot reach. That's correct at the moment.

MFM: So right now there are no plans to open up PIMCO Low Duration or a PIMCO Low Duration-type portfolio at lower minimums?

BG: No.

MFM: There just aren't very many good short-term bond funds. Vanguard has the only ones you can really look at. I think PIMCO Low Duration would compete very favorably.

BG: I do too. The Vanguard complex, I think, is really the wave of the future. You can talk about Fidelity all you want. But Vanguard's expense ratios, the fact that they are completely no-load, and the quality of their products make them really top notch. If I couldn't invest in my own funds, that's probably where I would go.

MFM: Let's talk about how the way you manage your portfolios sets you apart from other bond fund managers. You buy governments and corporates, but a lot of funds buy governments and corporates. What sets you apart?

BG: Well, I think it's several things. One is what we talked about earlier, taking the longer-term approach of 3 to 4 years. Trying to position the portfolio on a longer-term basis as opposed to a shorter-term outlook. Secondly, we also take a highly quantitative approach. If you came into our trading room,

you'd see our systems and our quantitative programs that allow us to slice and dice and take sort of a Vegamatic, bottoms-up approach to analyzing bonds.

MFM: Did you say Vegamatic bottoms-up approach . . . ?

BG: Yes. That followed from my slice and dice remark. In other words, we take a very analytical approach to valuing bonds. We are heavy computer users. And we look at rather esoteric issues, such as analyzing the adjusted spreads between different types of bonds . . . or the average life of mortgage-backed bonds such as Ginnie Maes [bonds issued by the Government National Mortgage Association]. We start with the big issues, such as the global economy, interest rates, and so on, but we also come at investment decisions using a bottoms-up approach to determine whether or not an individual bond is attractive, compared to any other bond on the marketplace.

MFM: You also take a hard look at creditworthiness for corporate bonds, right?

BG: Yes, exactly. We've got 4 fine people on the credit side as well. They have done such good work that we eventually ventured into the high-yield or junk bond market. We now have a fine high-yield bond fund with one of the best records for the past 3 years.

MFM: In other words, you build up your skills in an area and then you are also willing to move into new areas as well.

BG: I think that we've always been willing, as a firm, to look at new ideas. For instance, in the mid-1970s, we were one of the first to buy mortgage pass-through bonds—the GNMA or so-called Ginnie Mae bonds. Nobody wanted to mess with them because of the complexity of mortgage prepayments and so on, but we thought they made sense because they were yielding 200 basis points or 2% more than Treasuries at the time. So we set up a back office to take care of the monthly payments, and it was onward and upward from there. We invested in financial futures in the early 1980s because they were attractive from the standpoint of being at a discount relative to a straight purchase of bonds. We started investing in international fixed-income back in 1987, when that was still an undiscovered market on the bond side—and, I guess, even on the equity side. So we've been willing to look at new ideas and to be there relatively early. We've also looked at a lot of ideas and rejected them. We've been willing to look for new ideas which our competitors weren't looking at yet—ideas that provided additional yield and additional total return to the bottom line. I think that attitude has pervaded the company for the 26 years I've been here.

MFM: In other words, you've been quicker or more aggressive in employing new ideas or new quantitative or computer methods than some other bond investors?

BG: I think so. Computer technology was an idea we adopted very quickly in the early 1980s, when it became apparent that the bond market had changed. High tech was in, and unless you had computers, you were going to become quickly outdated. So even our entry into technology was an innovative strategy.

MFM: What are the characteristics of the perfect bond manager?

BG: I think the perfect bond manager should be a conservative investor, but an innovative thinker. You have to invest conservatively, but innovate aggressively.

MFM: You mentioned financial futures. That's a good lead-in to the discussion of derivatives. Maybe you could explain what a derivative is and how derivatives should be used. There has been a lot of publicity about the cases where derivatives were misused or abused. What about legitimate uses of derivatives?

BG: A derivative, in a general sense, is either a piece of an original bond or some innovative, rather surrealistic, duplication or image of an existing bond. A financial future is technically a derivative because it mimics the behavior of Treasury bonds.

Collateralized mortgage obligations (CMOs), which are pieces of mortgage loans, are derivatives simply because they weren't originally securities in and of themselves. They weren't part of an original financing with a corporation or an individual. For instance, when people take out a mortgage on their house, they don't issue a CMO, but they sign up for a mortgage. And that mortgage ultimately becomes a derivative when it is packaged with other home mortgages and then split apart again into a new form.

Derivatives are not necessarily inherently evil because they are, after all, just pieces of the total pie. It's sort of like Humpty Dumpty. Nothing wrong with Humpty when he sat up on the wall, but when he fell he shattered into a thousand pieces and no one could put him back together again. It's the pieces that are the problem, because many managers don't exactly know what they are, and what they look like, and how they will perform in the bond market as interest rates go up or down. It was the pieces that got Orange County in trouble and the pieces that have provided the impetus for underperformance and, in some cases, bankruptcy for other investment managers.

MFM: So, user beware. When a securities firm buys a Treasury bond and splits out the interest payment to 1 person and the principal goes to another, that's a type of derivative. What are other examples?

BG: I mentioned CMOs, collateralized mortgage obligations. Treasury futures and options. Other derivatives are pieces of an original investment such as the Treasury strips you mentioned. The tough part is that derivatives do not necessarily mimic the price of the original investment they are based on. One would move in one direction, and one in the other.

MFM: Did people just not understand how volatile these were? I'm thinking of the Piper Jaffrey Short-Term Bond Fund. It was a short-term fund, but if you looked at the portfolio, maybe it was really long-term because of the use of derivatives.

BG: Derivatives allow a bond or money market portfolio manager to sort of supercharge the performance of the portfolio, under certain conditions. It's kind of like adding alcohol to the gasoline of an Indy 500 car. As long as the markets stay where they are, or move in one direction, then derivative use will outperform more conservative investments, and that investment manager will be a temporary hero. Then the problem is, when the market moves in the other direction, the results turn sour. That happened to Orange County, where the county government was driven into bankruptcy through the misuse of derivatives. Many of these derivatives—not all of them—simply change their duration far quicker than even the manager knows. Unless you keep up with it on a daily basis, which many managers did not, then you don't really know what you have.

MFM: So they move a lot and they move quickly. And maybe, sometimes, in surprising ways because they don't have a lot of history. And so, you're saying you use derivatives, and a lot of other responsible people do, but it's like saying you drive a car. As long as you do so responsibly, problems are unlikely. But if you drive it at 100 miles per hour, eventually the wheels will come off.

BG: I think that's true. I like to think we use conservative derivatives.

MFM: What's your personal benchmark for performance for PIMCO Total Return and the other two similar funds? At what point do you say, "Well, we've hit the *this* and we're happy?"

BG: Well, if it were the end of the year and if we were 100 basis points or 1% higher than the bond market, or the Lehman Brothers Aggregate Bond Index, I'd be happy. This index is the S&P 500 Index of the bond market.

MFM: Let me ask you a quick personal question. If you had to put all your money in a single bond fund and leave it there for the next 5 years, which one would you use?

BG: I'd use PIMCO Total Return Fund. Relative to my forecast for fairly stable interest rates, the intermediate- to long-term duration plus the ability to use various sectors would, in my opinion, provide the highest return. I also stress, in this type of a market, *going forward*, because of the fairly low fees. I know probably one or two out there have lower fees than we do, but, for the most part, we're less than 50 basis points or 0.5% for the Total Return Fund. And that makes a big difference too. If you're only going to make 7% or so for the year, you can't afford to pay 1% to the manager. You know, when you sell your house, you only pay a 6% commission. One percent out of 7% is a 14% spread. You can't afford that.

MFM: You'd be better off using an index fund.

BG: Exactly.

MFM: How do you view your personal investing? How do you go through the process?

BG: In much the same way. I was reviewing the other night some old memos I wrote, back when I first started at Pacific Mutual in 1971–72 and I had just read a book called *Investing in the Primary Trend*. It was about stocks, but nonetheless, it talked about primary trends as opposed to short or intermediate trends. I wrote down a number of rules for myself when it came to investing, but it was always to focus on where the markets are headed for the next several years and then to decide the various individual selections. My philosophy certainly doesn't mimic that of a Peter Lynch, in which he suggests going out to wherever you're shopping, whatever product you're buying, to take a look at that.

MFM: The Dunkin' Donuts sort of special, huh?

BG: Exactly. My philosophy starts with the market, and what the economy's going to be doing for the next several years, and what kind of vehicle makes sense in that kind of environment; and only after that: Which individual selections make sense within that environment?

MFM: Name 3 mutual fund managers you think do a good job that you admire.

BG: On the bond side, I think Ian MacKinnon at Vanguard does a good job. Also, Dan Fuss at Loomis Sayles, although he has an equity approach to it in the quality of bonds—high-yield or junk bonds—he uses sometimes. But I think he's done an excellent job. Those would be 2 on the bond side. On the stock side, I followed John Neff for years, but now he's gone. He used to be one of my heroes.

MFM: Personally, how do you decide, "I should have so much in equity funds, so much in bond funds." How do you make that decision?

BG: Well, the primary criteria have to start with how much money you have to invest, how much you're willing to risk, and, I suppose, how old you are in terms of your ultimate objectives. I'm 52 now, not 22, so it's a little different now than it was. But having said all that, I'm still relatively young and think in terms of trying to maximize return relative to risk. My willingness to take risk might be a little diminished, but I'm still trying to find that particular niche where I can make the most money relative to the risk I'm willing to assume in the environment I see ahead. My longer-term view is that economic growth on a global basis is going to be the highest in the emerging market nations, but not necessarily across the board in all of them.

From an equity standpoint, you have to go where the growth is and, obviously, where the value is as well. My sense is that the emerging nations, from a growth standpoint, have a hands-down advantage over and above Europe and over and above the United States. So my equity focus is in that direction as opposed to the U.S. or Europe. My fixed-income focus is a bit different. There, you're not necessarily looking toward growth, you're looking to security of income

over time. And the U.S. has wonderful advantages from that standpoint, in terms of its political system and currency. Though it fluctuates, the dollar is regarded as the dominant world currency. The U.S. is still a great market to invest in from the standpoint of bonds and security of income. So most of my fixed-income investments tend to be here.

MFM: If you're making a fixed-income investment, one part of that equation is safety to some extent?

BG: Oh, yes.

MFM: So you're saying, if you're going to be safe, then be safe, and don't say I'm going to buy fixed-income but I'm going to buy Third World debt to try and maximize my return.

BG: Well, I think you could do that, but you just have to know it's really an equity type of investment as opposed to a bond type of investment. If I can get a 15% return from a bond in Argentina, then that's great, but I would have to compare the risk and return of that bond to stocks in Argentina.

MFM: It would be closer to the risk of a stock even though it's called a bond.

BG: Exactly.

MFM: That brings us to the point of the whole high-yield issue or junk bonds, as they are more often called. You have a PIMCO High Yield Fund that has been around for 3 years and has done very well for that amount of time. How does the high-yield sector fit with whether it's an overall bond portfolio or just an investor in general?

BG: Well, high yield is not as risky as emerging markets debt, but it certainly is in between conservative Treasury bonds and stocks. When you have a dynamic economic recovery and corporations are doing well, then high-yield bonds do well in turn, simply because the prospects for the corporations are much better than they are in a recessionary type of environment. So they have equity types of characteristics. An individual who buys high yield has to recognize that it's not a stock, but it will be more volatile than bonds over time and will probably mirror the path of the stock market to a certain extent in terms of the return. That having been said, I think high yield is an attractive alternative but only in bits and pieces. We use high-yield bonds to a small extent in PIMCO Total Return and Harbor and Fremont. But it's much like a chef allocating spices to the main meal.

MFM: It's not a pound of pepper . . . .

BG: Maybe a dash. In terms of specifics, it would be 5% or less of the portfolio, so if you have a disaster in any particular issue or if you have a disaster in the sector—and that happened as recently as 1990—then you're still OK.

MFM: Would you only tend to buy high-yield bonds if you were in a recession? That's when those types of bonds have more pressure on them. Would you wait until that point?

BG: That's the ideal time, but that's when it takes nerves of steel and the guts that even professional managers sometimes find lacking. I throw myself in that same category. It's the hardest thing in the world to buy a junk bond or a distressed investment at the bottom, simply because that's when it looks the darkest. And your fear, even though it's countered to some extent by intelligence, your fear is what you have to fight against. Really, one of the best characteristics of the professional investor should be this ability to understand the psychological nature of investing and recognize fear within himself or herself. But, recessions are the best time to buy corporate bonds because most investors do not want to own them.

MFM: You mentioned fear and emotions in managing money. What do you fear most? A real spike in interest rates, where they just go up really quickly, or a steady rise in interest rates, where they keep hitting fixed-income investments?

BG: Well, I don't know which one of those 2 I fear the most. From a personal standpoint, what affects me the most is that I don't like to lose money for clients. When interest rates go up, bond prices go down. If interest rates go up a lot, you tend to have close to zero or even negative returns, like most bond managers had in 1994. I not only like to think we're outperforming the bond market, but that we're bringing lots of dollars to the bottom line for our investors. The best thing is—if there were four quadrants of investing—you'd always want to be in the upper quadrant, where you're outperforming the market by 100 basis points and the market itself is doing very well. The worst time, obviously, is when the market is doing very poorly and you're underperforming the market. That's when you think you've really blown it.

MFM: Should of stuck with playing poker, right?

BG: Exactly. I think if you're a conscientious manager, those are issues you carry with you all the time. And that's not to ask for sympathy, because this is a well-paid business, more than well-paid, and if that's the only albatross you carry, then it's well worth it. If you are conscientious, it tends to affect you when it's moving in the wrong direction.

MFM: Has that emotional side ever led you into an investment cul-de-sac or dead end?

BG: I've avoided it, although there have been times I've been down and depressed; not clinically, but sour, I guess.

MFM: Bummed out.

BG: Yes. You have to avoid dwelling on things by returning to the fundamentals and moving forward. By simply knowing yourself and having confidence in your ability to perform, and by looking to the future, not to the past. That's how most of us human beings get over small or even large tragedies in our lives. If you could equate poor performance to a minor tragedy, you would need to look to the future and make plans to not only survive but to outperform going forward.

MFM: You mentioned those rules for investing you wrote down 26 years ago, when you first joined PIMCO. I don't know if you still have those, but what would your rules for personal investing be?

BG: Well, I guess my primary rule would be to either know what you're doing or find someone who knows at a relatively cheap cost. This is not a business for fools, and it's not a business for individuals who even know a lot but aren't aware, don't have personal knowledge of themselves or of human nature. But if you're going to invest a substantial portion of your net worth in financial markets, then you'd better acquire the knowledge. If you're not willing to spend the time, if you don't have the interest, the time, the knack, or all of that in combination, to pursue it steadily through the years, then it's probably best to search out and find a portfolio manager that does.

As Bill points out, this is not a business for fools. He also suggests that you would do well to seek out portfolio managers who know what they're doing.

In the next chapter, we are going to show you a list of good mutual funds run by people who definitely know what they're doing.

CHAPTER 5

Brouwer & Janachowski's Short List of Good Funds

One drawback to putting out a list of good mutual funds is that we get indignant calls from fund families asking why their mutual fund or funds were not included. But that's our problem, and we're used to it. Another drawback is that any list can become dated fairly quickly as changes occur at the funds. For example, a good fund can become questionable if the portfolio manager who built the great track record moves on, or if the mutual fund management group sells out to a larger firm such as a bank, insurance company, or brokerage firm. From time to time, good funds close to new investors and new funds come along. We hope you will put this list to good work, but we also hope that you will learn to identify good funds yourself.

As much as we wish the process were easy, in truth it is not. It is always easy to look at a fund's historical track record and show why it *was* a solid fund. It's quite a different thing to determine which funds are going to do well in the future.

One factor that makes it difficult is that no fund will turn in superior numbers every quarter or even every year. As much as we would like funds to consistently beat their index and their peer group every year, most good funds do not. They can be out of favor for as much as 2 or 3 years. But the difference between mediocre funds and good funds that have erratic performance is that over longer time periods—5 or 10 years—the good funds really pay off by turning in stellar performance to offset the subpar years.

Are All Good Funds Appropriate for You?

Each of the funds listed has had excellent performance. Each has significantly outperformed the majority of peers in its category and also has outperformed its benchmark index. For most stock funds, this means the S&P 500; for small company stock funds, it means the Russell 2000. For taxable bond funds, the usual measure is the Lehman Brothers Aggregate Bond Index. We have also provided the applicable Morningstar benchmarks as a point of reference for performance. Each Morningstar benchmark reports the average return for all of the mutual funds in that category, so you can see how a fund stacks up against its peers.

And all of these funds may not be appropriate for you. Based on your individual investment objectives, certain categories of funds on our list will match your needs while others will not. Stick with the categories that match your needs.

One Final Note

This list includes funds that you might not be able to purchase. We have included some of our favorite funds, which are currently closed. They are good for comparison purposes and they might even re-open some day. Also we have included funds that are designed for specific types of portfolios, such as retirement plans, foundations, or institutional investors. Unless your portfolio meets the fund's guidelines, you might not be able to purchase it. Check these restrictions through Morningstar or by contacting the fund directly. Funds designed for institutional investors usually have steep minimums and would be out of reach for most investors, but sometimes they are available at more normal minimums through discount brokerage firms.

Aggressive Growth Funds

Funds in this category seek rapid growth of capital. These funds often invest in small or emerging growth companies, including initial public offerings (IPOs) and companies with high price/earnings and price/book ratios. These funds may concentrate their holdings in one or more sectors, use leverage, and short-sell.

Aggressive Growth Funds	Investment Style	Total Return			Manager Tenure (Years)	Portfolio Turnover	Expense Ratio	Minimum Initial Investment	Total Assets (in Billions)
		1 Year	3 Year*	5 Year*					
American Century—Twentieth Century Ultra Fund Investor	Large growth	13.1%	20.9%	18.5%	16	87%	1.0%	$2,500	$20.1
Kaufmann Fund	Small/Medium growth	1.5	23.7	21.8	12	72	1.9	1,500	4.9
PERFORMANCE BENCHMARKS									
Standard & Poor's 500		29.4	25.9	18.4					
Morningstar Aggressive Growth Objective		−1.2	17.1	15.2					

*Annualized.   as of May 31, 1997

Growth Mutual Funds

Funds in this category seek capital appreciation by investing primarily in equity securities. Current income is not a consideration. These funds may invest in small, medium, or large-sized company stocks. They also tend to emphasize stocks which have higher earnings' growth rates and valuation multiples than value mutual funds.

Growth Mutual Funds	Investment Style	Total Return			Manager Tenure (Years)	Portfolio Turnover	Expense Ratio	Minimum Initial Investment	Total Assets (in Millions)
		1 Year	3 Year*	5 Year*					
Brandywine Fund	Medium/Large growth	16.4%	22.9%	22.2%	12	203%	1.1%	$ 25,000	$7,000.0
Brandywine Blue Fund	Medium/Large growth	16.5	22.9	23.3	7	197	1.1	100,000	398.3
CGM Capital Development Fund	Medium/Large blend	23.1	19.1	19.6	20	178	0.8	Closed	631.6
Founders Growth Fund	Medium/Large growth	13.6	24.5	21.0	28	134	1.2	1,000	1,300.0
Harbor Capital Appreciation Fund	Large growth	21.9	25.7	20.0	7	74	0.8	2,000	2,100.0
Mairs & Power Growth Fund	Medium/Large blend	25.9	30.0	22.4	18	3	0.9	2,500	243.9
Morgan Stanley Institutional Equity Growth Portfolio—Class A	Large blend	24.0	28.8	19.2	6	186	0.8	500,000	477.2
Papp America-Abroad Fund	Large growth	34.0	31.6	20.2	6	12	1.3	5,000	63.1
PBHG Growth Fund	Small/Medium growth	-17.1	19.5	25.6	12	45	1.5	2,500	5,400.0
PIMCo Capital Appreciation Fund— Institutional Shares	Medium/Large blend	25.9	23.8	19.2	7	83	0.7	200,000	474.4
Spectra Fund	Medium/Large growth	10.6	27.6	25.0	24	197	2.5	1,000	36.1
Strong Common Stock Fund	Small/Medium blend	20.7	21.3	21.2	7	91	1.2	Closed	1,300.0
Torray Fund	Medium/Large blend	30.5	28.6	20.3	7	21	1.3	10,000	262.3
Vanguard/Primecap Fund	Medium/Large blend	26.5	27.0	22.4	13	10	0.6	3,000	5,000.0
PERFORMANCE BENCHMARKS									
Standard & Poor's 500		29.4	25.9	18.4					
Morningstar Growth Objective		16.7	20.0	15.6					

*Annualized.   as of May 31, 1997

Value Mutual Funds

Funds in this category seek capital appreciation by investing primarily in equity securities. Current income is not a consideration. These funds may invest in small, medium, or large-sized company stocks. They also tend to emphasize stocks which have lower valuation multiples than growth mutual funds.

Value Mutual Funds	Investment Style	Total Return			Manager Tenure (Years)	Portfolio Turnover	Expense Ratio	Minimum Initial Investment	Total Assets (in Millions)
		1 Year	3 Year*	5 Year*					
Clipper Fund	Large value	25.4%	25.5%	19.5%	14	24%	1.1%	$ 5,000	$ 629.2
First Eagle Fund of America	Medium/Large value	24.7	22.6	20.6	10	93	1.8	5,000	220.7
Oakmark Fund	Medium/Large value	23.5	22.9	25.5	6	24	1.2	1,000	4,900.0
Sequoia Fund	Large value	34.5	26.4	20.4	27	15	1.0	Closed	2,800.0
Standish Equity Fund	Medium/Large value	29.0	24.8	21.0	7	159	0.7	100,000	119.2
Third Avenue Value Fund	Small value	25.0	21.6	20.1	7	14	1.2	1,000	916.2
PERFORMANCE BENCHMARKS									
Standard & Poor's 500		29.4	25.9	18.4					
Morningstar Growth Objective		16.7	20.0	15.6					

*Annualized.   as of May 31, 1997

Small Company Stock Funds

Funds in this category seek capital appreciation by investing primarily in small company stocks with market capitalizations of less than $1 billion. Some funds also include company stocks of more than $1 billion market capitalization. Income generation is not a consideration.

Small Company Stock Funds	Investment Style	Total Return			Manager Tenure (Years)	Portfolio Turnover	Expense Ratio	Minimum Initial Investment	Total Assets (in Millions)
		1 Year	3 Year*	5 Year*					
Acorn Fund	Small/Medium blend	10.5%	15.5%	17.7%	27	33%	0.6%	$ 1,000	$3,100.0
Baron Asset Fund	Small/Medium growth	6.3	25.1	21.9	10	19	1.4	2,000	1,700.0
Barr Rosenberg Series Trust U.S. Small Capitalization Series— Institutional Shares	Small value	19.7	25.8	23.1	8	72	0.9	1,000,000	88.6
Columbia Special Fund	Small/Medium growth	-1.0	15.9	16.4	10	150	0.9	2,000	1,400.0
Lazard Small Cap Portfolio— Institutional Shares	Small/Medium value	20.9	20.1	20.3	6	51	0.8	1,000,000	1,000.0
Loomis Sayles Small Cap Value Fund— Institutional Class	Small value	18.6	22.7	18.1	6	73	1.2	1,000,000	180.3
Parkstone Small Cap Fund— Institutional Shares	Small growth	-13.3	22.0	21.6	9	67	1.3	100,000	430.6
RSI Retirement Emerging Growth Equity Fund	Small growth	-4.5	25.7	22.9	8	150	1.9	0	71.7
Skyline Special Equities Fund	Small blend	27.9	20.4	21.1	10	130	1.5	Closed	272.5
T. Rowe Price New Horizons Fund	Small/Medium growth	-2.7	23.6	20.7	10	41	0.9	Closed	3,900.0
T. Rowe Price Small-Cap Value Fund	Small value	14.5	18.7	17.7	6	15	0.9	Closed	1,400.0
UAM ICM Small Company Portfolio	Small value	18.9	20.3	20.3	8	20	0.9	5,000,000	364.2
PERFORMANCE BENCHMARKS									
Russell 2000		7.0	17.1	15.8					
Morningstar Small Company Stock Objective		4.5	18.1	15.7					

*Annualized.

as of May 31, 1997

Growth & Income Funds

Funds in this category seek capital appreciation and current income by investing primarily in large company equity securities. Investments are chosen for both their growth potential and their ability to generate current income.

Growth & Income Funds	Investment Style	Total Return			Manager Tenure (Years)	Portfolio Turnover	Expense Ratio	Minimum Initial Investment	Total Assets (in Millions)
		1 Year	3 Year*	5 Year*					
Dodge & Cox Stock Fund	Large value	24.7%	23.8%	19.4%	30	10%	0.6%	$ 2,500	$2,700.0
MAS Funds Value Portfolio— Institutional Class	Medium/Large value	28.9	26.8	21.3	10	53	0.6	Closed	2,600.0
Mutual Shares Fund—Class Z	Medium/Large value	22.0	21.0	19.4	23	58	0.7	Closed	6,800.0
PIMCo Value Fund—Institutional Shares	Medium/Large value	22.7	23.0	17.9	6	71	0.7	200,000	69.7
Retirement System Core Equity Fund	Large blend	26.1	26.5	20.0	6	25	0.9	2,500	12.2
Selected American Shares	Large value	37.5	25.8	18.1	2	29	1.0	1,000	1,600.0
PERFORMANCE BENCHMARKS									
Standard & Poor's 500		29.4	25.9	18.4					
Morningstar Growth and Income Objective		23.7	21.4	15.8					

*Annualized.   as of May 31, 1997

Balanced Funds

Funds in this category seek both capital appreciation and current income by investing in a blend of equity and fixed-income securities. Usually, at least 25% of these funds' assets are held in fixed-income securities.

Balanced Funds	Investment Style	Total Return			Manager Tenure (Years)	Portfolio Turnover	Expense Ratio	Minimum Initial Investment	Total Assets (in Millions)
		1 Year	3 Year*	5 Year*					
CGM Mutual Fund	Large value/ Intermediate bond	21.1%	14.5%	13.7%	17	192%	0.9%	$ 2,500	$ 1,200.0
Dodge & Cox Balanced Fund	Large value/ Intermediate bond	18.0	17.5	14.9	30	17	0.6	2,500	4,200.0
Jurika & Voyles Balanced Fund	Medium/Large value/ Intermediate bond	17.3	16.3	15.6	6	69	1.4	250,000	59.1
Vanguard/Wellington Fund	Large value/Long bond	21.9	19.2	14.9	3	30	0.3	3,000	17,500.0
Westwood Balanced Fund—Retail Class	Medium/Large blend/ Intermediate bond	18.9	19.6	16.1	6	111	1.3	1,000	49.5
PERFORMANCE BENCHMARKS									
Standard & Poor's 500		29.4	25.9	18.4					
Lehman Brother's Aggregate Bond Index		8.3	8.0	7.2					
Morningstar Balanced Objective		15.7	14.9	11.7					

*Annualized.   as of May 31, 1997

Foreign Stock Funds

Funds in this category seek capital appreciation by investing primarily in equity securites of issuers located outside of the United States. These funds may invest in small, medium, and large-sized company stocks. They tend to have more than 60% of the portfolio assets invested in countries with developed markets. A smaller portion of the portfolio assets may be invested in less-developed markets.

Foreign Stock Funds	Investment Style	Total Return			Manager Tenure (Years)	Portfolio Turnover	Expense Ratio	Minimum Initial Investment	Total Assets (in Millions)
		1 Year	3 Year*	5 Year*					
Artisan International Fund	Medium/Large blend	18.6%	n/a	n/a	2	n/a	2.5%	$ 1,000	$397.7
Harbor International Fund	Large value	24.8	18.4	16.2	10	10	1.0	Closed	4,600.0
Hotchkis & Wiley International Fund	Medium/Large value	16.6	14.9	13.7	7	12	1.0	10,000	727.9
Janus Overseas Fund	Medium/Large growth	24.4	21.4	n/a	3	71	1.2	2,500	2,300.0
Morgan Stanley Institutional International Equity Portfolio—Class A	Medium/Large value	19.2	14.8	16.4	8	18	1.0	Closed	2,700.0
Warburg Pincus Emerging Markets Fund—Common Shares	Small/Medium/Large value	8.6	n/a	n/a	3	62	1.6	2,500	256.3
PERFORMANCE BENCHMARKS									
MSCI EAFE		7.5	7.7	10.6					
Morningstar Foreign Stock Objective		12.9	8.3	10.5					

*Annualized.

as of May 31, 1997

World Stock Funds

Funds in this category seek capital appreciation by investing primarily in equity securities of issuers located throughout the world. Usually 25% to 50% of their assets are invested in companies domiciled in the United States.

World Stock Funds	Investment Style	Total Return			Manager Tenure (Years)	Portfolio Turnover	Expense Ratio	Minimum Initial Investment	Total Assets (in Millions)
		1 Year	3 Year*	5 Year*					
Founders Worldwide Growth Fund	Medium/Large growth	9.5%	15.3%	13.4%	8	72%	1.5%	$1,000	$ 336.2
Janus Worldwide Fund	Medium/Large growth	21.4	21.1	19.1	5	80	1.0	2,500	8,300.0
PERFORMANCE BENCHMARKS									
MSCI EAFE		7.5	7.7	10.6					
MSCI World Index		17.1	15.0	13.7					
Morningstar World Stock Objective		13.2	13.1	12.2					

*Annualized.

as of May 31, 1997

Bond Funds

These funds seek current income by investing in various types of fixed-income securities. Tax-exempt municipal bond funds invest primarily in municipal fixed-income securities, while taxable bond funds invest primarily in corporate, U.S. Government and Agency fixed-income securities. Funds are categorized into two groups: taxable or tax-exempt municipal bond funds. Each group is then divided into short-, intermediate-, or long-term bond funds.

Bond Funds	Investment Style	Total Return			Manager Tenure (Years)	Average Credit Quality	Average Maturity (Years)	Expense Ratio	Minimum Initial Investment	Total Assets (in Millions)
		1 Year	3 Year*	5 Year*						
Fidelity Institutional Short-Intermediate Government Portfolio	Short-term bond (taxable)	6.9%	6.7%	5.7%	10	AAA	3.6	0.5%	$ 100,000	$ 344.8
PIMCo Low Duration Fund II—Institutional Class	Short-term bond (taxable)	8.3	6.9	6.1	6	AAA	2.6	0.5	5,000,000	339.9
PIMCo Low Duration Fund Institutional Shares	Short-term bond (taxable)	9.0	7.4	6.9	10	AA	3.4	0.4	5,000,000	2,800.0
RSI Retirement Trust Intermediate-Term Bond Fund	Short-term bond (taxable)	7.1	6.5	5.9	13	AAA	3.2	1.0	0	67.0
Bond Portfolio for Endowments	Intermediate-term bond (taxable)	8.8	7.5	7.3	22	AA	6.3	0.8	50,000	31.8
Clover Capital Fixed-Income Fund	Intermediate-term bond (taxable)	7.9	7.8	7.6	6	AA	10.6	0.8	2,000	22.5
Dodge & Cox Income Fund	Intermediate-term bond (taxable)	8.3	8.4	7.8	9	AA	12.8	0.5	2,500	603.7
Harbor Bond Fund	Intermediate-term bond (taxable)	9.6	8.6	8.1	10	AA	8.1	0.7	2,000	303.2
MAS Funds Domestic Fixed-Income Portfolio	Intermediate-term bond (taxable)	9.0	7.8	8.3	10	AAA	9.0	0.5	5,000,000	103.8
MAS Funds Fixed-Income Portfolio II	Intermediate-term bond (taxable)	9.6	8.3	7.9	7	AA	9.0	0.5	5,000,000	196.1
MAS Funds Fixed-Income Portfolio—Institutional Class	Intermediate-term bond (taxable)	10.5	9.3	8.7	13	AA	9.2	0.5	5,000,000	2,600.0
MAS Funds Special Purpose Fixed-Income Portfolio—Institutional Class	Intermediate-term bond (taxable)	10.7	9.6	10.0	6	AA	9.5	0.5	5,000,000	478.3
Pegasus Bond Fund—Class I	Intermediate-term bond (taxable)	9.4	9.0	7.7	6	AAA	6.3	0.7	1,000	828.0
PIMCo Total Return Fund II—Institutional Class	Intermediate-term bond (taxable)	10.0	8.5	8.1	6	AAA	7.1	0.5	5,000,000	486.0
PIMCo Total Return Fund III—Institutional Class	Intermediate-term bond (taxable)	10.5	8.9	8.4	6	AA	8.8	0.5	5,000,000	202.8
PIMCo Total Return Fund—Institutional Shares	Intermediate-term bond (taxable)	10.4	8.8	8.3	10	AA	8.4	0.4	5,000,000	13,000.0
Smith Breeden Intermediate Duration U.S. Government Series	Intermediate-term bond (taxable)	8.8	8.0	7.8	6	AAA	3.9	0.9	250	38.4
Strong Government Securities Fund	Intermediate-term bond (taxable)	8.2	8.1	8.1	7	AAA	8.0	0.9	2,500	686.5
Warburg Pincus Fixed-Income—Common Shares	Intermediate-term bond (taxable)	9.3	8.4	7.8	6	AA	7.2	0.8	2,500	180.1
Western Asset Trust Core Portfolio	Intermediate-term bond (taxable)	8.2	8.4	8.1	7	AA	10.0	0.5	1,000,000	461.2

*Annualized.

as of May 31, 1997

Bond Funds	Investment Style	Total Return			Manager Tenure (Years)	Average Credit Quality	Average Maturity (Years)	Expense Ratio	Minimum Initial Investment	Total Assets (in Millions)
		1 Year	3 Year*	5 Year*						
Loomis Sayles Bond Fund— Institutional Class	Long-term bond (taxable)	14.7	14.6	13.3	6	BBB	19.1	0.8	1,000,000	785.8
Managers Bond Fund	Long-term bond (taxable)	12.1	11.4	9.0	13	BBB	20.9	1.4	2,000	32.5
PIMCo Long-Term U.S. Government Fund— Institutional Shares	Long-term bond (taxable)	10.4	10.2	10.3	6	AAA	21.6	0.6	5,000,000	22.1
MAS Funds High-Yield Portfolio— Institutional Class	Intermediate-term high yield bond (taxable)	17.3	13.3	13.9	9	BB	10.4	0.5	5,000,000	407.3
PIMCo High-Yield Fund— Institutional Shares	Intermediate-term high yield bond (taxable)	14.9	13.4	n/a	5	BB	6.6	0.5	5,000,000	661.6
Vanguard Municipal Bond Fund Limited-Term Portfolio	National muni short-term (federal tax-exempt)	4.9	4.8	5.0	10	AA	4.0	0.2	3,000	1,800.0
Morgan Grenfell Municipal Bond Fund	National muni intermediate-term (federal tax-exempt)	6.9	7.2	7.6	6	A	8.0	0.6	250,000	296.6
Vanguard Municipal Bond Fund Intermediate-Term Portfolio	National muni intermediate-term (federal tax-exempt)	6.8	6.2	7.0	16	AA	7.9	0.2	3,000	6,400.0
Safeco Municipal Bond Fund	National muni long-term (federal tax-exempt)	8.9	7.4	7.1	16	AA	n/a	0.5	1,000	469.8
Scudder Managed Municipal Bonds	National muni long-term (federal tax-exempt)	8.2	7.0	7.1	11	AA	10.4	0.6	2,500	716.9
Vanguard Municipal Bond Fund High-Yield Portfolio	National muni long-term (federal tax-exempt)	8.3	7.2	7.5	16	AA	14.0	0.2	3,000	2,100.0
Vanguard Municipal Bond Fund Long-Term Portfolio	National muni long-term (federal tax-exempt)	8.6	7.5	7.6	16	AA	13.2	0.2	3000	1,200.0

PERFORMANCE BENCHMARKS

		1 Year	3 Year*	5 Year*						
Lehman Brother's 1–3 Year Government Bond Index		6.6	6.2	5.5						
Lehman Brother's Aggregate Bond Index		8.3	8.0	7.2						
First Boston High Yield Index		13.4	11.6	11.5						
Lehman Brother's Long Term Government Index		9.0	9.3	9.0						
Lehman Brother's Long Term Corporate Bond Index		9.9	10.1	8.8						
Lehman Brother's Municipal Bond Index		8.3	7.3	7.2						

*Annualized.

as of May 31, 1997

"Investing Isn't Gambling—It's About Putting Your Money to Work"

An Interview with *Charles R. Schwab*

Charles Schwab seems to be everywhere. His friendly smile has appeared in pretty much every financial publication we can think of. Plus, every Schwab client must feel like he is one of the family by now since he (his face, that is) has been hanging around in their den, living room, or kitchen for years.

Compared to people who are merely famous for being famous, Charles Schwab is well-known because he is a brilliant financial innovator. He practically invented the discount brokerage business, which has transformed the investment landscape during the past 23 years. Charles Schwab & Co., Inc. is the nation's largest discount broker, serving millions of customers through a branch network of 234 (and growing) offices.

In addition, Charles Schwab pioneered the idea of buying and selling mutual funds of many different fund groups through one central point when he created the Schwab Mutual Fund Marketplace®. He followed that up several years later when he established the innovative Schwab Mutual Fund One-Source™ program, which is a no-transaction-fee way for investors to buy and sell mutual funds.

Chuck Schwab has been a forceful advocate of the individual investor for many years. In 1984, he wrote a best-selling book, *How To Be Your Own Stockbroker* (Macmillan), to help ordinary investors do a better job of investing. Chuck has always been a strong voice for the investor, and he has always believed in mutual funds, even during his undergraduate days at Stanford University.

He has also done a lot for investors, by shaking up the stodgy Wall Street establishment.

Mutual Fund Mastery: Over the past 8 or 9 years, Charles Schwab & Co. has developed several innovations that benefit mutual fund shareholders—The Mutual Fund Marketplace and Mutual Fund OneSource. Why are mutual funds such an important part of the development strategy for the Charles Schwab Corporation now?

> **Charles Schwab:** Well, it's not just now. I've been a believer in mutual funds for many years. They are among the better investment vehicles for the American investor. I say *American* because, in other countries, they do not have our system of mutual funds or investment companies. To the average American investor beginning his or her investment life, or, for investors later in life, I think they should focus on the no-load mutual fund area. Since my earliest days, I've been thinking about personal finance for investors—about ways to make it better.

MFM: You also wrote a book on how to do this in, I think, 1984. It was called *How To Be Your Own Stockbroker* (Macmillan). It had a lot of information about no-load funds. But Schwab, as a company, did not go heavily into supporting mutual funds or starting its own funds until the late 1980s.

> **CS:** We were subject to banking regulations due to our ownership by Bank of America, so it was not until that ended and we became independent again that we began moving aggressively in that area.

MFM: Let's talk about the Schwab mutual fund family. What's the plan for the Schwab family of funds?

CS: It's in line with, I guess you might say, the indexed style or market-based style of investment management. Our approach is to identify a strategy and then carry it out using quantitative investment techniques. Like index funds or enhancements to index funds. There are funds out there with all kinds of objectives and purposes. Some do very well, and some are inconsistent versus an appropriate index. For our customers, we try to provide services with relatively less volatile outcomes. Whether it is discount stock brokerage, Mutual Fund OneSource, the Schwab IRA, or anything else, we try to deliver predictable service. That same philosophy underlies our mutual fund offerings. There are funds that are at the top of the hit parade one year and next year they're at the bottom. That's not our style. So, I'm very comfortable with this positioning of providing mutual funds that seek to be relatively consistent performers.

MFM: What about the Mutual Fund Marketplace and Mutual Fund OneSource? How do you decide which ones to add?

CS: Well, the mutual funds that go into both the Marketplace and Mutual Fund OneSource are based, for the most part, on customer demand. And demand comes from the fact that the funds had historically good performance or some other feature that makes them appealing.

MFM: You mentioned that one of the prime things that attracts people to a given fund is performance—very often, performance in the short run. How do you think people should select mutual funds?

CS: To start with, you have to consider your investment objectives. In my mind, I think of tax-deferred accounts, such as my IRA account, for example, where I don't have to pay taxes on gains each year. After all, one of the drags on investment performance is income taxes. Next, I think of any other accounts I have for which I have to pay taxes each year. In other words, I think of 2 different strategies for each of those broad types of accounts. Because the IRA (or any

other retirement plan) is tax-deferred, I might consider being somewhat more aggressive in my decision making in that arena than I can be in my personal accounts. So, I make different kinds of choices with respect to each of those.

MFM: What are examples of funds that you use?

CS: Well, in my IRA, I have used no-load mutual funds for years. I'm not claiming to be the greatest at picking funds, but you're welcome to hear about the ones I use. At times, I have had bad timing, and other times I took too long to make my decision. But it worked out. The performance is probably not too far from the S&P 500. To me, the amazing thing is how fast that money can accumulate in a tax-deferred account such as an IRA.

MFM: Yes, it's amazing, isn't it? Trying to save $100,000 is virtually impossible for many people, but in an IRA or, even better, a 401(k) plan, your assets can accumulate very fast.

CS: I made some mistakes along the way—primarily, because I was not always paying as much attention as I should to my own account. I missed some of the early stages of the bull market that started in 1982. Just being sloppy.

MFM: I'm sure many people reading this will feel better knowing that even Chuck Schwab occasionally procrastinates. Then they won't feel so bad if they make an error in judgment.

CS: We all do.

MFM: I think a lot of people feel guilty—that they should be perfect somehow. We should call every market move, pick every great fund, and so on. Speaking of picking funds, what are some of the ones you use?

CS: I'm hesitant to talk about my specific fund picks, since they're based on my personal objectives and since I'm talking to you long before this will be published. Objectives and situations change, and performance from one period of time won't necessarily continue in the future. But with that said,

Charles Schwab's Personal Approach to Investing

Investors often ask Charles Schwab about his personal approach to investing. Here are the basic principles that he has followed for over 35 years:

1. All of us need to develop a sound, long-term plan to prepare for a comfortable retirement. Social Security and company pension plans alone are not enough to do the job.

2. Every year you put off investing makes accomplishing your ultimate retirement goals even more difficult. As a rule of thumb, for every 5 years you wait, you may need to double your monthly investing amount to achieve the same retirement income.*

3. Understand yourself psychologically as an investor: your emotions, your fears and your tolerance for risk. Make sure you choose the kinds of investments you're comfortable with and that are appropriate for your long-term goals.

4. I am a firm believer in the wealth-generating power of stocks. Over time, stocks have outperformed all other types of investments and compensated for inflation, although stocks do have greater risks and price fluctuations than other investments.

5. Cash and bonds don't grow; they only pay interest. I include fixed-income investments and money market funds in my portfolio only to satisfy my needs for diversification and liquidity.

6. Patience is a virtue. Invest for market returns year in and year out. Maintain the discipline to hold on to or add to investment through down markets as well as up markets.

7. Use asset allocation and mutual funds to create a broadly diversified portfolio. By doing so, you can minimize and spread your risk over a variety of investments. This approach will lead to more consistent and reliable outcomes.

8. Investing doesn't stop when you retire. To make your money work for you throughout your retirement years, don't shift all of your money automatically into fixed income and money market investments too early.

* Based on monthly savings invested at 6, 8, and 10%.

Berger 100, Columbia Growth, and Columbia Special are some of the funds I use. But I also encourage all investors to conduct their own research about funds that look interesting to them. I recommend that investors look at a fund's prospectus and read it carefully before investing. Schwab provides investors with prospectuses on any of the funds we make available.

MFM: I think you hit on a good point. That it's not a matter of doing everything perfectly, it's a matter of having a strategy, sticking to it, and bouncing back from any problems or setbacks.

CS: Yes. In the long run, commitment and persistency are terribly important.

MFM: You mentioned IRAs; what about taxable investments?

CS: On the taxable side, it's been interesting. Over the years, I wanted an easy-to-use equity investment that was efficient in terms of taxes. Since no one had the ideal mutual fund, I designed my own—the Schwab 1000 Fund™. It is designed to be efficient with low portfolio turnover and capital gains, and has been historically very efficient in light of income taxes. Very little turnover.

MFM: If you had to put all your money in one mutual fund, what would you pick?

CS: Of course, this would apply only to my personal circumstances, but since I designed it, I have to go with the Schwab 1000 Fund. I kind of like the name. It has a ring to it, don't you think?

MFM: Funny you should mention that.

CS: Seriously, though, I like it because it is a fund that seeks to track U.S. market returns as measured by the Schwab 1000 Index®. It's very difficult to exceed market returns over a long period of time, as you know.

MFM: Why is it so difficult?

CS: In part, because of the nature of an index. A regular mutual fund has expenses to pay and an index doesn't.

MFM: What about trying to outguess or time the stock market?

CS: For individuals, whether they are using stock mutual funds or buying stocks, I think that there are great emotional issues that come into play. Let's say you're lucky enough to sell before there's a downturn in the market. So you're really brilliant. So then, you're sitting there waiting for the so-called next low before you buy back in. And then all of a sudden, something pops. The market turns, but you don't believe it. You think it's going to go down one more time. But it goes up. And up. You watch it go all the way back up to the point at which you sold. At that point, you might have trouble getting back in, and you continue to miss out.

MFM: Those people are not only missing out on the growth, they are also missing the point.

CS: Investing is about putting your money to work. It's not about gambling. It's not a zero-sum game; it's about putting your money into real companies that do real things that create value. Then everybody can win in investing. Real things are happening that impact your investment. I'm on the board of several companies, and I look for the executives to come in with growth plans. They don't come in with a no-growth plan, or a zero-growth plan, otherwise they'd be fired. Every company is seeking to grow. And that means they're making investments in different kinds of things, and when they grow, real value is created.

MFM: So growth in the economy has a compounding effect over time.

CS: Sure. You know, a firm like Schwab has had a tremendous growth over the last 23 years, because we take our cash flow and reinvest in new things.

MFM: We've talked about equity investing, so how should people make the asset allocation decision? Bonds and stocks, bond funds and stock funds—how should people make that decision?

CS: It all depends on the investment horizon. How far out, in years, can you invest? What is the nature of the money? Can you invest it for 7 or 10 years or more? Then stocks or stock mutual funds are the choices. If you need the money in 3 years' time because your child's going off to college, then you should be very conservative and think about more fixed-income types of investments.

MFM: So, for anyone not needing the money for 10 to 15 years, then a good choice . . . .

CS: May well be stock mutual funds. No substitute for it, for most investors. Potential protection against the ravages of inflation, which you need when you are on a fixed income at retirement. And, we're all living longer, collectively speaking. We're going to live beyond our parents' life spans in many cases, because of advances in medicine.

MFM: If you're 65 years old, say husband and wife, one of the two of them is probably going to be around until they're almost 90.

CS: Twenty-five, 30 years later. A big liability you've got to cover somehow, and you've got to do it through savings and investments.

MFM: Let's talk a little bit about the future, in the sense that, even though you don't have a crystal ball, you've thought a lot about what the future of mutual funds is going to be. What do you see happening in the next 10 years in this broad area of personal finance, and what are you thinking about at Schwab?

CS: I would like to see government policy make it even more advantageous for the individual to increase tax-deferred savings through an expansion and liberalization of the IRA account or something like it. Also, a capital gains tax reduction would be beneficial for investors.

MFM: Capital gains reduction has been somewhat demonized in the sense that people say it's only for the rich. Why would the reduction of capital gains taxes benefit society as a whole, not just the so-called fat cats.

CS: I don't want to make this too lengthy, but a reduction in capital gains tax would free up massive amounts of capital for job creation and economic growth. There are many people who own stocks or even businesses that they have held for a long time. As a result, there is a large gain that would be subject to income taxes. Because of that hefty tax, those people just hang on. If there were a low or even no capital gains tax, they would be more inclined to sell and to then redeploy that money. Largely because of taxes, $8 to $10 trillion of capital that is held in private hands is stuck. It takes about $70,000 of capital to create a new job. If you are in the electronics industry, it might be $100,000 per job. In a small service or retail business, it might be $10,000 to $15,000 of capital per new job. And, it's always the people who have the capital who can create the jobs. So we want to encourage those people to create more jobs and it really helps to have a liberal movement of capital in order to do that.

MFM: I think a lot of people don't understand what you mean by *stuck*. You're referring to

people who bought stock years ago and would have a lot of income taxes to pay so they just hold on to the stock.

CS: Let's take an example. You have $1,000 of stock and you have held on to it for 20 years. You bought it for $100 and now it's worth $1,000. You have $900 in capital gains, but a lot of that gain is really just the effect of inflation over time. If you sell that stock, you end up with maybe $700. You pay 30% or more in taxes. So, why would rational people sell that stock, unless they absolutely needed the money or unless they thought the company was in trouble? The tax structure tends to cause you to stay put.

MFM: One criticism is that a capital gains reduction only favors rich people. There are many people who own stock or real estate, or even a business, who could not be classified as rich. But many people do not want to do something, even if it makes sense, simply because people in upper-income brackets would benefit.

CS: We all know ordinary people who have owned homes for many years. Primarily through the impact of inflation, those people now have a large capital gain. Dollars today are worth much less than they were 20 or 30 years ago. So taxing that gain is very unfair.

MFM: Switching topics a bit, are mutual funds going to become the dominant providers of services, as opposed to banks?

CS: Well, I think banks will try to add more mutual funds as the format for providing more services for their customers. One of the problems with banks is that they have tremendous conflicts of interest. They love to take your money and put it into a CD, or put it into a money market account as they'd call it, and pay you 2%.

MFM: So, the old banking institutions of America are under pressure. Banks must provide better value and more convenience and efficiency. That's one thing that you've been a champion of for many years. Obviously, you started discount brokerage in 1975, but besides that, you've done a number of things with 24-

hour trading and electronic trading. What's the philosophy behind all the innovations?

CS: We try to be—it's our goal to be—the most useful and also the most ethical company in the brokerage and financial service industry. We will go to almost any length, do any number of handstands, if that's what it takes, to make the customer happy. We back up our operations with a set of rules and standards for treatment of the customer. Wall Street often doesn't think that way. They think about what's best for the firm.

MFM: The past 10 years or so have been amazing in light of the changes we have seen in discount brokerage, mutual funds, and all aspects of personal finance.

CS: That's right. I have to say that we've been fortunate as a company to have been in this business at such an explosive time for growth in the personal finance business because of our devotion to service, devotion to customers.

MFM: Let's talk a little bit about mutual fund expense ratios, which are an important issue for investors. The expense ratio amount comes right off the investor's return. In *The Wall Street Journal*, there was an article last year that suggested the Schwab OneSource program leads to higher expenses. Is that true?

CS: No, it's not. I generally find *The Wall Street Journal* to be pretty accurate, but in this case, they're just wrong. Over time, expense ratios for funds at Schwab have come down slightly. We've tried to monitor this very carefully. This is a competitive industry, and it's not in our long-term interest to have expense ratios go up. We view our service as a win–win thing for the mutual fund companies and for the public. We provide the public with great no-load funds. For the funds, we do all kinds of servicing of these accounts: We send out prospectuses, monthly statements, proxy materials, we execute the trades, and so on. And we do it faster and more efficiently than the funds can. We net buys and sells so they have one big trade on a given day instead of many small ones. It saves the

mutual fund company a huge amount of costs. And, so, we felt if we brought that efficiency to the fund, then they could share with us a part of their management fee, some of their expenses, and the customer would benefit. So I would hope our record of 23 years of service for customers would at least give us the benefit of the doubt, but it doesn't always work that way.

MFM: Anybody who's watched what you've done over time would understand that. As a separate issue, I and many other people thought mutual fund expense ratios would go down over time, but they haven't. Why is that?

CS: In terms of the overall expense ratios of funds, generally speaking, you would think that there would be economies of scale there, and some competition in that respect. You know, Vanguard is doing a very effective job out there, bringing the expense ratios to the attention of the public. We can control expense on our own Schwab funds, but we do not control other fund groups. Americans are basically trusting people. They have expected their financial vendors to have the highest integrity, and that has fallen down in a lot of spots. So, it's important for people to get engaged and to be more active. To look for these things, to analyze, to make choices. And that's a question everyone should ask: What expense ratio is reasonable, what should I pay for?

MFM: Has there ever been a better time to be an individual investor? Have investors ever had better access to inexpensive financial services than they do today?

CS: Absolutely not. And it's going to get even better. But with *better,* the word *complicated* comes into play, too. In the advent of the wonderful electronic world that we're seeing explode before our eyes, you're going to have more choices. More ways to analyze, more choices, and, as a result, more complexity. Firms like Schwab will have all kinds of services and programs to allow you to analyze your overall financial position in some meaningful way. That's going to be very helpful to people.

MFM: What about record keeping for income taxes? That is still very cumbersome with mutual funds. Do you have plans to make that easier?

CS: Well, I think firms like Schwab will provide investor solutions for things like income taxes. You would expect us to do that. We expect ourselves to do that. We have the people and the computers to do that. However, the magnitude of the records we would have is enormous. When you have, say, an average customer, you might have a lot of mutual funds and if you hold these for 10 years, you have a lot of records for all the different reinvestment dates, and so on. The more efficiently we can bring things like average cost forward, it'll become more efficient to track these things.

Charles Schwab has used no-load mutual funds for many years. And, he admitted that even he occasionally procrastinates. Perhaps the most important point he made is that investing is not a game. To Schwab, investing is all about putting your money to work.

When you turn the page, we will show you exactly how to put your money to work as you master the markets.

CHAPTER 6

Mastering the Markets

When Matt Millen was a tough, hard-hitting linebacker for the San Francisco 49ers, he said it best: "Things are never as bad as they seem when you're losing and never as good as they seem when you're winning."

The stock market has brought exhilaration and exasperation to investors for generations. At times, making good money is ridiculously easy; at other times, hanging on to what you have seems impossible. Markets rise higher and higher only to fall further than any sane person could imagine. Is there a way to navigate through these extremes without losing your mind or your nest egg? Fortunately, the answer is yes.

A rising or falling trend in the stock market can last so long that it seems permanent. Witness the long, relatively uninterrupted bull markets in the 1950s and early 1960s. Or, a long, nearly stagnant period from 1969 all the way to 1982, when the stock market lost ground to inflation. But, no matter how strong a trend seems or how long it lasts, it always—and we mean *always*—carries with it the seeds of its own reversal. A bull market for stocks may seem unstoppable, yet one day it will end and stocks will fall. The worst of bear markets may involve an unending stream of negatives, but it too will end. And when it does, with the benefit of hindsight, we can look back and see the factors that led to the reversal.

A winning stock market strategy need not be complicated, complex, or even completely correct. But it must take into account certain seemingly immutable rules of the road. To be successful, a strategy must be:

♦ Consistent.

♦ Correct (most of the time).

♦ Clear-cut.

Consistency Ralph Waldo Emerson said, "Consistency is the hobgoblin of small minds." Consistency, by itself, is of little merit. Consistently wrong or bad is no good. Nonetheless, when it comes to investment strategies, consistency in the planning and execution of your strategy is essential.

Let's say you have decided on a course of action that calls for a conservative investment strategy—one that may lag bull markets a bit, but gains considerable ground in flat or falling markets. Nonetheless, you have the good fortune to be in a sustained up market, one that lasts for several years.

During this period, your conservative selections have done reasonably well, but they have lagged behind the more aggressive funds as well as the stock market averages. Finally, in the face of this sluggish performance, you become impatient, dump your laggards, and jump on board the aggressive funds that have been doing well. Six months or a year passes, and you congratulate yourself—until the stock market tumbles. Your aggressive funds fall faster than the market overall, and, suddenly, you are losing a fortune. You quickly lose all your gains from the past few years, and maybe more. The slow-moving funds you dumped now look quite good, and you wonder what ever possessed you to change.

As you can see, making big strategic changes late in the game is dangerous both to your portfolio and to your peace of mind.

Correct (Most of the Time)   No stock market strategy is going to be correct all the time, but to be successful you must be correct more often than you are wrong. Charles Allmon, the editor of *Growth Stock Outlook*, became bearish about stocks over 10 years ago. During the 1987 Crash, his newsletter and a portfolio he managed did very well. Unfortunately, he never changed his mind. Allmon's allocation to stocks remained low through one of the longest stock market upswings in history, and he and his investors lost out on a huge profit opportunity. Being correct once is just not enough.

For a stock market strategy to work well, it has to have solid logic and good sense behind it. For example, the stock market goes up, on average, twice as much as it falls. Getting out before downdrafts is possible, though not necessarily easy. Getting back in for the ride up is the really hard part. Inflexible formulas and statistical rules seldom conform to reality, and they often lead to incorrect decisions.

Clear-Cut   The third and final factor is that your strategy must be clear-cut. If it requires making monthly portfolio changes, reading tea leaves, or patterns on stock charts, or any other methodology that is not simple and clear-cut, chances are you will not follow it at a critical time. The best investors have simple rules that are easy to understand and follow. They may be nothing more complicated than saving and investing more money every 3 months without fail—no matter what. Or, putting 20% in foreign stock funds with the remaining 80% allocated one-third in small company stock funds and two-thirds in large company stock funds. Or, buying nothing but technology funds or growth funds or balanced funds. Take the time to develop a strategy that could be easily communicated, in one or two simple sentences, to your children, your colleagues, or your grandmother. If your strategy cannot pass that test, it may need some refining.

Over time, as your skill and confidence grow, you will develop your own style as an investor. To start developing your own approach, you need to thoroughly understand the financial markets. And to help you do that, we turn to Benjamin Graham, the father of modern security or investment analysis.

In 1934, during the depths of the Great Depression, Graham co-authored (with David Dodd) the seminal work on stock or security analysis, called, appropriately enough, *Security Analysis* (currently out of print). In 1973, during the worst stock market crash since the Depression, he published a new edition of *The Intelligent Investor* (Harper & Row), a classic book with a preface by Warren Buffett. In *The Intelligent Investor,* Graham gave readers an excellent metaphor for the stock market:

> Imagine that in some private business you own a small share that cost you $1,000. One of your partners, named Mr. Market, is very obliging indeed. Every day he tells you what he thinks your interest is worth and furthermore offers either to buy you out or to sell you an additional interest on that basis. Sometimes his idea of value appears plausible and justified by business developments and prospects as you know them. Often, on the other hand, Mr. Market lets his enthusiasm or his fears run away with him, and the value he proposes seems to you little short of silly.
>
> If you are a prudent investor or a sensible businessman, will you let Mr. Market's daily communication determine your view of the value of a $1,000 interest in the enterprise? Only in case you agree with him, or you want to trade with him. You may be happy to sell out to him when he quotes you a ridiculously high price, and equally happy to buy from him when his price is low. But the rest of the time you will be wiser to form your own ideas of the value of your holdings . . . .

Taking Graham's philosophy and applying it is relatively easy. We believe (and we're sure Graham would agree if he were here) that time spent trying to determine where the stock market is going in the short run is time wasted. Time spent fretting about current market activity is also time lost. According to Graham, the only thing to consider is whether current stock prices are excessively high and therefore you should sell out, or whether they are so low that you should consider it a buying opportunity. Otherwise, Graham suggests you should ignore Mr. Market.

Since most people cannot resist talking about and reacting to the peaks and valleys of the stock and bond markets, let's take a short stroll through the terrain and separate fact from fantasy.

A Quick Primer on Stock Market Peaks and Valleys

The stock and bond markets are literally bazaars in which millions of investors all over the world carry out purchases and sales of securities. Individuals, corporations, charities, unions, governments, and even drug dealers all buy and sell in the same places. Decisions to buy or sell are made for a variety of reasons. For example, an individual may sell some stock because he or she needs to buy a house or invest in a new business. A government may sell bonds to finance an upcoming budget deficit. A company may sell bonds to finance a new manufacturing plant. And so on. What do all these buy or sell decisions have in common? In all these cases, the timing was dictated by an event that had nothing to do with the stock or bond market.

Whenever there is a significant rise or fall in the stock market, we can count on getting a call from a journalist or two, asking for a comment on why the market did what it did. We usually say the market fell yesterday because there were more sellers than buyers. The reporter then says, "Very funny. I know that, but what really happened?" The press is looking for a reason such as, "Fears over the budget deadlock led to profit taking on Wall Street today."

That may sound plausible, but it has no actual validity. All that happens on any single day is that there are tidal flows in and out of securities. Normally, the inflows and outflows are relatively equal, but occasionally they are not. Sometimes there is a triggering event, such as a statement by Federal Reserve Chairman Alan Greenspan that interest rates will be going higher. If the stock market tanks the next day, people attribute it to Greenspan's statement, when the two events may not be connected at all. Journalists know that their readers, listeners, or viewers want relatively simple reasons for things. And the public responds to stories of big shots who can move the markets. The list of big shots changes all the time, but who cares? In all the hot air, one point remains: Short-term movements in the stock market are meaningless, so don't get distracted by them.

Three key economic elements help determine the broad highs and lows of the stock market:

1. Corporate earnings. In the broadest sense, the stock market follows the trend of earnings. This is true for an individual company as well as the market overall.

2. The flow of liquidity (money) into or out of stocks (primarily determined by Federal Reserve decisions on short-term interest rates and growth in the money supply).

3. Stock market valuations (price–earnings ratios, dividend yields, book values, and so on).

Many investors mistakenly believe that the economy must be good before stocks can rise. Not true. In fact, throughout our history, there have been many long periods in which stocks and the economy have moved in different directions. Stocks often begin rising at the tail end of recessions, and they frequently weaken when economic expansions are going full speed ahead.

Stock market investors look ahead to companies that are having or will have growing corporate earnings. This activity may occur in two

---

If You're On the Sidelines

If you are on the sidelines now with money to invest, you need to establish a strategy for putting it to work. You can either invest it all at once or invest it in stages over a period of time. Since the stock market goes up more than it goes down, it is easy to make an argument for investing your entire portfolio as soon as possible. From our experience this has been the best strategy. But, many investors can't stand the thought of investing just before a correction, so we will offer another strategy called staging. It is really another form of dollar-cost-averaging. Here is how it works. Let's say that you have a $100,000 portfolio that is to be invested in stock mutual funds. Pick a time period over which to invest your portfolio. This could be as little as 3 months for the more adventurous to as long as 2 years for the very cautious. Divide the number of months in your time period into the portfolio to calculate the amount that will be invested each month. For example, if you were to stage the $100,000 portfolio into a 100% stock growth portfolio over a 1 year period, $100,000÷12 = $8,333. To make the math simple, you would then invest $8,000 every month in your selected portfolio. If there is a large market drop along the way, you could also accelerate the staging process.

It is important that you know exactly what your final portfolio will look like, before you start investing. You need to know which funds you will be buying and how much of each. You also must commit to carrying out your plan, no matter what happens. Many times we have seen investors abandon their regular investment strategy when the stock market falls. But if you believe in the adage, buy low and sell high, then you should be happy when stocks fall—as long as you have more money to invest. At that point, when each monthly investment comes up, you can confidently make your selection knowing you are on track.

---

types of companies: growth companies and more mature or cyclical firms.

To see how this works, imagine what the economy is like in the latter phase of a recession. Typically, the Federal Reserve moves to reduce short-term interest rates to give things a boost. Because of the recession, corporate profits are down, confidence is low, investors are depressed, stocks have been falling, and yet the stage is set for a bull market. Most people find that confusing, yet it is so logical. Why? Because everything in life—including the stock market—is cyclical. A pendulum swings one way and, by definition, it must swing back.

Expect the Unexpected, Part Two

In Chapter 1, we mentioned the concept of unexpected change. For example, the technological boom that began in the 1950s fueled growth in many companies and created whole industries that never before existed.

But unexpected change is often big trouble. The failure of a large Austrian bank in 1931—Credit Anstalt—contributed to the world events that precipitated the Great Depression, which was the worst stock market decline in this century.

In 1973, high interest rates and inflation would have caused a tough market anyway, but the Arab oil embargo deepened the misery and caused the worst stock market crash since the Great Depression.

Now that you know quite a bit about the factors that cause swings in the stock market, can you predict when changes will occur in a particular trend? Maybe yes, maybe no. Predictions are often made. Some are right and some are wrong. In our opinion, investors waste more time and money chasing the dream of market timing than they do on anything else. We can say with certainty that no single statistic, factor, or technique can predict the stock market's up and downs.

There are some obvious clues to the future, though. If price–earnings ratios are high (above 20), then stocks are expensive and further upturns will be more difficult. If price–earning ratios are low (below 10), then there is a lot of room on the upside. Neither of these indicators will tell you how long a particular trend will last. Periods of high valuation and low valuation can last for a long time.

One method is to invest until very high valuations become the rule and then simply move into cash and wait patiently on the sidelines until a buying opportunity comes along as happened in 1973–1974. In 1968, Warren Buffett stopped buying stocks. Several years later, when stocks fell, he made many of the purchases that cemented his reputation as a stock wizard. But, to wait while stocks are soaring requires great discipline, a keen nose for value, and the foresight to have built up a big pile of cash with which to take advantage of the buying opportunity when the time comes.

The best technique for buying low is to buy regularly. Whether you call it dollar cost averaging or just a disciplined period of regular purchases, that is the best way to deal with stock market peaks and valleys—simply ignore them.

Buy and Hold

One simple, easy, and remarkably successful investment strategy is the so-called buy and hold approach. A steady strategy of making solid investments and holding them for long periods is a very reliable way to make money. After all, an investor who buys and holds is simply letting returns compound over time and is relying on the proven propensity of our economy to continue growing. Let's look at a buy and hold strategy starting at the absolute worst time to buy stocks in the past 50 years—December 1972 (see Figure 6.1).

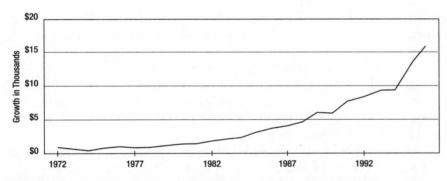

FIGURE 6.1 Investing Just Before the Worst Bear Market Since 1929. This chart illustrates the growth of $1,000 invested in the Standard & Poor's 500 in December 1972, just before the 1973 through 1974 bear market. (*Source:* Ibbotson Associates, Micropal, Ltd., Brouwer & Janachowski, Inc.)

Another really bad time to buy stocks was in October 1987. Let's see how a buy and hold strategy worked for someone unlucky enough to buy then, but smart enough to hold on (see Figure 6.2). As you can see, this strategy works, even if your timing is bad, as long as you have the patience to wait things out. If you are interested in a buy and hold strategy, mutual funds are an excellent vehicle because they have professional managers who are watching your investments when you are not. (No matter how dedicated you are, over a 20-year time span, there will

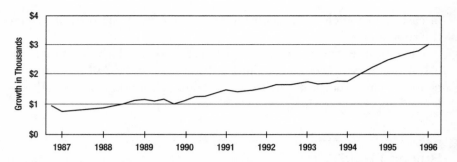

FIGURE 6.2 Investing Just Before the Stock Market Crash of 1987. This chart illustrates the growth of $1,000 invested in the Standard & Poor's 500 on October 1, 1987, just before the 1987 stock market crash. (*Source:* Micropal, Ltd., Brouwer & Janachowski, Inc.)

be a time or 2 when you simply get distracted by life and put your investments on the back burner.) Another plus is that the mutual fund structure is an enduring one that you can be confident will safeguard your assets for many, many years.

Buy and hold investors are people who have a great deal of confidence in themselves and in their investment strategy. They believe that the U.S. economy and the world economy will naturally grow over time, and that recessions, depressions, corrections, and crashes are all temporary events not worth bothering about. Sounds great and it is. If you faithfully follow this strategy, you will have a lot more time and energy to do all the things in your life you enjoy more than investing. That is, if there is anything you enjoy more—stuff like hanging out with your friends and family, traveling, working, kayaking, reading, drinking bubbly beverages . . . .

We have a confession to make, though. Our investment approach is not a strict buy and hold. We have to factor in significant changes for a given client's situation, changes in a particular mutual fund, and, of course, the ebb and flow of the financial markets. In other words, things change. Portfolio managers come and go, long-term investment trends arise and fade away, and, of course, investors' objectives and situations change too.

Modified Buy and Hold

The strategy we use should really be called a modified buy and hold approach. If you like researching investments and paying attention to the financial markets, you should consider a modification of the strict buy and hold strategy. You can periodically review new mutual funds for inclusion in your portfolio, and you can consider modest changes in how much you allocate to large company stock funds or small company funds. You may reposition some of your portfolio from domestic stock funds to international, or from stocks to bonds.

Dr. Kroopf's Personal Prescription

In 1986, Dr. Stanford Kroopf, a retired physician, asked us to manage his retirement account and some personal assets. After spending time with him, we determined that his key investment objective was conservative growth. He needed solid investment returns, but he was also concerned about keeping portfolio volatility to a manageable level. Balancing risk and return, in his case, worked out to 80% in stock funds and 20% in bond and money market funds. To maintain that 80–20 ratio, we planned to periodically rebalance the portfolio. If a rising stock market pushed the market value of the commitment to stocks beyond 80%, we would take some profits and move them into bond funds to bring the portfolio back to the original 80–20 allocation. Or, if falling stocks knocked his percentage in stock funds down, then we would move money from bond funds to stock funds. That was the plan.

The stock market crash on October 19, 1987, turned the plan into reality. That day, the Standard & Poor's 500 tumbled 22.5%, and Stan's portfolio fell 9.6%. That Wednesday, we bought stock mutual funds to bring the allocation back to 80–20. We heard from Stan on Friday. "I knew you would be busy during this crash, so I didn't call. But I'm dying to know, what did you do?" We explained that we had purchased more stock funds to rebalance his account. "That sounds good," he said. "I'm glad you did it, but I'm also glad that I didn't have to decide whether to buy or sell. I'm just glad that we had a system in place."

AND THE MORAL IS . . .

The stock market always fluctuates. Be forewarned, as long as you invest: Stocks or stock mutual funds can have electrifying runups and scary plunges. You can either react to what happens, or you can have a plan of action figured out ahead of time. Guess which approach we recommend?

Rebalancing

One important aspect of investing is setting an initial asset allocation. For example, you may choose to be 50% in stock funds and 50% in bond funds, or 70–30, or any other ratio of stock funds to bond funds. Once that ratio is set, you would do well to revisit it periodically because your percentages will change over time. If stock funds have done well, the percentage in stocks will creep up and eventually it could be much higher than you originally intended. Or, a crash in the stock market could reduce the percentage in stock funds significantly. In either case, you should consider rebalancing. Once a year, take a look at your portfolio and determine what the current percentage in stock funds and bond funds is *at that time*. If there is a significant change from when you started, we think you should rebalance. In some years, you may have to move assets from stock funds to bond funds in order to get back to your 50% (or 70%, 40%, etc.) allocation to stock funds. In other years, you may have to reverse the process. When you rebalance on a consistent basis, you automatically apply a solid discipline of buying low and selling high to your portfolio.

Developing a Style of Your Own

Develop an investment strategy that takes into account your own situation, your personality, and your emotional makeup. As we said, your strategy has to be consistent, correct (most of the time), and clear-cut. Fortunately, this is easier than it sounds. In fact, we suspect you already have a very good idea of what will work for you, even if you are still in the throes of an internal debate. If you still have some doubts, review Chapter 1 and read Chapter 7. The upcoming interview with Richard King should give you some useful insights too.

INTERVIEW

"Buy a Great Stock, Regardless of What Country It's In"

An Interview with *Richard King*

Richard King heads up international investing at the Warburg Pincus Funds. He is the lead portfolio manager for Warburg Pincus International Equity Common, International Equity Institutional, and Emerging Markets Funds.

King's international experience dates back to 1968, when he first joined W. I. Carr Sons & Company (Overseas), a London-based international securities firm, as an investment analyst.

Low-keyed and soft-spoken, King knows how to produce results. Under his leadership, the Warburg Pincus International Equity Fund has been one of the top-performing international funds since its inception in 1989. It averaged 13.5% per year, versus 5.3% for Morgan Stanley's Europe, Australasia and Far East Index (EAFE).

Mutual Fund Mastery: Richard, when it comes to international investing, you're an old hand, aren't you?

Richard King: Not that old actually; but yes, I've been at it a while. I moved to Hong Kong in 1970 as an investment analyst. It was exciting back then because those countries—Hong Kong, Malaysia, Singapore, and, of course, China—were completely unresearched. They were really emerging markets then. Any good fundamental research had great impact because these markets were imperfect.

MFM: You had to be a bit of a pioneer.

RK: Yes, a pioneer. You had to figure out reliable sources of information on the companies and use judgment to determine if a company's management was honest and straightforward and generally credible. And that was good training.

MFM: Given your track record, it's obvious you made a number of good moves, and good performance naturally followed. With good performance came an inflow of new investment. How have you responded to the growth in your fund?

RK: Well, we added a number of very strong professionals to work with me so that we can follow a broader universe of stocks with added intensity.

MFM: How do you retain a unified approach with so many high-powered analysts and associate portfolio managers?

RK: Fortunately, we were able to find people who approach investing in the same way as I do. The group also has to be tightly knit and disciplined.

MFM: To change things a bit, I want to ask about a term you use quite often. The term is *secular change.* From my early days in church, *secular* meant worldly and it was a pejorative term. What do you mean by it?

RK: Well, it is a grand-sounding phrase, which just means a long-term or once-in-a-lifetime type of change. Or a change that is going to go on for many years.

MFM: People talk about the normal business cycle, which, from the bottom of a recession to the peak of an expansion, is usually around 3 to 5 years. Are you saying this is a longer-lasting phenomenon?

RK: Right. Secular change might draw you to an emerging market because the first and greatest secular change is when a country begins to industrialize. People move from the countryside to the city. Manufacturing starts up. People who make cement and concrete and other similarly boring things do very well. Banks are formed. Electric utilities, steel companies—all these are growth industries and are quite exciting to invest in. You can invest for 10 years in such enterprises and they'll still be growing if they are well managed. Whereas, investing in Citicorp in the U.S., or a cement company in the United Kingdom, is a matter of timing.

MFM: So, in developed countries, these basic industries are more cyclical and tied to economic ups and down. They are no longer growth stocks.

RK: Absolutely. They are no longer growth stocks. They can still be a good business investment if you get in at the right time. Secular changes also occur in the developed markets. For example, there are many such changes in Japan, partly because the rather inefficient domestic part of the economy has lagged behind the export manufacturing sector, which is very efficient. There are huge changes to come in office automation in Japan, as well as in consumer spending and in areas like telecommunications.

MFM: Richard, let me ask you a quick question. Would you characterize the fund as either more value- or more growth-oriented?

RK: To me, the terms *value* and *growth* attempt to define an artificial distinction. I think growth can be good value. It all depends on whether the company's growth potential is fully reflected in its share price.

MFM: How would you describe the investment approach you developed?

RK: We're business investors. It is all basic commonsense stuff. We believe a company, or even the stock market, has a value you can determine by doing Graham-and-Dodd-type security analysis—kicking the tires, and

so forth. We believe the value changes with growth in cash flow, dividends, and so on; it is possible to work out the economic value of a company as a going concern with some degree of accuracy. This is what Benjamin Graham called intrinsic value. So, like our Warburg Pincus Venture Banking division, we are business investors looking for good businesses at the right price. Of course, stock market valuations are often too high when people are optimistic and liquidity is plentiful, and too low when people are depressed and credit is scarce. Therefore, searching out good business value can make us somewhat contrarian in our approach.

MFM: One advantage of international investing is that when one country's stock market is overvalued, another country's can be quite cheap, right?

RK: Yes. When Tokyo was at a record high in 1988, New Zealand was very depressed, having had years of poor economic growth and high inflation. But, New Zealand changed dramatically because a new government came into power and shunned the welfare state. They also had an independent central bank. There was extremely good business or economic value in New Zealand companies.

MFM: So you shorted Japan and bought New Zealand?

RK: No; that might have worked, but what we did was reduce our Japanese holdings and increase our holdings in New Zealand and other attractive stock markets.

MFM: How do you determine which countries are attractive for investment?

RK: There are 2 primary ways we decide to invest in a particular country. First, if we find a great stock that we want to own, we buy it regardless of what country it's in. Second, we also look at valuations across entire markets. If, for example, Argentina's stock market dropped 50%, we might reason that there must be extremely good values there and we'd be inclined to take a good look.

MFM: So, there would be 2 different streams of thought. One is simply finding some good stocks, and the other is deciding that a particular country looks interesting, and then looking at individual stocks in that country.

RK: That's correct. Ultimately, it still comes down to individual stocks. Even if a particular stock market has fallen, before we go in, we have to find stocks we want to own.

MFM: Good point. Do you think most investors who are in the stock market should have a portion of their money invested internationally?

RK: Yes, I think they should, because I believe growth will be greater overseas and, in the long term, growth is what will get you the higher returns. Investing internationally also provides diversification.

MFM: What is your personal benchmark for performance of the fund? Do you compare yourself to the Morgan Stanley Europe, Australasia and Far East Index?

RK: According to the prospectus; that is the main index we compare ourselves with. We also look at comparable funds. Comparisons are important, but essentially we don't forget our purpose, which is that we try to get our shareholders the best return possible, with a reasonable measure of risk.

MFM: The best return . . . ?

RK: The best return compared to the S&P 500 Index and inflation, and to whatever else is a reasonable return in today's world. Certainly, in the long term, we want people to feel that, by diversifying, they will be able to enhance their returns.

MFM: Warburg Pincus International Equity Fund is a diversified fund in the sense that it will go with both industrialized and emerging markets. How does that tradeoff between established markets and emerging markets occur?

RK: I think the fund has a major advantage because we can invest in the emerging stock markets, but we do not have to be in them if we think they're unattractive. So, I'd say there's an advantage in using a broad fund that has that flexibility.

MFM: What about a pure emerging markets fund?

RK: Since my days in Hong Kong 27 years ago, I've been a great believer in emerging markets. They are attractive because growth will be higher there. Obviously, it depends on which emerging market, because they are not all the same. But in the long term, emerging markets will give you better returns. Having said that, I would say an investor should put 80% of his or her international allocation in a diversified international fund and 20% in an emerging markets fund.

MFM: Great. People always like to know what you do. Do you invest in the Warburg Pincus International Equity Fund?

RK: Yes, I do. I hate to sound like an advertisement here, but I invest in most of our funds here at Warburg Pincus. For me, though, most of the investment is in the international funds because I think the growth in the long term is generally better there. I also have a decent exposure to the U.S. stock market as a Warburg Pincus partner.

MFM: For you, right now, do you think the best opportunity is in international mutual funds?

RK: I do. I don't really buy individual stocks any more. I used to when I was an analyst.

MFM: How do you determine your asset allocation for personal investment?

RK: Well, I'm not near retirement, so I'm prepared to take a long-term view of things. I tend to be equity-oriented because that's where I want to be in the long term. I have a certain amount in bonds, and I have something in Warburg Pincus Global Fixed-Income Fund, run by Dale Christensen. I keep bonds and cash to the minimum I need to make me feel brave enough to stick with stock funds.

MFM: So you have some ammunition on the sidelines, in case something falls.

RK: Yes. It helps to have a bit of cash when things begin to fall, so you feel more relaxed about things and do not panic. I like to buy a fund I can leave money in for 3 to 5 years and relax and take the view that, although it could be bumpy for a while, it will all work out over the longer term.

MFM: When you have a stock that has fallen, say 20% or even 50%, do you ask yourself if there is something wrong in the analysis?

RK: Yes, we do. If it has fallen that much, there has got to be something wrong. We obviously would get more suspicious of our original reason for owning that stock if it fell to such an extent.

MFM: What advice can you give to American investors who are a little bit leery about investing outside our borders?

RK: First, investing overseas provides diversification, which reduces risk. Also, the whole point of investing outside the United States is to potentially find areas of higher growth. In the long term, economic growth is what gets you higher returns and, generally, there are many attractive opportunities overseas.

MFM: I'll ask you a tough one now. If you had to put all your money into one single mutual fund and leave it there for 5 years, which one would it be?

RK: I suppose I'd go for our main fund, Warburg Pincus International Equity, rather then either our Emerging Markets Fund or our Japan Growth Fund, though the latter two stand to do quite well over time. If you had your choice of when you could take your money out of our Emerging Markets Fund, rather than having to sell exactly 5 years from now, I suspect you could do best in that fund. Japan is also a compelling story, and I believe that the country is in a recovery cycle that will last anywhere from 3 to 5 years. Emerging markets and Japan, in fact, will likely make up the greater portion of the International Equity Fund over the next 5 years. But if I wanted to sleep soundly at night, I'd choose our main fund, which provides the greatest diversification and, therefore, stands to be the least volatile.

MFM: What is an important lesson you've learned in 27 years of investment experience?

RK: Well, it's tough, but you have to look beyond the current market at times. You have to keep telling yourself that, when things look terrible, that's when the opportunity exists. For example, when the Chinese recently fired rockets in the Taiwan Straits, that was a good time to invest in Taiwan because many investors were selling and the Chinese will probably be sensible in the long run and life will continue. You have to keep telling yourself during a bad market that there will be a tomorrow and, during a bull market, you have to remember that you can't party forever.

Even though he has been working hard for many years, King still loves to look at stocks and talk about markets. In fact, if you're not careful, King will talk you under the table, because he loves what he's doing.

Despite his understated British style, King gave us plenty of words to live by: ". . . when things look terrible, opportunity exists. . . . during a bull market, you have to remember that you can't party forever." And he speaks from experience, because he has seen it all in his investing career. In fact, he was living and analyzing stocks in Southeast Asia when many of today's mutual fund managers were still in elementary school.

In the next chapter, we show you how to create a great portfolio of mutual funds.

CHAPTER 7

A Great Portfolio for You

Selecting good mutual funds is important, but creating a great portfolio that fits your needs is the ultimate goal. In this chapter, we want to help you do just that. Some investors may want to create a portfolio from scratch, while others may want to modify an existing portfolio. In either case, the way you construct and manage the portfolio is absolutely critical to your success.

Creating Your Own Great Portfolio

If you follow sports, you undoubtedly have witnessed teams filled with superstars who could not win the big one. Maybe it was a failure of chemistry or spirit or something else, but at a critical time the team's flaws were laid bare. Rather than being a team that worked together, they were really just a bunch of individuals who wore the same uniform. There are other teams filled with so-called underachievers. Teams that "had no chance" and yet they just kept winning.

We want you to develop a great portfolio the way a sport franchise develops a great team. You first start with a vision of what you want. You add funds that match that vision. Over time, you refine your approach and gradually weed out those that do not fit and put in those that do. Your portfolio may have some well-known, consensus superstar funds, but it may not. You may find that your needs are best matched by funds that do not garner a lot of media attention. Remember, your portfolio is your team. You are the coach, the general manager, and the owner so you can do exactly what you want. So let's get started building a great mutual fund team for you.

The investment approach we use is simple and straightforward. We spend the time it takes to understand our clients' financial and investment objectives. Once we know what the target or the goal is, then we create, manage, and track a portfolio of no-load mutual funds designed to meet the investment objectives for that client. We don't

Great Players Don't Always Make a Great Team

Hunting for Financial Independence

When Jim Hunter graduated from the University of Hawaii in 1969, he was not your typical student, either in age or experience. He had finished a tour of duty in Vietnam as a first lieutenant and psychological warfare specialist, working in the countryside alongside an elite Special Forces unit. When his tour ended, he took the first flight out of Vietnam and a courier flight to Hawaii. And that's where he stayed.

After graduating from the university, Jim tried a corporate job with IBM for a year, ran 2 car rental agencies, and, not incidentally, had a lot of fun. He and his wife, Marcia, enjoyed the Hawaiian lifestyle, but when their two children came along, they decided to chuck it all and leave. Instead of just settling somewhere, in 1984, Jim and Marcia packed up the kids and spent 3 months camping in several Western states, in search of the perfect place. They settled in Ashland, Oregon, which, according to Hunter, has it all: "Nice people, great climate, excellent schools, inexpensive real estate, and with the annual Shakespeare Festival, there is a nice, quirky cultural atmosphere. It's completely different from Hawaii and also from urban America."

He bought 15 acres and spent the next year building a beautiful family home. He now works as a rural route postman, and Marcia teaches in the local schools.

Their goal is to become financially independent, and Jim's approach is simple, though slower than it needs to be: "Save my way to financial independence; save as much money as possible." Jim's strategy of saving every nickel and putting it in the bank is admirable, but, unfortunately, he missed out on the tremendous growth in stocks over the past 13 years because of his ultraconservatism. Jim knew that, deep down, he should be investing for growth, but, as he put it, "I just couldn't pull the trigger." Despite his reluctance, he has built up some impressive savings and assets, including their Oregon home and a condominium in Hawaii worth $250,000. They also have $7,000 invested in stocks, $38,000 invested in bonds, and $310,000 in money market funds and bank accounts. In their retirement plans, they have $108,000 in stocks and $45,000 in money market funds. In addition, they are saving over 50% of their annual income, including $45,000 in personal savings and $10,000 in retirement plan savings.

BROUWER & JANACHOWSKI'S POINT OF VIEW

We pointed out to Jim and Marcia that their goal of financial independence had no deadline. The first step, then, would be for the 2 of them to set a deadline for independence and to decide how much money it would take. They set 10 years (when Jim turns 62) as the time period. Their home was paid off, so they decided they would need $30,000 (after income taxes) to pay for their modest lifestyle. We crunched the numbers and found their current strategy would work—but they could probably reach their goal much sooner if they were willing to step up the risk factor a bit. The increase we recommended was to bring their personal investment portfolio from its present 1% in stock funds up to a still modest 25%. If future returns are similar to the average for the past 70 years, then Jim could retire at age 55, 7 years sooner than his target. We recommended the following stock mutual fund allocation for their growth investments:

Artisan International Fund	15%
Harbor Capital Appreciation Fund	20%
Harbor International Fund II	15%
Selected American Shares	20%
Vanguard/Primecap Fund	15%
Warburg Pincus Emerging Growth Fund	15%

start until we know the goal. Then, and only then, do we start to build the portfolio.

Next, we are going to give you a system for setting up your portfolio according to the single most fundamental factor—time horizon. We think this will make creating a portfolio much easier. Thinking in terms of time horizon will also help you keep your portfolio on the fast track to investment success.

Time Horizon

We define time horizon as the minimum amount of time before you are likely to spend the money in a given portfolio or account. The easiest way to think of it is in terms of a specific event. You want to help pay for your child's college tuition. If the child is 10 years old, you have 8 years before college starts and 4 years over which the money will be spent. We will say the time horizon is 8 years because you will start spending the money then, and the spending phase is quite short.

For someone who is 57 and is planning to retire at 65, you might think the time horizon is also 8 years. Instead, it would almost certainly be much longer because very few people retire and blow all their money in the first year. To us, someone who is 57 and in reasonably good health would have a time horizon of 20 to 30 years at a minimum, because the person will probably live that long and will presumably need money during that entire time.

Spend a few minutes thinking this through. You will then be able to set some pretty accurate and realistic time horizons for each and every portfolio you have. Divide your accounts or portfolios into 2 types:

1. **Specific event investing** (buying a house or a car, paying for a child's education, buying a business).

If you are saving for a specific event, you generally know when it is likely to occur, or when you would like it to occur. For that reason, you can forecast how much you will need and your time frame for accumulating that amount. Select the period of time before that specific event, and the following guidelines will make sense. When you look at the suggestions, please bear in mind that we are assuming you have no need to spend money from this portfolio during the accumulation period.

We think of investing in terms of a scale from 1 to 10. If you have 1 year to go, you should be in cash, such as a money market mutual fund, Treasury bills, or a bank account. Beyond 1 year, you can allocate your assets according to our *Timetable for Specific Event Investing*.

TIMETABLE FOR SPECIFIC EVENT INVESTING

Time Horizon	Percent to Stock Funds	Percent to Fixed-Income Funds
2 years to go	20	80
3 years to go	30	70
4 years to go	40	60
5 years to go	50	50
6 years to go	60	40
7 years to go	70	30
8 years to go	80	20
9 years to go	90	10
10 or more years to go	100	0

Do you see a pattern developing here? If you picked it up, then you know that, beyond 10 years, you would also invest 100% in stock funds.

As you can see, the longer you can commit, the more confident you can be of a positive outcome in the stock market (see Figures 7.1–7.4). If you have at least 10 years before you will spend any money from an account, you can afford to be 100% committed to stock mutual funds.

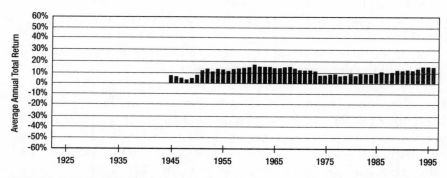

FIGURE 7.1 Twenty-Year Time Horizon. This chart shows the results of investing in stocks (Standard & Poor's 500) for any 20-year time period beginning in 1926. Each bar represents the average annual total return that the index earned for the 20 years ending in that year. Because long time periods smooth out the annual ups and downs of the stock market, there have been no negative return periods, and the historical returns for most 20-year periods have consistently landed in the 7% to 15% range. (*Source:* Ibbotson Associates, Micropal, Ltd., Brouwer & Janachowski, Inc.)

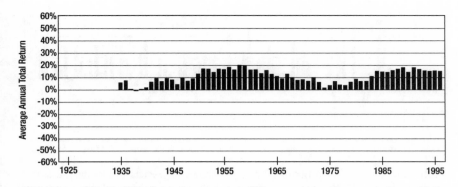

FIGURE 7.2 Ten-Year Time Horizon. This chart shows the results of investing in stocks (Standard & Poor's 500) for any 10-year time period beginning in 1926. Each bar represents the average annual total return that the index earned for the 10 years ending in that year. Because long time periods smooth out the annual ups and downs of the stock market, there have been only two negative return periods. (*Source:* Ibbotson Associates, Micropal, Ltd., Brouwer & Janachowski, Inc.)

But what about investing for your retirement many years from now? In that case, we would like you to think about that account or portfolio as long-term investing.

2. **Long-term investing** (generally, your retirement portfolio).

Long-term investing is a bit different from specific event investing. Investing for retirement or any other long-term goal is more open-ended

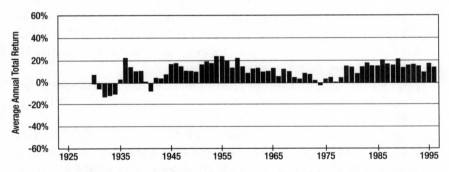

FIGURE 7.3 Five-Year Time Horizon. This chart shows the results of investing in stocks (Standard & Poor's 500) for any 5-year time period beginning in 1926. Each bar represents the average annual total return that the index earned for the 5 years ending in that year. Because 5-year periods smooth out the annual ups and downs of most stock market cycles, there have been only a few negative return periods. (*Source:* Ibbotson Associates, Micropal, Ltd., Brouwer & Janachowski, Inc.)

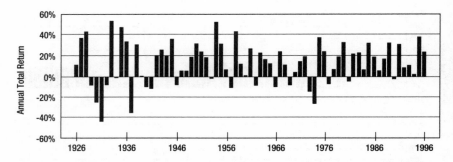

FIGURE 7.4 One-Year Time Horizon. This chart shows the results of investing in stocks (Standard & Poor's 500) for any year beginning in 1926. Each bar represents the annual total return that the index earned for that period. Short time periods have historically had dramatically volatile annual returns. (*Source:* Ibbotson Associates, Micropal, Ltd., Brouwer & Janachowski, Inc.)

because the event—retirement—is not an event at all. Rather, it is, ideally, a long period of time. Because it is open-ended, you have to account for changing needs, including income needs and the impact of inflation over many years. Fortunately, that's pretty easy to do.

We pointed out before that a healthy 57-year-old man or woman has many years of life to go, according to life expectancy statistics and, the actual time horizon for investing is much longer than you might imagine at first glance. Again, retirement is not an event that occurs the day you get that gold watch; it's a long time period. Most investors saving for retirement, and most retirees, have a time horizon of at least 10 years or more. On the *Timetable for Specific Event Investing,* we see that, for time horizons over 10 years, you should be 100% in stock mutual funds. Although 100% in stocks makes intellectual sense, for many people it may be too aggressive.

Let's go through the exercise, just to make sure you understand our thinking. First, we will show you how to set aside what we call Down-Time Money.

DownTime Money is a way to allow for the inevitable stock market crash, without getting so cautious that you miss out on the good returns that the stock market can generate. Second, we always want you to consider your own emotional makeup and your ability to sleep at night. Remember, these are guidelines or suggestions, not laws laid down from on high. Make your own decisions in light of your needs. Later on, we will give you a list of investment objectives that may help you determine your own personal retirement portfolio.

If you are already retired or about to retire, and you need to take income from your portfolio each year, then we'd like you to think about the process and about stock market volatility as follows.

First, are you an optimist about the future of the United States? If you are, then you have confidence that the best overall investment plan would be to take an ownership stake in a piece of America. It could be stock in a company, or a piece of real estate, or shares in an equity (stock) mutual fund. For our purposes, we'll say equity mutual funds.

Second, you have seen how, over 10-year-periods, the stock market has almost always had positive returns. And if you take any 20-year period, going back to 1926, all periods (even during the Great Depression) are positive. Therefore, any and all money with a 20-year time horizon should logically be invested 100% in equities or the equivalent (real estate, private ownership of a business, etc.).

Even looking at a 10-year horizon, for all but 2 periods since 1926, stocks have had positive returns. Therefore, we believe that any and all money with at least a 10-year horizon should also logically be invested 100% in equities or the equivalent (real estate, private ownership of a business, etc.).

Third, we believe that most people, of all ages, have at least a 10-year life expectancy, even if they are already retired. Someone who is 80 could reasonably argue the point, but people are living longer and longer, because of a better standard of living and advances in nutrition and medicine.

Fourth, since most retirees have at least a 10-year horizon, a goodly chunk of their retirement account should be invested in stock mutual funds. The only caveats relate to amounts you might need to take out of your portfolio for living expenses, your personal circumstances, and, of course, your ability to sleep well at night.

Calculate how much, if anything, you need to take in annual income from this portfolio. If you do not envision taking income out for at least 10 years into retirement, you can skip the rest of this section. If you will need income from your portfolio sooner, we want you to take it in a disciplined way. This is your DownTime Money.

The *longest* amount of time (since 1945) that the stock market has taken to fully recover (get back to even) is approximately 3½ years, so you might want to allow for a similar period for the future. If so, you would want to set aside approximately 4 years' worth of the annual income needs from your retirement portfolio.

The *average* time period to reach breakeven (since 1945) has been about 2 years, so that is also a reasonable number to select. In any case, we suggest you set aside 2 to 4 years' worth of annual income (Down-Time Money) that you would otherwise take from your portfolio. Put that money into a very conservative, short-term investment such as a money market fund, certificate of deposit, or very short-term bond fund. Then, you can invest the rest of the account as a long-term portfolio set up according to a specific set of investment objectives.

To do this, you need to pick your personal investment objectives, such as *balanced,* or *growth,* or any combination. (In a moment, we will give you specific portfolios for various investment objectives.) Another approach is to use the *Timetable for Specific Event Investing* and simply pick the time horizon you need to achieve your investment objective. As we pointed out, in most cases, you will be alive and kicking for at least 10 years, but you may want to pick a shorter time period. In that case, you can allocate your retirement portfolio accordingly.

As you can see, we consider time horizon to be a critical portfolio consideration. Another critical factor is portfolio diversification. If you select several mutual funds, but they all follow similar investment styles, you could be inadvertently putting your portfolio at risk. For stock funds, these types of portfolio diversification are very important. And they apply whether you use actively-managed funds or index funds:

1. **Market capitalization.** Create a balance between funds that invest in small, medium, and large companies.

2. **International stocks.** Add diversity by using international funds.

3. **Investment style.** Make sure you use both growth-oriented and value-oriented funds.

Pay Attention to Investment Styles

Diversify your portfolio with different investment styles. Stock funds come in two basic flavors—growth funds and value funds. Both are seeking growth or capital appreciation, but they do it in different ways. Growth funds invest in companies with rapidly growing sales, earnings, and profit margins. They will have hot short-term performance when this style of investing is in vogue. But eventually the hot streak will end and other types of stock funds will come into their own. The so-called value funds will begin performing well. Value funds also seek growth or capital appreciation, but they do so with different types of stocks. Value funds invest in companies with underpriced assets, unrecognized franchise value, or cyclical earnings. Both approaches can work very well, but they seldom do so equally at a given point in time. If you're loading up on funds based on recent performance trends, you're setting yourself up for an unpleasant surprise. Chances are, you're concentrating on a group (such as growth or value) that is just about to go into a lull while the other takes off.

A better strategy is to decide from the outset that you want to have participation in each style, both growth and value. If you are going to use growth funds, balance your selections so that you have some stock funds that have a growth style and some that have a value style. An easy way to accomplish this with a single fund is by using funds that have a "blend" style—usually defined as buying growing companies at a good price.

Diversify Among Different-Sized Companies

Investing only in large company stocks while ignoring smaller companies is a mistake similar to investing in only one investment style. We think your stock funds should have an emphasis on large companies, but not to the exclusion of smaller companies. But remember, small stocks can suffer through periods of underperformance that are several years long. Then, as in 1991, they boom.

Diversify Globally

Are you limiting your investments to U.S. funds only because you don't know much about international funds? If so, you are cutting out a large portion of the investment opportunities around the world. Better do the homework so that you can make an informed choice.

Just as value and growth investment styles are countercyclical, the various foreign markets often move up or down at a different pace than the U.S. markets. The reasons for this can be quite complex, but some of the most important aspects are differences in the political and economical climate. For example, the United States could be about to move into recession just as Europe is about to move into a growth phase. Another big factor is currency fluctuations.

Even though the international markets make up more than 60% of the global equities, it might be a stretch for you to allocate 60% of your portfolio to international mutual funds. Stay within your comfort zone. Many large institutional pension plans allocate 20% or so of their portfolio to international investments.

Bond Funds Need Portfolio Diversification, Too

For bond funds, portfolio diversification is also very important. The following also apply whether you use actively-managed funds or index funds:

1. **Maturity.** We generally recommend intermediate bond funds. If you are very concerned about interest rate risk, you can use short-term bond funds. We generally do not recommend investing in long-term bond funds.

2. **Diversity.** Use funds that purchase different type of securities (Treasury bonds, government agency bonds, and corporate bonds).

3. **Credit quality.** Use funds that generally buy high quality bonds. But you can invest a smaller portion in high yield or junk bond funds.

By utilizing bond funds that have these characteristics, you create a portfolio that is truly diversified. One that can withstand increases in interest rates, recessions, and even weakness in the U.S. dollar.

Neither the Rifle nor the Shotgun Approach Works Well

Most portfolios we have analyzed are either too concentrated or too scattered. They focus on a very narrow segment of the financial markets or they just blast away at everything. But good investing is not a battle, it's a building process in which you develop your skills, learn as you go, and, over time, create a strong, solid, and resilient team of mutual funds.

The truth is that many investors will buy a good fund or 2 but their overall portfolios have not been constructed for greatness and will probably only achieve mediocre results. Instead of stepping back to rethink and rebuild their portfolio from the ground up, they shuffle their investments periodically by selling a fund or 2 and buying replacements. When the results still don't improve, they blame it on their lack of skill in selecting funds. But the real problem lies in the person selecting the portfolio team members. Here is an excellent portfolio for investors who want a long-term portfolio of equity mutual funds:

10-YEAR PORTFOLIO

Funds	Region	Investment Category	Investment Style	Percent
Artisan International Fund	International	Medium/Large stocks	Blend	10
Hotchkis & Wiley International Fund	International	Medium/Large stocks	Value	10
Janus Overseas	International	Medium/Large stocks	Growth	10
Clipper Fund	U.S.	Large stocks	Value	10
Harbor Capital Appreciation Fund	U.S.	Large stocks	Growth	10
Selected American Shares	U.S.	Large stocks	Blend	10
Mairs & Power Growth Fund	U.S.	Medium/Large stocks	Blend	10
Torray Fund	U.S.	Medium/Large stocks	Blend	10
Acorn Fund	U.S.	Small/Medium stocks	Blend	10
Baron Asset Fund	U.S.	Small/Medium stocks	Growth	10
TOTAL				100

With this 10-Year Portfolio, our overall goal is long-term capital appreciation through a globally diversified portfolio. We allocated 30% to international stock funds and 70% to U.S. stock funds. Within the U.S. funds, we allocated approximately 71% to large and medium/large stock funds and 29% to small and small/medium stock funds. Overall we also created a balance between growth-oriented funds and value-oriented funds.

If you wish to choose a shorter time horizon than 10 years, simply take 10% for each year under 10 and move it into an intermediate bond fund. For example, using an 8-year time horizon portfolio, you could allocate 80% to stock mutual funds and 20% to bond mutual funds (see table on page 136).

In the 8-Year Portfolio, we used 80% of the same relative allocation made to the stock mutual funds used in the 10-Year Portfolio and added 3 intermediate-term bond funds to complete the 20% fixed-income portion of the portfolio.

If you are investing for a portfolio that is taxable, you may want to consider tax-exempt bond funds instead of taxable bond funds (refer to the tax-exempt income portfolio, which is illustrated later in this chapter). Many investors prefer tax-exempt bond funds, which come in 2 flavors: national and state-specific. National funds buy bonds from many different states and municipalities. State funds buy only bonds

8-YEAR PORTFOLIO

Funds	Region	Investment Category	Investment Style	Percent
STOCK FUNDS				
Artisan International Fund	International	Medium/Large stocks	Blend	8
Hotchkis & Wiley International Fund	International	Medium/Large stocks	Value	8
Janus Overseas	International	Medium/Large stocks	Growth	8
Clipper Fund	U.S.	Large stocks	Value	8
Harbor Capital Appreciation Fund	U.S.	Large stocks	Growth	8
Selected American Shares	U.S.	Large stocks	Blend	8
Mairs & Power Growth Fund	U.S.	Medium/Large stocks	Blend	8
Torray Fund	U.S.	Medium/Large stocks	Blend	8
Acorn Fund	U.S.	Small/Medium stocks	Blend	8
Baron Asset Fund	U.S.	Small/Medium stocks	Growth	8
TOTAL				80
BOND FUNDS				
Dodge & Cox Income Fund	U.S.	Intermediate bonds	High quality	7
Harbor Bond Fund	U.S.	Intermediate bonds	High quality	7
Strong Government Securities Fund	U.S.	Intermediate bonds	High quality	6
TOTAL				20

issued within a specific state. We generally do not recommend state funds because they have a much more limited selection of bonds to buy. Restricting the fund to only one state puts the portfolio manager in a bit of a straitjacket. A diversified national tax-exempt bond fund is a better bet.

As we said earlier, your long-term portfolio should be invested in stock mutual funds and/or intermediate-term bond funds. Anything with a short time horizon (such as your DownTime Money Account, once that's set up), should be in a money market mutual fund or a similar risk-free investment such as a very short-term bond fund.

Earlier, we said that if you prefer a portfolio structured by investment objectives, we would show you some examples. Here are several portfolios which are aimed at a particular investment objective:

AGGRESSIVE GROWTH PORTFOLIO (100% STOCK FUNDS)

Funds	Region	Investment Category	Investment Style	Percent
Janus Overseas Fund	International	Medium/Large stocks	Growth	14
Vanguard International Equity Index Fund Emerging Markets Portfolio	International	Medium/Large stocks	Blend	14
Harbor Capital Appreciation Fund	U.S.	Large stocks	Growth	12
Papp America-Abroad Fund	U.S.	Large stocks	Growth	12
Founders Growth Fund	U.S.	Medium/Large stocks	Growth	12
Spectra Fund	U.S.	Medium/Large stocks	Growth	12
Kaufmann Fund	U.S.	Small/Medium stocks	Growth	12
PBHG Growth Fund	U.S.	Small/Medium stocks	Growth	12
TOTAL				100

In the Aggressive Growth Portfolio, we did not use value funds. Value funds tend to add ballast to a portfolio that has been structured for steady growth. But here, we are going for maximum capital appreciation with funds that buy stocks in rapidly growing companies. The portfolio is diversified globally. Janus Overseas looks for fast-growing companies in developed foreign countries. The Vanguard Emerging Markets Portfolio is more aggressive, investing in many less-developed

GROWTH PORTFOLIO (100% STOCK FUNDS)

Funds	Region	Investment Category	Investment Style	Percent
Artisan International Fund	International	Medium/Large stocks	Blend	10
Hotchkis & Wiley International Fund	International	Medium/Large stocks	Value	10
Janus Overseas	International	Medium/Large stocks	Growth	10
Clipper Fund	U.S.	Large stocks	Value	10
Harbor Capital Appreciation Fund	U.S.	Large stocks	Growth	10
Selected American Shares	U.S.	Large stocks	Blend	10
Mairs & Power Growth Fund	U.S.	Medium/Large stocks	Blend	10
Torray Fund	U.S.	Medium/Large stocks	Blend	10
Acorn Fund	U.S.	Small/Medium stocks	Blend	10
Baron Asset Fund	U.S.	Small/Medium stocks	Growth	10
TOTAL				100

foreign countries. The domestic portion of the portfolio is diversified to cover small, medium, and large company growth stocks.

The Growth Portfolio is the same as the 10-Year Portfolio. The objectives are identical—a well-diversified global equity portfolio.

BALANCED PORTFOLIO (65% STOCK FUNDS, 35% BOND FUNDS)

Funds	Region	Investment Category	Investment Style	Percent
STOCK FUNDS				
Artisan International Fund	International	Medium/Large stocks	Blend	6.5
Hotchkis & Wiley International Fund	International	Medium/Large stocks	Value	6.5
Janus Overseas	International	Medium/Large stocks	Growth	6.5
Clipper Fund	U.S.	Large stocks	Value	6.5
Harbor Capital Appreciation Fund	U.S.	Large stocks	Growth	6.5
Selected American Shares	U.S.	Large stocks	Blend	6.5
Mairs & Power Growth Fund	U.S.	Medium/Large stocks	Blend	6.5
Torray Fund	U.S.	Medium/Large stocks	Blend	6.5
Acorn Fund	U.S.	Small/Medium stocks	Blend	6.5
Baron Asset Fund	U.S.	Small/Medium stocks	Growth	6.5
TOTAL				65
BOND FUNDS				
Dodge & Cox Income Fund	U.S.	Intermediate bonds	High quality	9
Harbor Bond Fund	U.S.	Intermediate bonds	High quality	9
Strong Government Securities Fund	U.S.	Intermediate bonds	High quality	9
Warburg Pincus Fixed-Income —Common Shares	U.S.	Intermediate bonds	High quality	8
TOTAL				35

The Balanced Portfolio uses the same mutual funds as the 8-Year Portfolio but the allocations are different. 65% of the portfolio is allocated to stock funds, while 35% is allocated to bond funds.

TAXABLE INCOME PORTFOLIO (100% BOND FUNDS)

Funds	Region	Investment Category	Investment Style	Percent
Dodge & Cox Income Fund	U.S.	Intermediate bonds	High quality	25
Harbor Bond Fund	U.S.	Intermediate bonds	High quality	25
Strong Government Securities Fund	U.S.	Intermediate bonds	High quality	25
Warburg Pincus Fixed-Income —Common Shares	U.S.	Intermediate bonds	High quality	25

The Taxable Income Portfolio utilizes primarily, high quality, intermediate bond funds. They maximize current income while reducing the risks associated with gyrating interest rates and economic cycles. The very conservative investor might want to substitute one or more short-term bond funds (see list in Chapter 5) with the intermediate-term bond funds listed above. This will make the portfolio even more immune to the effects of gyrating interest rates. The adventurous investor, might consider incorporating high yield bond funds in their portfolio. But be cautious. These funds tend to be very cyclical, so be careful. The key point to look at is the spread or difference between the yields of Treasury bonds or high quality corporate bonds and high yield bonds. When the economy is in recession, the spread widens because investors are concerned about the creditworthiness of companies. As the economy improves, the spread generally narrows. A good time to buy a high yield bond fund is during a recession.

For the extremely adventurous, or those who like to live on the edge, you might consider international bond funds and even emerging market debt funds. We don't feature a list of funds in either of these categories in Chapter 5, because these funds aren't a good fit for most investors' long-term portfolios—they are best for those who follow these markets closely.

TAX-EXEMPT INCOME PORTFOLIO (100% BOND FUNDS)

Funds	Region	Investment Category	Investment Style	Percent
Scudder Managed Municipal Bonds	National Muni	Long-term bonds	High quality	33
Vanguard Municipal Bond Fund Intermediate-Term Portfolio	National Muni	Intermediate bonds	High quality	33
Vanguard Municipal Bond Fund Limited-Term Portfolio	National Muni	Short-term bonds	High quality	34

In the Tax-Exempt Income Portfolio we don't use state tax-exempt bond funds. We prefer national municipal bond funds, which are only exempt of Federal income taxes. The overall blend of funds is structured to achieve an intermediate-term, high quality tax-exempt bond portfolio. The references to the very conservative and adventurous investors in the taxable income portfolio above apply to the tax-exempt income portfolio also. Use additional short-term bond funds to reduce risk, or add spice with high-yield municipal funds.

10-YEAR INDEX FUND PORTFOLIO (100% STOCK FUNDS)

Funds	Region	Investment Category	Investment Style	Percent
Vanguard Index Trust 500 Portfolio	U.S.	Large stocks	Blend	40
Vanguard Index Trust Extended Market Portfolio	U.S.	Small/Medium stocks	Blend	15
Vanguard Index Trust Small Capitalization Stock Portfolio	U.S.	Small stocks	Blend	15
Vanguard International Equity Index Fund Emerging Markets Portfolio	International	Medium/Large stocks	Blend	10
Vanguard International Equity Index Fund European Portfolio	International	Large stocks	Blend	10
Vanguard International Equity Index Fund Pacific Portfolio	International	Large stocks	Blend	10
TOTAL				100

The 10-Year Index Fund Portfolio seeks long-term capital appreciation. We allocated 30% to international stock funds and 70% to U.S. stock funds. Within the U.S. funds, we allocated approximately 57% to large stock funds and 43% to small and small/medium stock funds. Since all these funds have a "blend" investment style, we achieved overall balance between growth and value for both the domestic and international funds.

To reduce volatility, you can add an intermediate bond fund by using the Vanguard Bond Index Fund Total Bond Market Portfolio or the Vanguard Municipal Bond Fund Intermediate-Term Portfolio.

The final point we want to make is that you control all the elements of your portfolio. You cannot control the stock market, nor can you control the portfolio decisions a particular mutual fund makes. But you can decide what funds will be in your portfolio. You can decide the balance between stock funds, bond funds, international funds, and even value or growth funds. Creating a great portfolio is possible because you control the strategy and you control which funds you use.

But now, we think it's time to pause and see how you're doing. Are you pretty comfortable with what you've learned in this chapter? With the importance of paying attention to your time horizon and to portfolio diversification? Or, do you have more questions than answers? If you're OK, then just keep on going. The next interview, with Jane Bryant Quinn, is very interesting. If you're feeling a bit overwhelmed, then now is a good time to take a break. Do something else that is totally different and get back to mastering mutual funds in a day or so. We'll see you then. And, remember, you've actually absorbed a lot more information than you think. You're doing great, just hang in there.

Creating a Great Portfolio

"I Can't Guess When Stocks Will Tumble, but I'm Happy to Exploit It When It Happens"

An Interview with *Jane Bryant Quinn*

Characterizing Jane Bryant Quinn as a consumer advocate is like calling Colin Powell a retired soldier. A true statement, but it leaves out some important facts.

Jane Bryant Quinn is *the* consumer advocate. Best-known. Most prolific. Longest tenure on the beat. But when you meet her, it is very hard to believe she began covering the growth and development of the consumer movement way back in the early 1960s, before there was an official consumer movement. Back then, she wrote for a small newsletter called *The Insider's Newsletter,* which was published by *Look Magazine.* Now, her twice-weekly column appears in 250 newspapers nationwide. She covers a broad range of consumer issues, and she is best known for her clear, lucid, and compelling advice on personal finance.

She also writes a regular column for *Newsweek* and another for *Good Housekeeping* magazine. She has been a regular on *CBS News* and once hosted her own public television show, *Take Charge.* Now, among other things, she is working with Intuit Corporation to help create financial planning software that really works.

But wait, there's more. She is also the author of two best-selling books, *Everyone's Money Book* (Dell) and *Making the Most of Your Money* (Simon & Shuster). She is presently completing a new and revised edition of *Making the Most of Your Money* due out in November.

Mutual Fund Mastery: Jane, this is a new one for you, because someone is interviewing you instead of the other way around.

Jane Bryant Quinn: That's right. It feels strange, being on this end.

MFM: To start with, everybody reads your columns in their newspaper, but nobody really knows how you started doing this. We read what you say, but we don't know that much about you. You've been writing your newspaper column as long as I can remember.

JBQ: I'm still writing and I can laugh at how long it's been. When I started at *The Insider's Newsletter,* I was low man on the totem pole. Since nobody wanted to do the money stories and since I was the newest hire, I got them. Fortunately, I thought they were fascinating and interesting, and I got very involved in money issues. A friend of mine who worked for *Look Magazine* asked me if I read the *American Banker* and I said, "No, why should I read that?" He said, "Well, if you know where the bankers are putting their money, you know a lot about what's going to happen in this country and you'll get some really good stories." So I started reading it, and he was right. Over time, one thing led to another. I did a newsletter then for McGraw-Hill, about personal finance, and I left them to start my newspaper column in 1974.

MFM: You have seen tremendous progress in personal finance and consumer issues in general. What are the major changes and the major battles that have been fought on behalf of consumers?

JBQ: When I started covering this field, Congress had in front of it the Truth in

Lending Bill, which brought us the ability to compare loans by looking at the annual percentage rates. Back then, you couldn't do that. Everyone had a different kind of interest rate and you had no idea how much your loan really cost. Truth in Packaging, Truth in Labeling, and many more laws we simply take for granted were being presented to Congress back then. I was covering that process. All of those bills have since been passed. Truth in Savings passed most recently. It took almost 30 years to get that one through. So we now have comparable interest rates on our savings accounts. We can now tell which bank is paying more than other banks. One battle we still have not won, is for truth in life insurance pricing. At the rate this bill is moving, 30 years and counting, I may not live long enough to see it passed.

MFM: The life insurance industry probably hopes that's true, but we think you'll be dogging their heels for many years to come. Consumer protection regulations have improved a lot, but what changes have you seen in the attitude people have toward personal finance and investing?

JBQ: Two very clear trends. One is away from individual stocks and toward mutual funds. Individual stocks are much more an investment of the older generation. These days, mutual funds are the investment of choice for the younger generation. And the other is toward investment in equities generally.

MFM: Away from bonds.

JBQ: Away from bonds and away from bank accounts. A lot of people, of all ages and backgrounds, are buying equities now. Most people wouldn't have considered owning equities 25 years ago. They would have had a bank account. They would have prepaid their mortgage. They would've had life insurance and that's about it. It didn't occur to a lot of people 25 years ago that they should be thinking about the stock market. The tremendous awareness of stocks and stock prices, mutual funds, and investing is an

enormous change. I think if you went back 25 years, you'd be stunned at how different the climate is today.

MFM: Back then, most mutual funds were stock funds. We did not have the diversity of bond funds and money market funds. And people who bought stocks or mutual funds in the 1970s did not do well because the stock market plunged almost 40% in 1973–74.

JBQ: You had a long period of time when the stock market didn't go anywhere. But real estate was doing well and that's something people thought they understood, because they had houses, which were something they could get their minds around. They didn't think they had to analyze it. They learned the hard way that they should have analyzed real estate like any other investment, but back then, they didn't think so. So the period from 1965 to 1982 was a stagnant time for the stock market overall. Just looking at the stock price appreciation alone, not counting dividends, the market didn't go anywhere.

MFM: Right. Certain sectors did well, such as natural resources, but overall, the stock market was not very exciting.

JBQ: It went up and down and up and down and there were no net gains. Your gains came entirely from dividends. So that put you in a different frame of mind when you thought about fixed-income investments or when you thought about income-paying real estate. There was a different attitude about what was a sensible investment for the average person. Stocks just didn't make sense in the common view. You had to be, or attempt to be, a market timer during those years, or you wouldn't get anywhere at all.

MFM: Or a good stock picker like Warren Buffett. After all, the 1970s was when he made his best buys.

JBQ: But then you had to move from stock to stock and you couldn't just buy something like an index fund and put money into it regularly and shut your eyes and go away. Which I think is one of the great things you can do nowadays in the current climate. That helps people come into the market. Even if you were a good stock picker, you had to change stocks from time to time.

MFM: What's the difference, in your mind, between how someone should invest in mutual funds or stocks versus investing in real estate? Neither one can be counted on as a sure win, at all times. How should people look at those 2 broad types of investing?

JBQ: First, people need to look to their asset allocation, which is something they weren't doing when they were piling into real estate. If you own a house, you already have an awful lot of your money tied up in real estate. If you then proceed to buy raw land, or an apartment building or houses and rent them out—you are putting all of your future into a single asset class, which, I hope by now, we've learned is not a good idea. So one thing is, when you're looking at how you're allocating your investments, you have to remember to count your house toward your real estate allocation. Which I think a lot of people just plain didn't do. And the second thing is, you have to understand that investment real estate, in many ways, is like stocks, in that you must analyze it. You must think about it. A lot of people just thought real estate goes up, and they never thought, "I have to look at the cash flows, I have to analyze the market, I have to look at my costs, I have to look at percentage returns." These kinds of things all have to be done when you're analyzing a stock. You have to do the same in spades for real estate. What is the demand? What else is being built? Can I raise this piece of property to a higher and more valuable use? All kinds of questions that people never asked, because they didn't think real estate needed analyzing. So, in that way, real estate is much more like stocks than people think. It is different in that houses, buildings, and land are not nearly as liquid as stocks. You can always sell real estate quickly if you sell it well under the going price, but that's not what we have in mind when we talk about liquidity.

MFM: That's right.

JBQ: Anything will sell quickly, if you cut the price. But it won't sell quickly if you want the market price. That's why people get caught in a lot of illiquidity. This is a part of investing that doesn't occur to many people—to look at how liquid their position is. Whether it is real estate or your 401(k) plan or even a tax-deferred annuity—these things are not liquid. In order to sell quickly, you are going to have to take a hit, whether it is a lower price or a tax penalty or something else.

MFM: Let's just start at the beginning and go through the investment process the way you think it should be done. People who are in their 40s or maybe early 50s: What should they do? How should they start the whole process of looking at their overall investment needs and situation, and liquidity needs, and move forward?

JBQ: Oh, there's a big question.

MFM: I'm good at asking really big questions.

JBQ: Right. You start by taking stock of where you are. That, in itself, would be an eye-opener for many people. People in their 40s or early 50s usually own a little of this and a little of that. They've probably never tried to put it all together and look at how everything is allocated. So, the first step is to see where you are, look at everything you have—look at your cash in the bank, your house, your retirement accounts. If you're married, look at those of your spouse. Many couples nowadays manage their money separately, but they are assuming they will go into retirement together. What you do, or don't do, will affect your spouse and vice versa.

MFM: Are you saying they should do this together?

JBQ: Yes. You've got to look at your investments together. Look at everything both of you have and see how it's allocated among stocks, bonds, real estate, cash. What is the balance between liquid and illiquid investments? Figure out how much you need to have readily at hand and how much you can invest for the long term. When people allocate their assets, they must do it for their personal situation. Something you read in a magazine or get from your broker or a mutual fund may be too generic. They produce nice little pie charts that say you should have so much here and so much there. That can indeed be very helpful as a guideline. But, one thing those pie charts can never consider is your personal situation.

MFM: Can you give us an example of why this is important?

JBQ: Sure, I'll give you a personal example. About 7 years ago, I had a piece of real estate and I was all set to sell it. At the last minute, the sale fell through. Shortly thereafter, the real estate market crashed. It was frustrating and I was very sad about what might have been.

MFM: Yes.

JBQ: I thought I was selling at the peak and then something went wrong. The point is, real estate's not liquid. You can't sell it in 3 days. And when something happens, you might get caught in a bit of a bind. I was in a financial position that was quite illiquid for me, and I didn't like it. Since I'm a freelancer and could lose a paycheck at any time, I took stock of my position and said, "I need to be more liquid in my other investments since I am so locked up in real estate." So I cut back on stocks and went more into short-term Treasuries. Purely from an investment point of view, I was quite sure stocks would do well. So if I were just looking at statistics, I wouldn't have made a change in my allocation. But because of my real estate holdings, I knew I was highly illiquid and I was not comfortable with that situation. Even though I did not expect a terrible stock market or that something bad would happen to my income, I couldn't take that chance. If it did, I'd be stuck. So I lowered my allocation to stocks—not because of my opinion on the market but because of my opinion of my own personal situation.

MFM: It was a prudent move to make sure you stayed within your personal comfort zone.

JBQ: People need to find a comfort zone related to their own liquidity, their own job situation, their own need for money at any time. There's a lot of things in this mix that are not in the pie charts or statistics you'll get from your mutual fund company. And you need to think about those.

MFM: In other words, there is the logical side of asset allocation, which comes from historical information, charts, and graphs, but you still have to temper that with information from your own . . . .

JBQ: Exactly. Because the pie charts or statistics or rules of thumb don't know if you're sick, or if you have a kid with a problem that has to be taken care of, or if your company was just merged and you may lose your job. They don't know if you got stuck in the real estate crash. Yet, these are things you need to factor into your own situation.

MFM: What's an easy way to get started?

JBQ: Write down, on one side of a yellow pad, where your money is—all your savings and investments. On the other side, write down what that money is supposed to fund—retirement, college, or anything else. Then see how well your assets match up with your objectives. I think many people will find they have a terrible mismatch. Perhaps too little money that's liquid and guaranteed, for near-term objectives. Perhaps too little invested for growth, for objectives that are years away.

MFM: You mean one particular account may be allocated fine—say, an IRA account—but the rest of the money may be allocated very poorly, given the overall situation.

JBQ: That's right. They may think they are 60% in stocks, but they may not be counting a fixed annuity they bought at a bank, or money they have in a savings account. Plus, they may have a whole life insurance policy. All of a sudden they realize they don't have 60% in stocks at all. Counting all of their money, they may have 70% in fixed income.

MFM: Rather than just taking a wild guess, you're saying people should take a few minutes and jot everything down and classify it as real estate, bonds, and other types of fixed income such as bond funds or annuities, stocks, stock funds, and cash, whether it is in a bank account, credit union, or money market fund.

JBQ: That's right. That's the value of putting everything on a page and taking a look. And I think that will be an eye-opener for a lot of people. When people are having trouble with their credit cards, they're always advised to sit down and see how they're really spending their money. The same thing applies to people who are trying to allocate their assets properly. Start by getting a better understanding of where they are now.

MFM: Once you know where everything is, how do you figure out what it should be, in light of your objectives and your personal situation? Is there a way to come up with a number or percentage?

JBQ: Well, most pension plans [not 401(k) plans, but rather defined benefit pension plans] traditionally use a balance of 60% stocks and 40% bonds. So that's a good starting point, 60–40. Then, let's say you're in good shape personally. Nobody's sick. Your job is sound. You have enough put aside in a money market fund so that you're sufficiently liquid—all that's out of the way. Then you ask yourself how you feel about the stock market. Are you prepared to take the risk? I asked Ibbotson Associates to tell me how long it takes to break even—from a market peak, down to the bottom, and then back up again—assuming dividends were reinvested. From 1945 through 1995, the breakeven time, on average, for the S&P 500 was 2.5 years. The worst period was in the early 1970s, when it took 3.5 years. So, if you are not going to touch some money for 4 years or longer, then I believe you can put that money into a well-diversified stock portfolio with reasonable confidence. But if you are going to need that money in less than 4 years, stocks are a tremendous risk.

You'd be wiser to put it into a money market fund, or in the bank, or in Series EE Savings Bonds, so that when you want it, it will be there, plus interest, guaranteed.

MFM: So if you're saving for a purpose, one critical factor in determining how you should invest is your time horizon.

JBQ: Absolutely. If you had to look at only one factor, your time horizon is the big one. You can be 60 and have a 30-year time horizon, as I expect to be with my retirement investment. So, I'm going to put it in stocks or stock mutual funds. Or you could be 40, deciding how to invest money that's for your daughter's tuition in 2 years. That 2-year money should probably go into Series EE Savings Bonds, whereas that 30-year money should go into stocks or stock mutual funds.

MFM: Why Series EE Savings Bonds?

JBQ: I like savings bonds for short-term money because they are exempt from state income tax and because they generally pay a little more than most certificates of deposit for a 2-year period. The point is that you need to know when you'll want your money back. When you are putting things down on your yellow pad, make sure you consider those that are long-term goals and those that are short-term goals.

MFM: In other words, whether you need the money in 2 years for college funding or a down payment on a house or to start a new business, that money is 2-year money—regardless of the actual purpose. Is that right?

JBQ: Absolutely. What matters is how soon you need the money.

MFM: Earlier, you said that younger people are tending toward mutual funds and away from buying individual stocks. Also, that people are buying more equities than they used to. Is that because there's been so much media attention to the stock market, or because returns have been good, or a combination?

JBQ: Well, returns have been good. And people have learned from their reading that, over the long term, stocks do much better than bonds. The baby boomers are starting to save for retirement now. This is a generation that tended to have kids late, so they will be paying for college at the same time they are thinking of retirement. Therefore, this is a generation that wants to get the most bang from its buck. They are increasingly going toward equities. Also, in their experience, stock market drops are brutal, but short, and then the market rises to stunning new highs. They have not gone through a down market like we had in the 1970s. They have a different view of things. They're willing to put the money in and ride out the downturns.

MFM: Hopefully, the stock market cooperates and continues its recent behavior, but financial markets don't always cooperate.

JBQ: So true. But what is this generation going to do?

MFM: Good point. It's not a perfect world, but the stock market stands a better chance of getting a 10% or 11% return than bonds or money market funds. From the viewpoint of a younger investor, say 50 years old or less, wouldn't you hope the stock market would have its poor returns now, when you don't have much invested and are accumulating money, rather than in your later years when you are much closer to retirement?

JBQ: Perhaps. My best guess is that we probably have a good 10 to 12 years while all this baby boomer money is pouring in. In today's market, for example, they can't bring out IPOs fast enough to keep up with demand. There's a strong generational upward bias in the market right now. . .

MFM: More buyers than sellers?

JBQ: Yes. Lots of demand. Yet the question remains: When the baby boomers start to sell, who will they sell to? If we're going to have a flat or up and down market, a period like 1965–82, we're going to have it then. So the strategy would be: Get in the market with everything you have right now. Get it

while you can. But be aware that things will probably flatten a lot by the time you're ready to sell. The question of who the boomers will sell to arises because the next generation is relatively small. But the globe does a wonderful job of recycling money. Surpluses in one place seem to be shortages in another. The best argument for free trade is that we want to make Southeast Asia and Latin America and other countries with young populations as rich as they possibly can be. So when they get older, they'll have mutual funds and will want to diversify into stocks, both here and abroad.

MFM: About the time baby boomers here need to sell.

JBQ: They'll buy our stocks. There is also increasing pressure to invest part of the Social Security trust fund in the stock market—either the trust fund itself would invest in stocks, or individuals would invest part of their Social Security accounts. So there is another potential source of funds that would be supportive of equities.

MFM: With everything you have said, I think investors have an idea of what they need to do. How important time horizon is; the fact that mutual funds are a very good vehicle; why equity funds are so important. The one point we have not covered is index funds and actively managed funds. How do you feel about index funds?

JBQ: I love index funds. I think they are an absolute must for many investors, but I don't love *all* index funds. A lot of so-called index funds have odd things in them. But the plain vanilla, wonderful, low-cost index fund . . . .

MFM: Like Vanguard?

JBQ: Like Vanguard. Vanguard is the leader and the best, when it comes to indexing. The Vanguard Index Trust 500 Portfolio is never going to be the number-one performer in a given year, but it is almost always in the top 25%, and there are very few other funds that can say that. I ran a whole series of names once, a year ago or so, against the Vanguard

500 Portfolio over various periods of time, looking for funds that could usually beat it. And you know, there are hardly any.

MFM: There are some, but not very many. You're talking about an elite group of funds.

JBQ: So, since you're never quite sure that your own fund will be on top of the S&P 500 next year, it's a good bet to have core investments in domestic index funds.

MFM: So, for you, you'd have your core portfolio in index funds and you might have some other money in something a little racier.

JBQ: Yes, for fun. Emerging markets funds, for example. There's a good example of an interesting place for some of your racy money. Or an aggressive growth fund, maybe.

MFM: Once investors understand what they need, and have made the decision to use index funds or actively managed funds, how do they get started? Let's say that, at the time, the stock market is high. If they're not heavily in the stock market, what should investors do?

JBQ: The dollar-cost-averaging question is an interesting one. Because the stock market has an upward bias, the chances are 2 out of 3 that you would be better off investing a lump sum all at once rather than feeding in the money over a year. The odds are that the market will rise more often than it will fall. Therefore, dollar-cost-averaging will hurt returns more often than it will help them. If you're putting money in once a month and the market is going up, then you're not going to do as well as if you put it in all at once. Dollar-cost-averaging is for risk control. You're willing to give up some possible gains in order to limit the risk of investing just before a market drop.

MFM: The key point with a regular investment program is that you must keep on doing it even when the market falls.

JBQ: When a given market falls, that's when I jump in. In fact, I bought some emerging markets mutual funds back in 1994 when the crisis in Mexico caused so

many problems. And did the market go lower after that? It sure did. But the market is now going up and I have a lot of confidence that, given my time horizon, it was a great time to buy emerging markets mutual funds. That's one piece of market timing I would indulge in—jump in with both feet when a market crashes.

MFM: If you had a sum of money and it had a long-term investment horizon, you would jump in when stocks tumble?

JBQ: Yes, I just have no confidence in my ability to guess when that tumble is going to occur, but I'm happy to exploit it when it happens.

MFM: What do you think about the industry as a whole, in terms of its health, or if the stock market fell, or if interest rates went up a lot?

JBQ: If the stock market fell, there would certainly be less cash flowing into equity mutual funds. But it would flow into money market funds and bond funds. I would think, at that point, there would also be a lot of mutual fund mergers. If you had a long period of poor performance and less money went into equities, you would end up with fewer mutual funds over time.

MFM: And people might move some money out stock funds and into bond funds.

JBQ: Sure.

MFM: But, that doesn't really hurt the mutual fund industry.

JBQ: No, it does not. It will simply consolidate. Sponsors with small funds will combine them with other funds. Maybe some banks will get out of the business. Some people talk as if a mutual fund is somehow a special kind of investment, like a single stock. And maybe this one stock has gotten inflated and will crash. But that's not the way mutual funds work. The trend is indeed for people to use mutual funds. If they don't use stock funds, they'll use bond funds. So, I think the mutual fund industry itself is healthy at this time. There are probably more mutual funds than we eventually need in this country, and when we hit that moment, the industry will shrink.

MFM: There are still fewer mutual funds than there are banks, for example. We probably have more banks than we need, also.

JBQ: A perfect analogy. We have many more banks than we need. Ten years from now, we may have half the number of banks we have today, because money is going in different directions. Businesses are using other intermediaries. The same kind of thing will eventually happen to mutual funds, and there will be a great consolidation.

MFM: What about mutual fund operating expenses, expense ratios? Do you have any thoughts on that?

JBQ: People pay insufficient attention to expenses because the ratio looks so small. Why worry about expenses when you're making 20% or 30%? But no matter what you're earning, if you don't care what you're being charged, you're going to pay too much.

MFM: Whether you're buying gas, mutual funds, or anything else.

JBQ: That's right. Not until investors become more price-sensitive is this going to change. There are, of course, low-cost mutual funds that are indeed price-sensitive. Vanguard clearly sets the standard in that area. In fact, they just cut their expenses. I feel reasonably certain there are other large mutual fund groups that could function on lower expenses if the shareholders said, "I'm not paying that." But, at the moment, individuals are so blinded by their performance that they're willing to pay whatever they're charged. I don't think they even know what they're charged.

MFM: In many cases, they don't, I'm sure. Let's talk a little about the things you're doing with Intuit and Quicken: the CD-ROM and the other things you're working on. How do those work?

JBQ: You enter your income, your spending, your savings and investments, your age, your pension, the year you expect to retire. Then you press a button and the software tells you whether or not your current level of saving is going to give you enough to retire on. If not, you can create scenarios where you change your asset allocations, save more, change your retirement age, and so on . . . to see how you can make your retirement work. Quicken Financial Planner includes a college planner, which tells you the costs of all the colleges. You can put that into your long-term plan, to see how you're going to pay for it. There's a life insurance needs analysis. You'll find a Quick Plan up front, so you can do a down and dirty analysis of how you're doing, before going on to the full-fledged plan. I think it's a terrific program.

MFM: Sounds like it.

JBQ: It's a clear, good, well-thought-out piece of software for people who want an answer to the question, "Am I saving enough?" which is a good question to ask.

MFM: With millions of people using Quicken and Quicken Financial Planner, Intuit is in a good position to help people find the answers they need. Before we wrap this up, we heard you are working on a new edition to your book, *Making The Most Of Your Money.* Is that right?

JBQ: I am, and in fact, I'll be calling you for a repeat of your successful mutual fund choices, which I published in the first edition.

MFM: Uh-oh. Can we expect the same outstanding compensation?

JBQ: You mean my eternal thanks?

MFM: That's what we were afraid of. When will this edition hit bookstores?

JBQ: I'm typing as fast as I can, and reporting on all the new forms of investing around. It's supposed to be in bookstores soon, but we will see. While I have you, I'm doing a column on bond funds and I want to ask you a few questions. Can we turn this interview back to its natural order?

MFM: Same deal? Your eternal thanks?

JBQ: What else? What I'm looking at is a story on . . . .

That's Jane Bryant Quinn. When you write as much as she does, you just never miss a chance to get a good quote. We think it's safe to say we all owe her for tirelessly championing the cause of fair play, full disclosure, and access to objective information. She has helped remove some serious roadblocks to investment success for all of us. Speaking of roadblocks, the next chapter covers some of the serious ones. Turn the page and find out how to avoid them.

CHAPTER 8

Fear, Greed, Impatience, and Other Roadblocks to Success

In 1841, Charles Mackay wrote a fascinating book, *Extraordinary Popular Delusions and the Madness of Crowds* (still in print from Harmony Books). Mackay spelled out several speculative frenzies that occurred when passion prevailed over prudence. For example, the normally frugal Dutch became swept up in a mania over tulips, which were bought and sold on Dutch stock exchanges, corner bars, store counters, and, apparently, everywhere else during the roaring 1600s.

Mackay writes, "At first, as in all these manias, everybody gained. The tulip-jobbers speculated in the rise and fall of the tulip stocks, and made large profits by buying when prices fell, and selling out when they rose. Many individuals grew *suddenly rich*. A golden bait hung temptingly out before the people, and one after the other, they rushed to the tulip marts, like *flies around a honey pot*. Everyone imagined that the passion for tulips *would last forever . . .*" (italics added).

This mania ended in 1636, when tulip prices began falling. The fact that prices would fall eventually should have been no mystery; everything—even tulip bulbs—is subject to supply and demand. Initially, demand for tulip bulbs outstripped supply as more and more ordinary people became buyers. But then came a day when all those greedily hopeful tulip owners looked around and beheld very few tulip buyers willing to pay higher prices than the sellers had paid.

Mackay continues, ". . . prices fell, and never rose again. *Confidence was destroyed*, and *a universal panic* seized upon dealers" (italics added).

So what does tulip mania have to do with you? Let's analyze the critical elements in Mackay's tale, which we have conveniently emphasized. Note the words that we italicized:

Suddenly rich	*Confidence was destroyed*
Flies around a honey pot	*A universal panic*
Would last forever	
GREED	FEAR

The emotional content of these words can be boiled down very simply to GREED and FEAR.

Before we go any further, we want to get one thing straight. We think greed is OK. Fear is OK, too. In fact, any emotion you have is fine, if your response is appropriate for the particular circumstances.

Long before there was money, or tulips, or gold watches, or even gold itself, there was greed and there was fear. Both were highly appropriate responses to life. In prehistoric times, life was pretty basic. Cavemen and cavewomen concentrated on the necessities of life— food, clothing, and shelter. In those days, if a starving person came across a hunter cooking a piece of venison, the starving person probably experienced a strong craving for that meat. The hunter who was grilling dinner probably experienced fear (or anger) at the thought that some hungry stranger was about to charge in, wielding a knife, to take the meat. The 2 of them may have fought it out, or perhaps they decided to barter for supper and that was the beginning of the first meat market.

Uncontrolled greed leads to problems for you and for others. Remember the normally frugal Dutch and their tulips. But controlled greed can help you reach your financial goals. And a little fear of loss does not hurt, either. You may not believe these types of emotions come into play in your life, but we beg to differ.

J. P. Morgan said, "Men have 2 reasons for the things they do. A good reason and the real reason." Old J. P. was only partially right. All of us—women, men, and children—make decisions for reasons that may be emotional, irrational, or even illogical. Yet, once the decision has been made, we use logic and reason to rationalize our actions. We create an "explanation" that sounds good to others. Occasionally, naked fear or greed is so overpowering that people actually own up to their "base emotions," as in the tulip bulb mania. Mass hysteria or the instinct of the crowd takes over because everyone "knows" something. Everyone knows tulip prices will go up forever. Or, everyone knows the stock market can go up forever.

Groups of like-minded people do things no sane person would do. Dallas Cowboy football fans have been known to wear their team's football uniform to work, even though a flabby office worker seldom looks good in skin-tight pants, knee socks, and football cleats. More seriously, rabid soccer fans in England periodically run wild and trample each other, at times because their team won, and at other times because they lost.

Benign examples of crowd behavior are fads like Pet Rocks, Hula Hoops, Barney, Cabbage Patch Dolls, or the Mighty Morphin' Power Rangers. For some inexplicable reason, a particular product or person becomes very hot. You see it everywhere for a while. And then, just as inexplicably as the fad appeared, it fades away.

When we were teenagers (think back—we *know* you can remember that period in your life), many of us were very attuned to the rules and requirements of our friends. Parents, teachers, and other adults receded in importance. Earning and retaining the acceptance of our friends often seemed of paramount importance.

Later on, as we matured, those intense concerns about belonging to the group seemed quaint. In fact, that whole teenage period seems long ago and far away. When reminded of our past behavior by friends or relatives, we may be a bit chagrined. "Gee, honey, look at these shoes. Wow, you just don't see too many lime-green platform shoes these days. Remember when you always wore them with the paisley print bell-bottoms?"

How about that tattoo you got after downing a bottle of Southern Comfort with your Navy buddies. Seemed like a good idea at the time.

"Yes, Doctor, it's about this tattoo . . . I'd like it removed."

"Hmmm . . . it says 'I Love Mary.' It's actually very well done."

"Unfortunately, now that I'm married to Joan, the tattoo is a bit awkward."

We think you get the point: Peer pressure can encourage you to make long-term decisions you later regret, at your leisure. It can make even silly or dangerous things seem OK.

When it comes to investing, the results of crowd behavior are often very pronounced. And because we are human, it is very difficult to avoid being suckered into going along with the crowd.

Stampeding Investors Rush for the Exits

The stock market crash of 1987 was a good example of crowd behavior. Professional and amateur investors alike stampeded for the exits, all at the same time. With lots of sellers and very few buyers, the market crashed 508 points in one day.

In the aftermath of that cataclysmic event, news media of all types wrote articles about the event and the likelihood of an economic depression being triggered by Wall Street. Many individual investors witnessed this "consensus" of opinion and headed for the exits themselves over the next few months.

The Tale of Mordred

A couple of weeks after the Crash of 1987, one of our clients (we'll call him Mordred) came in to see us. Until his recent retirement, he had been a senior vice president of finance in a very large corporation and had regularly made decisions that involved millions of dollars and affected many people worldwide. He owned his home and had an investment portfolio worth several million dollars.

Because of his professional experience and qualifications, we considered Mordred to be one of our more sophisticated clients. When he came in that day, we knew something was wrong. He looked haggard, as though there had been a loss in the family. His eyes were dull and they were not focusing very well.

Turns out that he was in mortal fear of losing all of his money. After retiring, he had purchased subscriptions to most of the business and financial publications. Because he was retired and had few outside interests, he read them all, cover to cover, every day. At that time, most publications were uniformly negative about America's economic future. Many predicted a general economic depression. And Mordred bought it. He was no longer working, so he did not realize that businesses were open. Kids were still going to school. Farmers were still farming. Factories still pumped out cars or detergent or computers. In short, life went on.

Mordred's fears grew until they overwhelmed his normally logical mind. On the day of the Crash, his account fell about 7% while the S&P 500 plunged 22.5%. He asked what our plans were, and we said we were buying more stock funds. He listened to us and then said he had decided to sell everything and go into Treasury bills. When we gave our reasons why that would be a mistake, he listened, but he told us to sell anyway.

So we did. The next year, 1988, stocks were up 16.5%, and 1989 brought another 31.6% rise. We lost touch with him, so we do not know when, or if, he ever went back into stock funds. We do know that Mordred panicked, and because of that strong emotional reaction, he left a lot of money on the table.

For us, it was a valuable lesson. Because of Mordred's sophistication, we *assumed* he would react well in a market downturn. He was a very intelligent and experienced investor, yet his emotions got the better of him. Later on, if he saw his mistake, it would have been very difficult to get back in. We hope he did, but admitting a mistake and buying back in at a much higher level are never easy.

Some of the smartest people become the worst investors because their emotions override their strong reasoning powers. Brains alone have nothing to do with investment success—or any success beyond IQ tests. Why is that? And why do almost all of us suffer through difficult periods of self-doubt and anxiety over our investments? One answer may be found in the phrase emotional intelligence.

Emotional Intelligence?

In his best-selling book, *Emotional Intelligence* (Bantam 1996), Daniel Goleman makes a persuasive argument that the emotional centers of the brain predate development of the so-called rational or analytical mind. He also believes that certain mechanisms allow the emotional centers to bypass the analytical portion of the brain.

Goleman gives us a valuable and thoughtful explanation for a phenomenon investors have recognized for a very long time: *Emotion easily overrules reason.*

We can all remember times when we reacted emotionally and, in retrospect, it was totally inappropriate—even scary or dangerous. At other times, our emotions have helped us break through a barrier or just have a great time. We cannot downplay emotions in our lives because emotions *are us.* As investors, we need to make sure our emotions serve us well rather than leading us into danger.

Tale of the Reluctant Investor

We have an acquaintance who sold his business for an after-tax profit of several million dollars in the early 1980s. Although he was an excellent businessman, he turned into an indecisive investor. We suggested he put a portion of his profit into stocks. He said he planned to do so, but stocks were too high. At the time, the Dow Jones Industrial Average ("the Dow") was just over 1000. He wanted to wait until the average fell back under 900. We said, "Why wait? Invest some now and some later."

Time passed, and he asked us for advice. We said the same thing: Buy stocks. He said the same thing, except the Dow was then at 2000. He was waiting for 1500.

When the Dow tumbled in 1987, he was about ready to make the big plunge, but he was quite certain it would go even lower. Last time we talked, with the Dow over 7000, he was still waiting for the buying opportunity.

Our friend, the reluctant investor, just could not bring himself to move. As a very successful businessman, he understood risk and reward, but the arena of investing confused him. He was afraid of buying just before a stock market crash, and that fear apparently unnerved him.

As you can see, taking control of your emotions means taking responsibility for your actions, but it also means being realistic. Develop a plan for investing that will serve you for life. Create it and follow it. Make changes only when cool, calm reflection suggests that a change is required. If you must change your plan, do so reluctantly and never in reaction to recent events.

Investment Self-Assessment

We all have strengths and weaknesses. Instead of fighting our weaknesses, we need to accept them and, in doing so, to also recognize our strengths. The following is a brief list of aptitudes that relate to investing. We want you to rate yourself and then have 2 people evaluate you. It is vital that these 2 people rate you objectively, so do not show them your self-rating or each other's ratings. Then, without arguing or questioning or challenging their results, simply average the three ratings to determine your grade in each category.

Assign a rating of 1 to 5 for each answer: 1 = None, 2 = Low, 3 = Medium, 4 = High, 5 = Very High.

1. **Investment knowledge and experience.** How much proven knowledge and experience do you have in investing, whether in mutual funds, real estate, stocks, bonds, or other types of securities?

2. **Patience.** How do you stack up in terms of your ability to wait calmly for events to unfold and to demonstrate other qualities of patience and fortitude?

3. **Discipline.** Do you regularly exercise discipline over your desires in order to achieve a long-term goal, whether it is physical fitness, dieting, success at work, sports, music, or any other important activity?

4. **Emotional stability under stress.** Do you display "calmness under fire" or are you very reactive to stressful situations? Does your personality change radically when exposed to fear, anger, or anxiety? When things are going your way, do you change and become overconfident, careless, arrogant, or prone to errors of judgment?

5. **Math skills and detail orientation.** Do you feel comfortable with numbers, or do you tend to "lock up" when faced with a sheet of numbers, facts, or figures? Are you apt to take extra time to make sure small details and relatively unimportant matters are seen to properly?

6. **Greed or desire for riches.** To what extent are you motivated by money or by wanting to be rich? Answer carefully, because greed may or may not take the form of wanting or having lots of possessions. Some people who desire wealth do not care much for material possessions. To them, money means freedom and choices.

7. **Desire to win.** Do you have a strong desire to succeed? To win at whatever you do?

8. **Work ethic.** Have you demonstrated a willingness and even a desire to work hard over long periods of time?

9. **Reading comprehension.** Do you like to read and to absorb information from reading, no matter what the source (books, magazines, reports, newspapers, online services, and so on)?

10. **Clear, long-term goals.** Do you have clear, long-term goals that you regularly talk about, work toward, and dream about? Are you passionate about theses goals?

Using your answers to these questions, write a short, detailed description of yourself as an investor. List your tendencies, strengths, and weaknesses.

If you are investing with your husband or wife (or anyone else), each of you should first create a personal description and then let the other investment partner critique the self-assessment in writing.

Be as candid as possible in your assessments. When your evaluation comes back to you with comments, go off by yourself, read it, and think about what you have learned. After a brief time, take the test again. Ask someone else whom you respect to evaluate your second version.

If your second version is still substantially different from those of your evaluators, you have to face the fact that you are probably writing what you wish were true rather than what really is true. Continue this process until you have agreement or until you can't go through the process anymore. The goal here is not to arrive at certain answers that will determine your success or failure. The key point is that you must understand and accept your investment strengths and weaknesses. Only then can you find ways to strengthen your weak areas and make yourself a better investor.

Remember, fear and greed are useful when they are appropriate to the circumstances and when you are in control. If there comes a moment where you feel out of control, that's OK. Just make sure you do not take any significant actions when you are in the grip of either emotion.

Even though tolerating risk is an issue that many investors agonize over, it is not the main reason why many investors fail to reach their goals. The primary cause of investment failure stems from bad thinking and nonexistent or ineffective planning. In Chapter 1, we discussed the fact that many people plan their vacations better than their investments. Now, let's go over the step-by-step approach to investing that we call our bottom-line basics.

BROUWER & JANACHOWSKI'S BOTTOM-LINE BASICS

♦ Set clear investment objectives.

♦ Allocate your assets in line with your objectives.

♦ Build a great portfolio.

We are going to flesh out exactly what these 3 steps mean and how you can use them to create your own investment master plan. But first, we have to make one very important point. Many investors ask us how to maintain an investment program through the mood swings of the stock and bond markets. The simple answer is the topic of the next section.

If you have a burning need to prove something or to get rich quick, your frustration and envy of others will cloud your judgment. The best way we know of to stay in control is to take a long-term view. What is a long-term view? How do you develop one? If we are such emotional creatures, how can we possibly change? These are all questions that must be answered, and this is the time to start.

When people buy a house, they generally do so for the long haul. Many considerations and careful planning go into the purchase: size, location, condition, distance to schools, monthly payments, down payment, and so on. Credit applications are filled out. Once they are approved, a down payment of 10% to 20% is made, loan documents are filed, the

Buy Mutual Funds the Way You Buy Real Estate

new owners take title, and all the furniture and other possessions are moved in.

At this point, the last thing on a normal homeowner's mind is moving out. Years go by, payments are made, and the homeowner's equity fluctuates wildly because of changes in the local real estate market.

Despite all this activity, the homeowner blithely ignores valuations because they are not easily calculated; he or she has no current intent to sell the home. Some 20 years later, when a new job requires a move, the lucky homeowner is pleasantly surprised at how much the equity in the home has grown.

Contrast this sequence with a typical stock or stock mutual fund purchase. Investors often buy just because the mutual fund made the cover of a magazine or was recommended by a friend, or because the investor thinks stocks are going to do well this year. Usually, very little research or planning has been done. If the purchase is made on a Monday, the investor begins, on Tuesday morning, the daily ritual of checking the fund's current price in the newspaper. Today, +4 cents. Tomorrow, −3 cents, and so on. Day after day.

On plus days, our lucky investor feels a bit richer. On minus days, poorer. If the mutual fund moves up quite a bit, the inevitable question is raised: "Should I sell?" If it tanks right after the purchase, the investor bemoans his or her fate while asking, "Should I sell?" This daily obsession continues until, finally, the pressure builds, or the wretched fund has not moved for 2 months, or a hotter fund comes along . . . and a sale is made. Total average elapsed time: 10 months.

Can you imagine buying a house or an apartment building because you think real estate is going to go up *this year?* Not very likely. Real estate is illiquid, expensive, and highly leveraged. Yet, despite the obvious risk of a highly leveraged purchase and all the disadvantages of illiquidity, owners confidently hold on through all the ups and downs. Why? One reason is that real estate purchasers feel like OWNERS. This is *their* home or apartment building or condominium.

Mutual funds are very liquid, not leveraged, highly diversified, and well managed. Yet, despite these incredible advantages, many investors buy and sell at the drop of the Dow. Why? Because they do not feel like OWNERS.

Another factor in the patient approach to real estate investing is that real estate is tangible. We can see it, feel it, walk through it. And, everyone else does it, so we feel a sense of validation from our family and friends. If everyone else is doing it, it must be right, right? Real estate was an outstanding investment in the past; therefore—the thinking goes—it will be again in the future. And it *will* be. Carefully chosen real estate bought at the right price will always do well. Unfortunately, how do you know what the right price is?

We are *not* down on buying a home or any other piece of property. The intangible value of owning your own home is definitely worth something. And the potential investment value is also good, if you made a good purchase. But it is far from a sure thing.

Our point in bringing this up is that we would like you to take the "real estate" approach when you buy mutual funds. How many home-owners check the price of their home every day? None. How many think about selling if the price falls 10%? None. Even more absurdly, how many would consider selling because there was a report that real estate prices *might* fall? Again, the answer is: None. So please, use a similar level of patience and fortitude with your mutual funds. Follow these simple guidelines:

♦ Invest with a long-term time horizon.

♦ Investigate your purchase carefully, *before* you buy.

♦ Ignore short-term market fluctuations.

Now that we have gotten that off our chest, let's go through the Bottom-Line Basics, one at a time.

1. Set clear investment objectives.

Simply put, having clear investment objectives is like going for something you really love. If you dearly love coffee first thing in the morning, it is pretty obvious what to do, right? You get up, stagger to the kitchen, and make coffee. Or head out and buy a cup, or finagle someone to get it for you. Bottom line: You get your coffee. You know what you want, you know how to get it, and everything else just has to wait. Children. Work. Food. World War III. No matter what, it waits.

That same clarity and certainty are necessary for your investment success. Figure out what you want, when you want it, and how much you need. Once you know exactly, precisely, down to four decimal points, what you need, the rest is simple.

2. Allocate your assets in line with your objectives.

Once you know your goal, the next step is to allocate your assets to get what you want. To start, recognize that you have different types of money (we are not referring to drachmas, pesos, or francs). One way to understand this concept is to use an investment timeline.

Right on Target

Kathy Kueneman is the North American Sales Manager for a Singapore-based printing company, Tien Wah Press. Before that, she headed worldwide licensing for Charles Schultz's Snoopy toys for Determined Productions in San Francisco. Despite her fast-paced life, Kathy has a very simple and clear-cut goal.

She told us, "I want to move from New York to California and to retire comfortably by age 60 or before. That's 14 years from now and my biggest financial concern is not knowing whether I'll have enough money to retire when I want to." Kathy had a pension plan and an IRA, and, 2 years ago, her company set up a 401(k) plan.

Unfortunately, she has a lot of ground to make up because of poor investment decisions. "I had an IRA rollover with Merrill Lynch for about 10 years, but there was almost no growth in the account, even though it was a great time for stocks. Because my account was small, I think my broker looked at me as someone he could sell some stock to when he needed to unload something."

A couple of years ago, she picked a basket of Fidelity mutual funds, and things began looking up.

Kathy owns a small apartment building in Berkeley, California, with approximately $240,000 of equity for the two units. She also has about $130,000 in personal savings currently parked in a money market fund. She has been saving $30,000 or more a year and leaving it in this account. "I feel guilty about not having invested it more wisely; this money should be invested for long-term growth," she says. For retirement savings, she has a $47,000 IRA rollover, invested in seven Fidelity stock funds. The $14,000 in her new 401(k) plan is invested in a handful of no-load stock mutual funds. She is contributing about $6,000 each year and her employer makes a matching contribution of $3,000.

BROUWER & JANACHOWSKI'S EVALUATION

Kathy's strategy of investing her IRA rollover and 401(k) plan in growth mutual funds is right on target. She is 46, and she has an investment time horizon of many years. But because Kathy's personal portfolio is invested primarily in money market funds, she could run out of money by her early 80s, if she retires at age 60.

We recommended that she invest the personal portfolio for long-term growth. If future returns come in at around the historical averages, this new asset allocation would allow her to retire on time at age 60 and maintain her current lifestyle throughout her retirement. We recommended allocating her portfolio into the following funds:

Baron Asset Fund	15%
Brandywine Fund	15%
Harbor Capital Appreciation Fund	20%
Janus Overseas Fund	20%
Selected American Shares	20%
Warburg Pincus Emerging Markets Fund	10%

INVESTMENT OBJECTIVE	INCOME	INCOME & GROWTH	GROWTH & INCOME	CONSERVATIVE/ MODERATE GROWTH	AGGRESSIVE GROWTH
YEAR	1 2	3 4	5 6 7	8 9 10	11 →
Percent Equities	0	30 to 50	50 to 80	80 to 100	100
High dividend yield, quality large cap		OK	OK	OK	OK
Growth—quality large cap		OK	OK	OK	OK
International diversified		OK	OK	OK	OK
Growth—quality small cap			OK	OK	OK
Emerging growth				OK	OK
Emerging markets					OK
Foreign—single country					OK
Venture capital / other illiquid					OK
Percent Fixed Income	100	50 to 70	20 to 50	0 to 20	0
Short—good quality	OK	OK	OK	OK	OK
Intermediate—good quality		OK	OK	OK	OK
Long—good quality		OK	OK	OK	OK
High yield				OK	OK
International diversified				OK	OK
Foreign—single country					OK

FIGURE 8.1 Timeline Allocation. Your investment timeline determines your investment objectives and asset allocation.

From Figure 8.1 you can see that you have some assets that need to be liquid because you will be using them soon, and you have others that you probably won't touch for many years. Therefore, common sense says you should invest those assets differently.

Come with us to a large shopping mall, where we meet Suzie, who is facing an interesting asset allocation challenge. Suzie is staring at a pair of inline skates. They cost $49.95. The sports store is next to the candy shop, and therein lies temptation, because Suzie also loves lemon drops. She has 72 cents in her pocket. Suzie faces a serious time-line and asset-allocation problem. She wants the skates, but she would have to stuff her money back in her jeans and ignore the lemon drops if she decided to save for the skates. It could take forever. Even if she saved her pennies and nickels and wheedled some more from the adults in her life, it would still be a long stretch. Or, she could go in right now and walk off with some candy. A tangible handful of sweets now, or an intangible but much bigger thrill from saving up and buying a great pair of skates?

We do not know what decision she will make, but we do know that her choice will say volumes about Suzie. In fact, from the choice she is about to make, we could make a pretty good bet on how she will deal with money later in life. If she is willing to defer spending on something small today so that she can save up for a larger prize later, then she has a saver's mentality. If she decides to go for it today because tomorrow's skates may never come, then she has a spender's mentality. Or, she could be somewhere in between—saving most of her cash, but indulging a little bit too. One thing is certain: People have to save some cash before they can become investors.

Investors Are Successful Savers

Somehow, in some way, you scraped together some money that you can now invest. You banked, instead of spending, $50 or $100 each week or each month. You put some of your salary into a tax-deferred 401(k) plan. You took an extra job. After all this effort, you do not want to lose your hard-earned cash. But if you don't take some risks, you won't get the maximum benefit.

Because you worked so hard to save this money, doesn't it make sense to keep your money working hard after you've saved it? That is the sole point of asset allocation. This capital is yours. It was obtained by great effort. So let's make sure it works for you as hard as—or harder than—you worked to get it in the first place. For professional investors, asset allocation is a vital step that must be taken before specific investments are selected. Yet, many investors buy quickly, without thinking through this issue. To illustrate the importance of this step, let's take a little quiz.

Pop Quiz

Two women decide to become investors. Each invests $1,000. It's 1926 (junk mail, nuclear weapons, color television, and other hallmarks of the 20th century have not yet been invented). One investor puts her money into stocks, and the other investor buys government bonds. Both investors make arrangements to reinvest all dividends and interest and then they fall into a deep Rip Van Winkle-type of sleep. They snooze through current events such as the Great Depression, World War II, the rise and fall of Richard Nixon, the Beatles, European reunification, hair transplants, global warming, and O.J.

They both wake up exactly 71 years later. Miraculously, despite their inattention, they have done quite well financially. The first question is: Which one has more money? The one who bought stocks or the one who bought government bonds? Next question: How much more money does the winner have, compared to the loser? Two times as much? Four times . . . ? Look at Figure 8.2 to find out.

Because of the magnitude of the difference, you can see why asset allocation is important. Over short periods, stocks and bonds fluctuate wildly. No one knows which will be ahead. But over longer periods, history shows that stocks will usually win out. Stocks have an inherent advantage that should beat out bonds or other income-oriented investments such as Treasury bills and certificates of deposit. What's the advantage? Stocks and stock mutual funds represent ownership of assets that produce a rising stream of earnings. Bonds are an IOU that represents a fixed and static stream of income. Guess which one does better during an inflationary time. And since we will always have politicians, we are very likely to have some form of inflation.

Asset allocation, then, is a logical and well-thought-out plan to use your assets in the most productive manner to reach your goals. Our knowledge of the future is, regrettably, less than perfect, so the past has to be our guide. It is our belief that, over a long time (20 years or

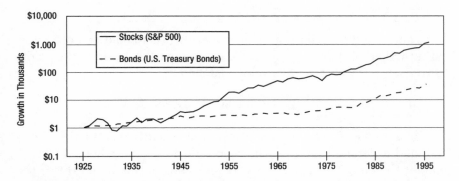

FIGURE 8.2 No Contest. The growth of $1,000 investments in stocks (S&P 500) and bonds (U.S. Treasury Bonds) over a 71-year period. Stocks have dramatically outperformed bonds. (*Source:* Ibbotson Associates, Micropal, Ltd., Brouwer & Janachowski, Inc.)

more), a mediocre stock fund will easily beat out even a good bond fund. Therefore, choose very carefully the asset classes you invest in.

3. Build a great portfolio.

Once you know exactly how much you need to invest in stock mutual funds, bond funds, and money market funds, you are ready to build a great portfolio.

But how do you select mutual funds that fit your objectives? What's the process, and how do you go about figuring out which ones are right for you, from among the many thousands of funds that clamor for your attention and clutter the pages of every business publication in the land? Reread Chapter 5, where we gave you a list of mutual funds and some tips on how to find good ones on your own.

Take the Time to Track Results

The final step is to track your results. Now that you have a great portfolio, you do not have to agonize over daily, weekly, or even monthly mutual fund share prices if you do not want to. In fact, it would be better if you ignored daily price changes. You already know that checking the daily per-share price changes for each mutual fund you own does not constitute an effective monitoring program. And it can actually be harmful if it tempts you to "micromanage" your portfolio by tweaking it every time the financial winds blow.

The best way to track results in your portfolio is to take an in-depth look every quarter. To be frank, you would get better results if you did your tracking only once a year, but, as a novice, the suspense would be killing you if you waited that long. So, a quarterly review would be fine.

Crash Control

In closing, we would like you to do something that could be both interesting and helpful during any dark days of a market crash. Write a note to yourself and put it in an envelope labeled:

To Be Opened in the Event of a Stock Market Crash

In the note, spell out your investment objectives, your time horizon, and a detailed plan of what you will do if, and when, the stock market tumbles. You now know enough to take a stand, and this is the time to do it—before such a dreaded day comes. Lay out your strategy in these areas by completing the following statements regarding what to do after a crash.

For Stock Fund Investors

Complete these two statements by picking one of the two choices given:

♦ If stocks fall 20% or more, I plan to

_____ buy more stock funds.

_____ hold tight with what I have.

♦ If stocks continue falling and go down another 10% or more, I will

_____ buy more stock funds.

_____ hold tight with what I have.

If you plan on buying more stock funds, the money must come from somewhere. Please specify the source of this money, which must be realistic and must be named.

♦ I will get the money to buy more stock funds from

_____ (savings, bond funds, the cookie jar, etc.)

For Bond Fund Investors

♦ If interest rates on intermediate- or long-term bonds go up

to _____%, I will buy the _____ (bond fund) and I

will invest at least $_____ .

For All Mutual Fund Investors

Please initial the following statements, as indication of your agreement:

♦ I will not make any decision to sell shares of either stock funds or bond funds when I am worried or depressed about current or future conditions.

♦ I know this is only a temporary setback and the U.S. economy and the stock and bond markets will survive this current downturn and come back stronger than ever.

- This downturn is a great buying opportunity. My job right now is to find more money so that I can take advantage of this opportunity.

These are guidelines that we think make sense. Feel free to modify them, but make sure you say whatever you think you will need at the time of a crash. Remember, when things go bad, we all need some reassurance. You will not be immune.

Before you put the statement sheet in the envelope, sign and date it. Also, have it witnessed by a friend or family member who will be your "conscience." Give that person a copy and ask him or her to help ensure that you stick to your plan.

INTERVIEW

"The Reality of Investing Is Taking Intelligent Risks"

An Interview with *Don Phillips*

Back in 1987, had you asked Don Phillips where he would be in 10 years, it's unlikely the answer would have been: president of the industry leader in mutual fund research (not to mention closed-end funds, variable annuities, and other types of investments). Morningstar, Inc. has been a huge success because the firm came up with a great idea and executed it very well. It did not hurt, either, that the mutual fund industry grew rapidly during that period.

Don was the first mutual fund analyst whom Joe Mansueto (Morningstar's founder) hired. Phillips got the job after answering an ad in the *Chicago Tribune.* Working for Morningstar was a great fit for Don because he is very bright, very thoughtful, and a good writer and researcher, and because he loves mutual funds. Always has, since he first bought shares in Templeton Growth Fund as a teenager.

Don is a great spokesman for mutual funds. He is straightforward, and he has acquired an enormous breadth of knowledge about mutual fund portfolio managers, investment concepts in general, the financial markets, and the forces that drive individual investors.

He has had one unique advantage. He came to the investment industry in an unlikely way—from the world of Shakespeare, Chaucer, and T. S. Eliot. He has degrees from the University of Texas and the University of Chicago in English literature, and, at one time, he envisioned a future as a Ph.D. candidate and, eventually, a college professor. Even though Don never made it into academia, we believe his erudite background helped shape Morningstar's standards for well-written, carefully researched reports about mutual funds.

Mutual Fund Mastery: OK, let's start with an easy one: What is the mission of Morningstar as a company?

Don Phillips: Our mission is very straightforward: To help investors make better investment decisions. We think we're part of a process we call the democratization of data. Getting more and better information out to a wider and wider audience. It's something that's happening in all areas of society because of the advances in technology, and we're just trying to play a role in that process—specifically, in the investment field.

MFM: And what about Morningstar Mutual Funds?

DP: Well, Morningstar Mutual Funds has become our most popular product and what we're trying to do is give someone the ability to make an informed decision about a mutual fund. To cut through the marketing hyperbole that mutual funds tend to surround themselves with and get down to the nitty-gritty—what risks the manager takes. Sometimes, when people think about investing, they think it is simply a matter of avoiding risk. The reality of investing is taking intelligent risks. But you can't take intelligent risks if you're not aware of the risks you are taking. And that's what we're trying to communicate. To give people an idea not only of what might go right with their investment, but also the knowledge of what might go wrong, because if you don't know that, then you're not going to use the fund wisely.

MFM: And you could get blindsided.

DP: No fund company took out an ad after the Crash of '87 saying, "Look at how much money we just lost for you." And yet, that's one of the most valuable things you can know.

MFM: To make an abrupt transition, I have to ask about the Morningstar rating system.

DP: We're known for our five star rating system for funds, and while I can defend that on one level, it certainly isn't all you need to know when you're investing in a mutual fund. We wanted to take the focus away from that rating system and move it more toward the work we're doing in really tearing apart the portfolio on a mutual fund.

MFM: So your rating system has been so successful, now you're trying to tell people, don't look at that completely, there's lots of other things to look at, right?

DP: Well, it's a long process. This is my tenth year with Morningstar, and the star ratings predate me. They've been there since the beginning and, while I think it's a useful tool, we've also recognized for a very long time that it isn't the be all and end all of investing. I think one of the problems investors are having today is that there are too many superficial screens, too many superficial types of research. I don't mean that in a pejorative sense so much as the literal sense; they're looking at the shell of the fund. They're taking an NAV at 2 different points in time and using that to calculate total returns or . . . risk figures. You're always looking at the shell of the fund. And I think that can separate good funds from bad funds on the whole. It can identify managers who have more merit, who have done better over time.

But I think it really falls apart when you get to the level of assembling funds in a viable portfolio. What you'll end up doing is buying a number of funds that have done well in the recent past without recognizing they have done so because they all took the same risks. That's why we have been focusing so much on fundamental research, tearing apart the

portfolio, really getting a feel for what makes the fund tick, and that's something we've been doing for a long time. Plus the ongoing interviews that we do constantly with fund managers. That's the kind of fundamental research you need to supplement the top-down research.

MFM: So the star ratings are really just past performance. There's some kind of volatility or risk factor measured in; how does that work?

DP: I think there's a place for the star ratings in investing. The fund industry is giving the investor an impossible task—here's 8,000 funds; pick the one that's right for you. The advantages to the star system, over other surface level measures, is that it's longer-term-oriented. We're not looking for the best fund for the last quarter. The minimum time we'll rate a fund is for 3 years. If we have 5- or 10-year performance numbers, then we'll weight that even more heavily in our calculations. The other advantage—it includes all costs. There's been a tremendous amount of creativity, as you know, in costs in the mutual fund area. Sometimes I wish some of the creativity that's gone into creating new sales charges and different share classes had simply gone into running the funds better.

MFM: Or picking and training better portfolio managers.

DP: Exactly. So we include all the costs, whether front-end sales charges or deferred sales charges, and that's a leveling of the playing field, making it a little easier to understand. So it's a measure of the load and expense-adjusted return relative to the risks the fund has taken. There's a volatility measure and it's a down-side volatility, measuring the chance of loss. And it's that combination—which funds have had the best returns over an extended period of time relative to the risks that they've taken—that drives the star ratings. I would say that's an intelligent way to start the search, but investors want easy shortcuts.

MFM: A way to get all the best mutual funds . . . in about an hour.

DP: Yes. And I think investors have the wrong paradigm for investing. They want to think of it as something simple and straight-forward, like a multiple-choice test. You circle a, b, or c—one answer is right and the other 2 are wrong. And I think Wall Street has perpetuated that misguided simplicity for a long time. We think the right paradigm for investing is the essay exam. There isn't necessarily a right or wrong answer; it's a matter of reaching and obtaining goals, and there are a lot of different paths you can take to come up with a successful answer. There isn't simply one. That's why we don't just print the star ratings in isolation. The star rating is just one piece of the information. I think someone in our graphics department counted something like 1,200 different pieces of information on each Morningstar page.

MFM: How did you happen to join Morningstar?

DP: I had been a mutual fund investor since I was a teenager. My father bought me shares of the Templeton Growth Fund when I was a kid. And that was a great thing for me because I got two role models out of it. One was Sir John Templeton, who was obviously a wonderful role model to have, but the other was my father. He showed me that he was an investor and it was something I could be doing. And I think that introduction at an early age is very valuable. When I go around and talk to groups like the American Association of Individual Investors, I always encourage people to go talk to their children and grandchildren, to let them know what they did that evening, that they're investors. I don't think there's a lot of role models for investing and saving in this country.

MFM: Not good ones, anyway.

DP: So we need to create our own role models and let people know that investing is something they can do and that it is a socially conscious act. It's taking responsibility for yourself. It's living within your means, it's frugality. A lot of things that are very beneficial to society as a whole.

MFM: It's almost like the mantra of the Libertarian party. It's almost what they say—people need to take more responsibility, not less.

DP: I saw these figures come in over the last couple months. Someone said the surge in money going into mutual funds over the last 3 months is roughly equivalent to the decline in spending over the last Christmas season. If there really is a link between those two, it's very interesting, because what it suggests is that Americans are finally doing what economists have been chastising them for years for not doing. We're not saving enough. This is going to hurt us relative to Japan. This is making us uncompetitive. And here you get the first 3-month period where there is real evidence this is happening. That investors have taken this to heart. They are saving more of their money, spending a little less on frivolous things. Economists then jump up and point at the assets going into mutual funds and say, "Ah hah! Speculation."

MFM: Exactly, and they say, "Mutual fund mania."

DP: This is what they've been telling us to do for years; we finally do it, and they call it speculation after just 3 months? I think it was about 2 years ago, when you saw the pendulum swing from all the positive stories on fund investing that were, frankly, often fluff pieces—"This is Bill; he manages a mutual fund and he likes trout fishing." But now it's swinging the other way and you're getting some articles that, I think, are being unfair in their criticism.

MFM: And there are, certainly, a lot of criticisms. You've made some of them yourself. But before we go too far into that, you didn't say how you happened to join Morningstar.

DP: As an undergraduate at the University of Texas, I was initially an economics major. But the prospects for graduating from UT with an economics degree in the early 1980s, and going to work in a Texas bank when the economy was in a horrid recession, weren't too attractive. So I stuck around and got an English degree and then went on to the University of Chicago to study literature. My thinking being, I'd be a college professor and an active investor on the side. I got through the Master's level of the program to where you had to make a decision to commit for the next 10 years, hunker down, and get the Ph.D.—basically, spend the most productive years of your life in a library. That wasn't really what I wanted to do, and it wasn't that much fun. When you get into graduate school in literature, you stop reading literature and start reading criticism of literature. And it's a very political environment. So, I said, why don't I see if I can switch this around. Get a job writing about and researching mutual funds, and read the great books on the side, rather than be a professor and do investing on the side. I met Joe Mansueto, who had started Morningstar and had begun to build the database. At that time, I think he had 3 full-time employees. I really liked what he was doing. I had other possibilities that could've paid me more, but I was in a good position because I got out of school without a lot of debt and was able to take a flyer on a young company and a person I believed in. And things have worked out very well for both of us.

MFM: It's interesting because your background in English and your writing ability really show up. I have always believed the Morningstar commentary and style were pleasantly intellectual. Literate without being stuffy. I think that's very unusual in this business. If you look at much of the literature, it's not that well written. Let's talk about the commentary and the newsletter—what's the editorial policy for the commentary for Morningstar Mutual Funds, and how do you develop topics?

DP: Well, the topics really come easily if you focus on the challenges facing investors. The nice thing about our business is that we've aligned ourselves so we don't have a lot of conflicts of interest. We don't accept advertising, we don't consult for fund companies, we're not in the money management

business, and we're not mutual fund managers ourselves. There's no Morningstar fund of funds. So I think we're in a position where we can be quite objective. What we do is go out and talk to investors. We get a feel for the sort of problems they're having and see if there are things we can do to push the industry and direct it in some way. We look for ways to further the interests and goals of investors, and of the financial planners and professional investors who use mutual funds. That's what we try to do. That's the goal of the commentary, to contribute in a meaningful way to the debate. Not to dominate the debate, not to pretend we're the only voice, not to pretend we have some magic system. But just to contribute in an honest and intellectually fair way to the debate.

MFM: Who should use mutual funds, and who should buy stocks and bonds directly?

DP: I think what's happening in our society right now is pretty healthy. Most people are starting off with mutual funds. I think the trend has changed. I think, historically, people started off with individual equities. They'd hear a tip at a cocktail party, or their brother-in-law would recommend a stock. They'd go out and buy this, they'd take some flyers, but they didn't do very well. And then they'd get frustrated about investing and leave it aside for 10 or 20 years and then come back and get serious about their investing and employ mutual funds to do that. And only then would they start making some progress toward their goals. I think that's changing largely because of 401(k) plans. I think more people are starting with mutual funds and getting their sea legs that way. To feel what it's like to be in investment markets. It's the only way to get that experience. You can't read about it in a book. But if you get those statements regularly, you begin to get a feel for how you react when markets go up and when they go down.

MFM: Right, and whether or not you like it . . . .

DP: If you like it and if you can handle it, right. I think what's going to happen is that a number of these people are going to get the bug and they are going to learn something you and I both know—that investing can be a lot of fun. And I think what's going to happen is that people will move from their 401(k) funds to other mutual funds and then perhaps add closed-end funds and individual securities. I think its a much healthier progression.

MFM: Rather than going the other way. Having all your money in one technology stock.

DP: Exactly. And so they'll use the closed-end funds and stocks as additions to their investments rather than the main thing. And I think they are likely to be more successful because of that.

MFM: Certain people love following stocks, and those people should do that. And some people may want to put money in a bond and know that in 10 years they'll have that money. You don't have a maturity date with a mutual fund. So there are cases where you can make the argument for individual securities over mutual funds.

DP: Frankly, if you become a good investor in individual securities, you'll also become a better fund investor. You'll appreciate more what the fund manager brings to the table, and you'll be more likely to use funds well.

MFM: Switching topics, who are 5 mutual fund managers you admire? Not necessarily that they are the best, but people whose process or approach you admire.

DP: One at or near the top of the list would be Jim Gipson from Clipper Fund. I really like the way they run that fund. There's no right way to run money, but his philosophies jibe very much with the approach I like to take to investing. He tends to buy very high-quality companies. He's willing to concentrate. His portfolio, I believe, has 19 stocks right now, but very high-quality companies. At times, they go out of favor. For example, a couple of years ago, when you had the healthcare scare, he owned no healthcare stocks. But when they sold off, he stepped in and bought names like Johnson & Johnson and Merck. He did very well. More recently, he's been buying some of the retail stocks—Wal-Mart and Toy "R" Us. They were Wall Street darlings a few years ago, but now they have fallen from favor.

MFM: They are still high-quality companies and they haven't stopped doing business . . . .

DP: Exactly. They're going to be around. They may have missed one quarter's worth of earnings. You go to the small towns and you look around, and Wal-Mart is still there and very viable. I like that style. Quality companies when they go out of favor, a contrarian investor. Gipson bought a lot of long bonds in the early 1980s and rode those as interest rates declined. More recently, the stock market has gone up, and he has a little more cash on hand. But it's a concentrated, contrarian portfolio that has some real character. And frankly, when you look at a lot of mutual funds, you see many that look like the S&P 500 with a higher expense ratio. It's nice to see some funds that are a real reflection of the manager's personality.

MFM: It's true in the bond area. So many bond funds are kind of an index clone with a higher expense ratio.

DP: Bond funds are strange because they started off using almost the opposite tack from that of equity funds. Equity funds started off with diversified funds and the sector funds came later. Bond funds, on the whole, tended to be sector funds to begin with. You know, short-term municipal, intermediate-term government, and so on. Only recently have you seen a little more creativity in bond funds, where some people are coming along—like the strategic income funds, which are a great idea, but for some reason don't sell very well. And instead of taking a lot of one type of risk like you do in a long-term government fund, these funds take a little bit of a lot of different types of risk, and, to me, that's a much more intelligent way to go about it.

MFM: One of the funds we use is PIMCO Total Return and Harbor Bond—they'll have a little foreign, some governments, Treasuries, some corporates, and a little bit of lower-rated bonds. They seem to be able to bounce from one area to another and always add real value.

DP: That's a great organization for exactly that. Two other managers I like in the fixed-income arena who have a little bit more creativity than the typical bond fund manager would be Dan Fuss at Loomis Sayles Bond and Bob Rodriguez at FPA New Income. Both of those funds have wonderful records. The Loomis Sayles record isn't as long as the New Income Fund, but by taking different types of risk around a basically conservative core, they're able to enhance their returns and provide a terrific investment opportunity.

MFM: What about some other equity fund managers you admire?

DP: One manager I admire, who is going through a tough time right now, is John Rogers, who runs the Ariel Growth Fund. John did sensationally well in the late 1980s. He had a shoot-out-the-lights year in 1988 and did very well over an extended period of time. More recently, his numbers haven't been as good, but it's explainable why they haven't been as good. One of John's philosophies is, you always stick to your knitting, and he's never owned a lot of high-flying technology companies. He tends to own a lot of Midwestern companies that don't have a lot of debt and are probably in more mundane businesses, but are good solid enterprises. And that's something, in a high-flying market like this, that doesn't capture the investor's fancy. You get everything remotely connected to the Internet trading at a huge premium . . . .

MFM: One hundred times earnings, no problem.

DP: Investors are often overly optimistic. These Internet companies often have little or no revenues and no earnings. You get these very viable companies in the Ariel Fund that maybe don't have the same sex appeal, but are really terrific investment opportunities. What I admire about John Rogers is how steadfastly he is sticking to his discipline. This is one of those dark nights of the soul for true value investors. I also like Ab Nicholas of the Nicholas Fund. I think he's going through the same sort of thing, and I admire both managers for sticking to their guns and staying with their strategies. And, I'm putting some of my personal money into the Ariel Growth Fund. Because I believe in what he's doing and like to see a manager who sticks to his or her philosophy even during times when it gets rough.

MFM: Let's talk a little bit about the load versus no-load issue. I don't know if you can call it controversy, but I think it's a little confusing to people. There are 2 issues I continually get asked about when you say no-load fund versus load fund. People ask how a no-load fund makes money.

DP: Right, it is getting remarkably blurred. Even 10 years ago, it was fairly simple—there were the load funds that had an 8½% load and the no-load with no sales charge and sold directly to the investor. The load is compensation for the financial professional to walk you through the investment process. If you benefit or would like to have that service, I think it's very wise to pay it. There are some terrific financial professionals out there who can help you assemble a portfolio of funds, and oftentimes, one of the key things they do is enforce discipline. They get you to answer questions honestly. In a bull market, everyone thinks they're the bravest investors ever. Sitting down with a financial planner who can say, "Here is what things might look like if things got bad; here is how much money you could lose," that could be money that is very well spent. Unfortunately, there's this debate that has raged about load vs. no-load. The no-load people assume the moral high ground, that load funds are seen as shifty or bad. And frankly, the load companies made a colossal mistake. First off, just the semantics of the debate—letting it be framed as load vs. no-load. How in the world do you defend an ugly, burdensome word like *load?* Yet, the process was very good. They could've just as well said service vs. no service.

MFM: They tried that a bit with contingent sales charges or back-end loads . . . .

DP: Different attempts late in the game. But I think they let down the financial planners and brokers in the field. The load fund companies, in effect, said, "Oh well, if you don't like this up-front load, we'll just hide it around back." But if you walk into a room and a child is playing with something and they put it behind their back immediately, what do you think is going on? You think they are doing something they weren't supposed to do. It really created this impression of, "Yes, these loads are bad, we'll do something about it." They didn't step up and say, "No I think these planners and brokers are providing a valuable service and it's one we think has merit and we're going to keep it up front." I see nothing wrong with the load, as long as it's candid and it's up front. Unfortunately, at a gut level, people who run load fund complexes don't really believe in the broker. I sat in the office of an executive of one of the 10 biggest mutual fund companies in America, and he was talking about our basic Morningstar page, and he said, "You guys do a sensational job in the analysis, writing up the fund, really capturing all of its characteristics, but you know the brokers, they are going to look at whatever has the most stars and sell that." And I looked him in the face and said, "If you really believe that, why do you let them represent your product?"

MFM: We talked a little about your fund choices. What funds do you use, and how do you pick those particular ones?

DP: When I look at funds, I look first and foremost at the portfolio manager. I'm a believer in active management. I also believe, as a fund investor, you need to have a certain amount of respect for the managers and for the process. I look for people who are fanatics. Warren Buffett talked about the one-question job interview—"Are

you a fanatic?" And that's what I look for, people who have a real passion for what they do. I meet hundreds of portfolio managers a year and, at some point, it's easy to tell which are the ones who really love this and which are here because when they got out of graduate school, this was paying more than management consulting. You look for people who believe in what they do.

MFM: Who'd be buying stocks even if they weren't getting paid.

DP: Yes. I like funds that have a lot of character. I'm not a big fan of the fund manager who is always trying to keep his or her sector weightings within plus or minus two percentage points of some index. I'm willing to take a little risk, have funds that are a little bit different. I think it was Sir John Templeton who said, "If you want to beat the market over time, you've got to do something different." Some of the managers I've had in my portfolio over the years are people like Mario Gabelli, Roger Engeman, Shelby Davis, who I think is a sensational manager. Ab Nicholas is another; I mentioned John Rogers and Jim Gipson. Dick Weiss, at Strong, and Ron Ognar, who is also at Strong; also, Ralph Wanger and Don Yacktman.

MFM: Can you say you know very clearly what Ralph Wanger does?

DP: I don't think anyone can say they know Ralph Wanger. I shared a cab with him from O'Hare Airport back into the city and it was 45 of the strangest minutes of my life. But it was also 45 of the most fascinating.

MFM: I remember talking to him years ago, and he was saying he was going to buy Hildebrand, the company that makes caskets, because there were all these diseases making people die. And I was, like, how can you? It was a theme, he said.

DP: You'd just as soon not play, right? If you go to dinner with the better portfolio managers, they'll ask you more questions than you ask them. I've had dinner with Mark Mobius, who runs the Templeton Developing Markets Fund, and Mark Holowesko, who runs Templeton Foreign and two other funds of theirs. I have both managers in my portfolio. They'll say, "Oh, you use that product; why did you choose that over another? How is your business doing? Are there new needs you have?" They are always asking questions—what's the investment angle? And getting back to Ralph Wanger, there's a classic story about him when he worked at Harris Associates. An analyst for the firm came in bemoaning the fact that Ford and GM were doing so poorly, relative to their Japanese competitors. The guy was a domestic stock analyst; that's all he could see. There wasn't an opportunity in the domestic stocks and, as I've heard the story, Ralph was sitting there doodling pictures of airplanes, and he muttered under his breath, "Don't bitch, switch." At that time, in the Acorn Fund, he had Nissan and Toyota. If someone's losing, someone else is winning. It may not be the most pleasing idea to think he's seeing new diseases and running out to say, "Ah hah, I'm going to buy a coffin manufacturer," but I'm sure it made sense to him. And given his record, who is going to knock it?

MFM: I think he has to be intellectually open. He's not stuck in the narrow-minded approach. A good portfolio manager will look at anything that could make money.

DP: You've got to understand what your job is as money manager. It's not necessarily to go out and make the social calls for people. There are some funds that do that and there's a place for that. It's very valuable, but that's not the role of the typical fund manager—to be enforcing his or her social beliefs.

MFM: You brought up an interesting point, when you said you believe in active management. Does that means you don't invest in index funds?

DP: No, I don't use index funds because I'm in a position where I can identify good active managers. I spend a lot of time thinking and reading about this topic every day in my work. The debate is often misplaced— passive or index vs. active—as if there was a right and a wrong answer. The advantages of passive investing are low expenses. I got a letter from Jack Bogle [Chairman, The Vanguard Group] in which he made the point that index funds make little or no sense unless they are no-load funds with very low expenses. And he's right. Unfortunately, the average mutual fund, index or active, is overpriced. You would expect the median mutual fund manager to get the median return, which, in stocks, is the S&P 500. Unfortunately, fees have gone up over the last decade and so, instead of aiming for 70 basis points, which funds did 2 decades ago, they aim for 150 basis points per year in expenses. And what that does is, it shifts the line over. Meaning more and more managers are going to be below the median return. You've really got a fairly elite group of managers who, over time, are going to beat the market. And the great majority are going to trail the market. So the way I think of the investing options that you have is as a horseshoe as opposed to a straight line. On one prong you've got low-cost, no-load index funds—a viable approach to money managing. The other prong represents funds with great managers and reasonable costs. Unfortunately, the great majority of the fund industry is in the U-shaped part of the horseshoe, where you've got overpriced, uninspired mutual funds. And that's the bulk of the fund industry. And that morass is the enemy to the individual investor and the financial planner. That's what we have to purge from our portfolios. I prefer active management, but I think, for many investors, a combination of both index funds and actively managed funds makes good sense too.

MFM: Getting back to your personal investments, how do you determine your own asset allocation?

DP: I don't spend a lot of time thinking about asset allocation. I think one of the disservices the academics have brought to the investment arena in recent years is this notion that over 90% of your variability of returns comes from asset allocation. I think people take that study to mean you should spend 90% of your time thinking about what your asset allocation should be, which is absurd. You don't wake up in the morning and say, "I'll change my stock weighting from 26% to 27% today. And let's see, maybe bonds should move down to 14% of assets." That's not something you can add a lot of value to. Where people make real mistakes is when they try to do their asset allocation based on broad macroeconomic themes. I think it was Peter Lynch who said, "I think the investor who spends 15 minutes a year on macroeconomics, wastes 10 minutes." To me, the central investment paradox is that the questions that could yield the greatest theoretical benefit tend to be the ones least worth asking about because they are largely unanswerable. What I'm referring to is, asking which way is the market going, or where is the Dow going, or are interest rates going up or down. If we knew the answers, we could all go down to the Chicago options pit and be millionaires by the end of the week. The problem is, you can't answer those questions with any degree of certainty. Therefore, the questions you need to be focusing on are the ones you have a unique ability to answer. Such as, "When is the tuition check due? When do I plan to retire? How much risk can I handle?" These kinds of questions ought to guide your asset allocation and your big-picture thinking, not the dollar–yen relationship. That's the mistake I think most investors make. Unfortunately, it is a mistake that the overall discussion about investing in the financial press tends to encourage, because it's sexy to talk about political relationships or the Federal Reserve Board's latest move.

MFM: Unfortunately, the media, the investment industry, and even our wonderful government regulators have a tendency to make things more complex than they need to be. Because they have to fill space, well-intentioned journalists are continually asking what should we be looking to do now? The answer is, you probably shouldn't be looking to do anything different in 1996 than you did in 1995—assuming you did a good job.

DP: That's what I always loved about Sir John Templeton when I'd watch him on Louis Rukeyser's show. Here was this incredibly successful, wise man and he'd talk about investing in such plain and straightforward terms. I've started to realize that all the great investors do that. It's the bad investors that have all of this complexity, all these theories, and are focusing on the short term. The great investors recognize that, at heart, investing is very simple—buy low, sell high. This is not the most complex thing. It's next to impossible to master, but it's not a complex concept.

MFM: It's actually easy to master if you have time on your hands. Buying low and selling high is easy to do if you're willing to take 10 years to do it.

DP: If you are disciplined. The problem is that, when the stock market is high, investors are happy about adding to their investments, but when the market is low, they are less happy and less willing to buy more. That's the basic problem with low-risk mutual funds. There are wonderful ones out there that are very good at keeping risk down. The problem is, they look best compared to other funds at those moments in time when no one wants to buy mutual funds—when you really should buy them. Which is one of the reasons I think Ariel Growth is an interesting fund to be looking at now.

MFM: That's a good point. Things are never as good as they seem when you're winning and never as bad as they seem when you're losing.

DP: The great investors balance the 2—the classic fear-and-greed story.

MFM: Who are some other great investors? Not necessarily mutual fund people, but people you could listen to, read about, learn from.

DP: Anyone interested in investing needs to make a point to get to know what Warren Buffett has achieved. There's a bit of a cottage industry these days on Warren Buffett books. I think the one by Roger Lowenstein is far and away the best (until Mr. Buffett writes his own book). Lowenstein's book is called *The Making of an American Capitalist* (Random House). I'd also recommend subscribing to *Outstanding Investor Digest*.

MFM: What other ones?

DP: John Train has a couple of good books called *The Money Masters* and *The New Money Masters* (both published by Harper Business Books). Those books are very valuable. I like to read about portfolio managers. One of the things you learn is, there is no one right philosophy on how to invest money. Peter Lynch and Warren Buffett have very different methods. At heart, they may share things in common, but how they go about and do their investing is quite different. Templeton does it a different way, Roger Engemann or Mark Holowesco might bring different things to the table. That's an important thing as an investor, not to get caught up in the debate about which discipline is better or worse than this one. What you have to do is find the discipline best for you.

MFM: That works for you and you'll stick to.

DP: Yes. John Templeton probably wouldn't do a great job trying to run a small-cap high-tech fund. The exception to that might be Lynch. I think his genius lies in looking at stocks through a lot of different perspectives. That ability to wear different hats and see different things in different stocks is his unique ability. But how many Peter Lynches have we found?

MFM: Is there anybody running a mutual fund now who has that similar ability?

DP: The closest counterpart I can think of is Jeff Vinik, who used to run Magellan. I think he is a brilliant investor. Unfortunately, he was in an almost no-win situation. There was so much scrutiny of every move he made. At Fidelity, there's an attempt to codify what it was that Lynch did well, and then to bring in technology and tools to help a whole series of fund managers do similar things. I know Fidelity gets criticized sometimes, but when I visit their managers, I find

them to be one of the most humble groups. At a more typical fund company I visit, they say we've got this magic or system, which means we'll always be great. You go to Fidelity and they say, "Look, we don't have anything special, we're just going to try to outhustle our competitors. Turn over more rocks, as Peter Lynch would say, and look at more opportunities and try our best." So far, they've done very well. I don't think they're going to be able to replicate what they did from 1990 through 1995 in the immediate future, but it was an absolutely spectacular run.

MFM: Speaking of the next few years, what do you think the world of mutual funds is going to look like 10 years from now?

DP: Well, I think there'll be more funds rather than fewer. A lot of the growth in mutual funds is simply additional share classes—the A shares, the B shares, and so on. And I think this has done a terrible disservice to investors because it has made something that was quite simple, needlessly complex. The great beauty of mutual funds was their simplicity, and that's the elegance of fund investing. When you start saying, "This is the fund and before we talk about what it does, let's talk about A shares and B shares and contingent deferred sales charges and redemption fees . . . ," well then you've just cluttered, unnecessarily, the investment landscape. I was talking with one regulator in Washington recently, and she sort of sighed and said, "My Lord, there's still a lot of letters left."

MFM: Has there ever been a better time in history for ordinary investors to have access to high-quality investments?

DP: Absolutely not. And that's the wonderful thing. It's the democratization of data and it's an empowering thing to individual investors. It's happening throughout our society. You look at what CNN has done. The leaders of the former Soviet Union can't pretend the world is one way when their people can turn on CNN or get on the Internet and find that reality is something different. For years, I think the people who have sold financial services had the upper hand because they had information and people they were selling to didn't. So the power was in the hands of the sellers. Increasingly, because of the increased flow of information, the power is in the hands of the purchasers or those intermediaries who represent and think like the purchasers. And that is a tremendously healthy thing.

MFM: Very healthy.

DP: There were firms who had mutual fund research, but they'd sell it only to the fund companies because they paid top dollar. It created an artificial barrier because these people had it and the other people didn't. And what you've seen is the democratization of data, and in the end the investor wins.

MFM: Can this get even better or are we peaking out?

DP: No. It will get better yet. There'll be more information. I think investors will put more pressure on mutual fund companies to release their portfolios in a timely and accurate manner and in such a way that more people can come in and do real research on the funds. See who is taking which risks and when. Right now, there is no accountability in the fund industry. We did a study in the wake of the Orange County scandal for *Fortune,* and we took all of the most recently available mutual fund portfolios and then did a listing of which funds had the greatest exposure to Orange County bonds. The good part of the story is, no fund had more than 8% of their assets there, which meant, on the whole, if you were a fund investor instead of an individual bond investor, you were probably better off. So it was a positive story for funds. But what happened is, when *Fortune* started calling up these fund companies, they said, "Oh, we sold those bonds, they're gone." You knew that couldn't be true. Someone still owned those things. They didn't decline before the fiasco. One fund group also called us up with thinly veiled threats of a lawsuit, saying it was

completely irresponsible of us to release that information [saying they held Orange County bonds] to *Fortune* because the information was out of date. The information was about 3 months old, but they hadn't published anything more recent. We said, "Is this the most recent portfolio you've released?" And they said, "Yes it is." And we said, "When's the next update coming out?" And they said, "Not for another 3 months." So we said, "How are we wrong in releasing this information? We didn't say you owned it on this day, we said you owned it 3 months ago and that's true." "Well," they said, "you shouldn't have said anything." We believe in releasing more, not less, information. So I'm happy that things are changing. Ten years ago, the problem was how to get information to make an intelligent decision.

MFM: It was an access issue.

DP: Right. Today, it is a very different issue. How can you make sense of this overload of information? The key issue in the future will be bridging that gap from data to knowledge. And that is going to be the key skill set. You're going to have plenty of data, but just having plenty of data doesn't mean you make good decisions. It's what you do with it. And that's where the financial planning and investment advisory profession can bring so much to the table. It's knowing what to do with this information to help investors make these decisions. You are getting more and more financial planners who define themselves as putting the customers' interests first. Independent money managers who do the research for them and make this leap from the data to the knowledge.

MFM: In fact, people will have to limit the information they take in. It's a matter of being more discriminating in what you look at and where you take sources of information.

DP: I think that's a very good point. One of my favorite quotes is from Pascal, who said, "I write this letter long because I lack the time to make it short." It's so easy to put together volumes of information in this day and age. It reminds me of the University of

Chicago, where I did my Master's thesis. They had a rule—your thesis could not be more than 25 pages. If you turned in a 26-page paper, they would not read the last page. I thought that was great. They wanted you to hone your argument and make it concise and straightforward. There was an analyst on our staff who went to a different school, and she also got an English degree. There, the requirement was, you had to turn in a minimum of 100 pages. Increasingly, it's going to be the ability to take all that data and hone in on what's important—what counts. I think that's the beauty of our one-page analysis. Look, it's easy to produce a ten-page document on a mutual fund; it's hard to produce a one-page document.

MFM: That was very well done, Don. How you got from Pascal to Morningstar in one thought. What new things are you planning?

DP: Well, we're trying to keep our ear to the ground and ask questions and seek out the problems facing investors. I've just praised our single page of research on a given fund, but I'll also be the first to concede I think it's fighting the last decade's challenge. It shows you what one fund looks like at one moment in time. And while that's a good starting point, it's not nearly enough. The real challenge facing investors today, I believe, is how funds combine. Because the typical story that's written about funds today almost seems to assume someone's starting with a blank slate. "Eight good funds to buy now . . . ."

MFM: "Five fund managers who may be the next Peter Lynch . . . ."

DP: Exactly. It's assuming you're starting with a blank slate, and no one is. That's not reality. Reality is that you've got some funds in your 401(k) plan. You've got some funds you bought from your broker a decade ago. A couple of funds you bought from Vanguard or Fidelity a few years ago. The challenge for investors is how to make sense of this mess they've already got. How do you understand collectively what risk you're taking and how do you then intelligently add to that? Or how

do you monitor this? Mutual funds aren't static. The portfolio managers come and go. Strategies change. Funds veer off into different ways. And what might have been a good solid portfolio at one moment in time, at another moment might not be that. You need to have tools to analyze the whole portfolio. And that's the way that we're moving. The beauty is that if you're analyzing mutual funds, you're already analyzing a portfolio, because you're looking at a portfolio of securities that a manager selected. What we're trying to do is create tools that will help investors understand their whole portfolio, not just the subsets. Not just the individual stocks, bonds, mutual funds, or variable annuities they've put into it.

MFM: How the portfolio is going to work as a whole. If I make this change or that change, how will it look?

DP: Precisely. And I think the solutions are going to be electronic. You really can't do a print product about all the different ways funds or investments might combine.

MFM: Tell us about your new Principia software.

DP: What we're trying to do is create a very open framework. Something that will combine stocks, mutual funds, closed-end funds, and so on, to let the individual investor, or the individual investment adviser, go in and make very high-level decisions. To move seamlessly between stocks and bonds. Our basic Principia program is a software program about mutual funds, and there are versions for closed-end funds and variable annuities. We're creating a couple of different modules too. One is called Portfolio Developer. And what that does is allow you to plug in different investments and then, in the aggregate, see what your exposure is to different sectors. What's your exposure to foreign versus domestic. . . .

MFM: So you could have 8 funds or 5 funds and find out what would this look like as a total portfolio?

DP: Exactly. And that's the challenge facing investors. Especially if you look at some of the auto manufacturers, where some of their 401(k) plans offer 40, 50, 60 choices. That's daunting. Sometimes too many choices is harder than too few. And what we're trying to do is give people an understanding that if they choose 5 out of a list of 50, what that collectively looks like. Because an inherent problem with fund investing is that people tend to look at the recent winners. And so they'll buy funds off the same leaders list. And almost by definition, the way you end up on the leaders list is because you took the same risks that other hot funds took. So a person buying 5 funds off the same list is really getting 5 different shadings of the same basic approach. In other words, it's not a diversified portfolio.

MFM: It may be an extreme portfolio because to be at the top you have to be somewhat of an extremist.

DP: That's exactly right. The way you end up on the leaders list in the short term is to have simply taken more risks than your competitors and, of course, you had those risks pay off. That's why top funds in one year can easily go to the bottom of the performance charts the next year. Which doesn't mean that looking at those performance charts is irrelevant, but oftentimes who did well in the short term is simply a measure of who took more risk. I think what a lot of investors should be focusing on is the consistency issue and perhaps ignore those funds that are in the top 5% and instead look at the ones consistently in the top half.

MFM: You were talking about the Principia, the first part, which is the Portfolio Developer and then . . . .

DP: There are 2 other modules that we're working on right now. One already exists—the Electronic Binder. And what we're doing now is giving you the ability to print the entire Morningstar page electronically. It's in a file where you can go in and print as many copies as you want of an individual page or just print out systematically these five pages

and then you can keep exactly what you want in a reference file—this is what I owned at this moment in time and I want to freeze that . . . .

MFM: Or show it to your family or . . . .

DP: Right, this might be a good investment for my son-in-law, maybe I'll send this off to him. It makes our existing service more flexible. And the other area we're doing that I think will be the most fun for me, as a mutual fund junkie, is called Advanced Analytics. And what we're doing there is really to further the push of fundamental analysis of mutual funds. As I mentioned earlier, I think the biggest problem with mutual fund research is that far too much is superficial. The reason people are embracing these superficial solutions is that they're easier. Frankly, doing the fundamental analysis is hard. And we're going to find ways to make it easier.

MFM: So you get a fund that, in the beginning, maybe was a small company stock fund and then, over time, has gotten bigger and had to become more and more a large cap fund—you'll be able to show that.

DP: Absolutely. Our page shows that to some degree now, because we have the historical-style boxes which can document this. But here, we'll be able to do it in even greater detail and you can look at a fund like 20th Century Ultra—5 years ago, the fund had $500 million in assets; today, it has $15 billion in assets. Something's got to change in that situation. We can, in fact, document that 5 years ago, they were a small cap fund with a median market cap in the $750 million range. As the assets grew, it became more of a mid-cap fund, and today it's a large cap fund. If you look at the portfolio today, you'll see Citicorp, you'll see Merck, IBM, Microsoft. These are not small stock names. It doesn't mean it's not going to be a good fund anymore, but it perhaps occupies a different place in your portfolio. And if that's still in your portfolio as your small company growth exposure, you don't have any more small cap growth exposure. There may be a very good chance you've doubled up on the large cap growth. Say you already had Vanguard U.S. Growth there, now you've got 20th Century Ultra that's really mining the same territory. You might want to rethink that.

MFM: What do you think about T. Rowe Price as a fund group? To us, it seems they have made kind of a comeback here. For a long time, you couldn't think of too many good equity funds at T. Rowe Price, but over the last few years, they've really made a comeback. Is that true and why do you think it happened?

DP: It's absolutely on the mark. You're dead on. T. Rowe Price has just made phenomenal strides. A decade ago, if you looked at their equity research department, it really wasn't hitting on all cylinders. They brought in a guy . . . named Jim Kennedy—I met him earlier this year and asked him exactly that question. What he did is to set about systematically upgrading their research capabilities. Instead of just jettisoning everything they had, he set about doing it slowly and surely. Building a few people a year. They put together a wonderful team there. The beauty of T. Rowe Price is that there are no weak links in the lineup. They are above average at everything. They are above-average growth investors, they are above-average value investors now with Brian Rogers and what he's doing with equity income. They're above-average large cap, small cap, and international. They don't have a weak link.

Speaking of that, I think that's why Fidelity recently made some changes in their fixed-income department.

MFM: Right; international and fixed-income for Fidelity have been very weak for years. I don't know why, but they have.

DP: For international, they're still trying to get that going on all cylinders. A couple of years ago, they said, "We're going to make our fixed-income funds more like our stock funds. We're going to try and find pockets of opportunity and exploit them." And that got tripped up in 1994. I think what Ned Johnson did then was very shrewd. He stepped back and realized that, even though this philosophy might work well in the long term, what the market is saying is that investors don't want the risk taking in their bond funds. They think of them as commodities. The very fact they brought in Fred Henning, who had run their money market funds, to head up the whole fixed-income department gives you a real idea of what direction they might be going in. I think they're making these funds much more stable. They still want to make them good—don't get me wrong on that. Good, but more stable.

Don Phillips told us Morningstar's mission is to help investors make better investment decisions. When it comes to your investments, we think you can take a lesson from Don and Morningstar—develop your own mission or goal. Turn the page to our final chapter which is all about the really important goals such as love, health, or even loafing.

CHAPTER 9

Love, Health, Money, Retirement, Loafing, and Other Worthwhile Goals

To make the most out of your portfolio and your future, you must have a clear and unambiguous goal.

What is your dream? No, not the one that sounds good, we mean the real one. Do you want to send your kids to Stanford University, all expenses paid? Or, have enough money to say "Basta" (Italian for "Have a nice day.") to your boss? Maybe you'd like to donate money to a charity that creates jobs for the poorest of the poor around the world. Maybe you're concerned about the rainforest or even a historic building in your hometown. How about buying an island in the Caribbean, or enough great works of art to endow your own museum? Perhaps you've always wanted to write novels, but you figure you also need to be independently wealthy and a resident of the Left Bank in Paris in order to be properly inspired.

What is your dream? None of that painfully shy, overly humble stuff. Just tell us. And then write it down.

We need to know, and so do you. It wouldn't hurt if your friends and family knew too, but that may be pushing it right now. If you find this a bit difficult, you're not alone. We do, too. For some reason, many of us find it hard to voice our dreams. And because dreams are not always the most concrete things, we find it hard to turn our dreams into clear, concise, and unambiguous goals. You need to set goals that are big enough and outrageous enough to carry you along until the day comes when you can honestly say, "I'm living my dream."

Back in the early 1980s, we began to dream about an investment process that was simple, clear-cut, and mutually beneficial for our clients and for us. We were working at Merrill Lynch back then, and we had to put up with a lot of pressure to sell specific investments. It took several years and some trial and error, but in 1985, we formed Brouwer & Janachowski, an investment advisory firm that did exactly what we had been dreaming about. There were lots of missteps, lots of problems along the way, but we began living one of our dreams in 1985.

It soon turned out, though, that we came up with other goals too—like reaching out to you. So books, articles, and speaking engagements became a way of doing that. We hope we will never stop carrying out our dreams. We also hope that, by living our dreams, we will be able to help you finance your dreams, whatever they may be.

Before we go further, we have another question: What is your biggest financial fear? We've asked you to tell us your dream; now we want you to dredge up and face your fear. Are you afraid of being broke? Of making bad investments and putting your family in financial jeopardy? Or, do you fear being left on the ground when stocks or real estate or international investments are soaring to the sky? No matter who you are or what you're like, there are times when you hear an inner voice or when your stomach tightens and you are confronted with an uncomfortable thought relating to your financial future. So tell us, just what is it? We want to help, but you need to make the first move.

We'll get back to this in a moment, so don't think you're off the hook.

A Quick Review   Let's refresh your memory and take a quick stroll through the investment process we have outlined.

In Chapter 1, we suggested:

1. You must invest your time before your money. In other words, figure out where you're going before you start out.

2. Hope for the best, but plan for the worst. If everything goes great, there will be no problems. But we want you to be financially fit no matter what happens, even if there is another economic depression.

We introduced you to The Laws of Investment Success:

1. **Invest for a minimum of 20 years.** Many investors have an outlook that is far too short. Their concern is with what stocks or interest rates are going to do in the next few months or years. If you adopt a longer time horizon, we believe your investing—and your sleep—will improve.

2. **Place your money with the investment pros, don't bet against them.** Mutual funds give you the opportunity of investing alongside Wall Street's best investment minds—people like Shelby Davis, Bill Gross, Mike Price, and many more. We think mutual funds are the best investment vehicle for most investors.

3. **If you want capital appreciation, be an owner and not a loaner.** For centuries, the big money has been made by those who own something—real estate, oil wells, companies. Stocks and stock mutual funds represent a share of ownership in a portfolio of well-managed companies. You are much more likely to get more capital appreciation from stocks than you will from bonds.

4. **You have to pay if you want to play.** To become a good investor, you have to first invest some of your time. Next, you have to get started and learn from both your successes and your failures. In most cases, what we call experience is really just the applied lessons of failure.

5. **What counts is what you keep—after taxes.** Income taxes take a bite out of your returns, and there is not much you can do about it. But by using tax-deferred retirement plans and mutual funds that practice reasonable tax efficiencies, you can at least minimize the unkind cut of the tax collector.

In Chapter 2, we covered the many wonderful attributes of mutual funds, with particular emphasis on the no-load funds. We believe that the modern mutual fund structure is one of the marvels of the 20th century.

Chapter 3 took you through our thinking on how to evaluate mutual funds. In Chapter 4, we showed you how to use Morningstar Mutual Funds as a resource to help separate the few really good funds from the also-rans. Chapter 5 is our list of solid funds in different mutual fund categories, and Chapter 6 showed you how to build a great portfolio.

Chapter 7 covered useful topics like fear, greed, and other roadblocks on the superhighway to success. For centuries, investors have suffered from emotional excess when it comes to investing. Way back in the 1600s, Dutch investors rode what may have been the first bull market—in tulip bulbs, of all things. They went way up and then crashed. When you read Charles Mackay's wonderful 1841 book, *Extraordinary*

Popular Delusions and the Madness of Crowds, you can still hear echoes of their despairing cries.

We also gave you a self-assessment quiz which we trust you dutifully took. As part of the effort, you were supposed to give your quiz results to a close friend or your husband or wife. Did you do it? We hope so. If not, why not turn back there right now and get started?

Chapter 8 helped you develop your own personal investment strategy. To be successful, we believe your approach must be consistent, correct (most of the time), and clear-cut. We also covered stock market peaks and valleys. For the most part, we think it is better that you ignore short-term stock market movements, but you still need a working knowledge of what actually causes the tidal flows in and out of stocks. And we covered 2 investment strategies that work:

1. Buy and hold.

2. Modified buy and hold.

The End of the Beginning

And now, here we are at the end of the beginning. We have given you all the tools you need to make your investment future very bright. We hope you now have the confidence and the resources you need to succeed.

The fact is, you have many resources available to you that were almost unthinkable even 10 years—much less, 100 years—ago. The flip side is that money is much more important now than it was 100 years ago. Back then, most people lived in a rural or semirural environment. Most families had close relatives who farmed, and at least there was food to eat. Now, we use money to buy everything we need, and that, in part, leads to a bit more anxiety for contemporary men and women.

We Want You to Succeed

To get what you want from your investments is relatively simple but not necessarily easy. To start, you have to face the natural tendency toward procrastination or its evil twin, hyperactivity. In addition, you have to avoid the belief that advice from family or friends is more useful than convictions you have developed from your own research. You have to be your own investment adviser. After all, it's your money.

There will always be challenges—inflation, deflation, recession, depression—and changes in your life situation—you lose your job, you get married, you have a child. Hindsight tends to soften hard edges, but looking ahead never has been easy. Sticking to a plan in the face of adversity has never been easy, either.

"It's a Toss-Up, You Can Either Go to Las Vegas or You Can Farm"

Twenty years ago, Gene and Mary Jo Cole tied the knot and began working the family potato farm in southern Montana. During the "easy money" days of the early 1980s, banks went out of their way to lend to farmers like the Coles. As Mary Jo put it, "They made it very easy to borrow and expand. Didn't even ask for financial statements." With easy credit, the Coles beefed up their spread to 350 acres.

In 1985, a hard frost killed half their crop and nearly destroyed their way of life. "I always say, 'It's a toss-up, you can either go to Las Vegas or you can farm,'" said Mary Jo. "And we knew that. But we took on too much debt and that, plus the devastating frost, wiped out our savings."

The Coles were stuck in a vicious cycle of living from year to year, crop to crop. After paying interest on the debt and paying taxes, there wasn't much left. They toyed with the idea of walking away from the farm, but they loved farming and country life too much. Then, in November 1993, they suffered a different kind of blow—Mary Jo was disabled in an auto accident. The insurance settlement allowed her to set up an investment fund to pay for future health care, but the accident had a different kind of sobering effect. They realized they couldn't rely on staying healthy and farming as their sole strategy for financial success.

BROUWER & JANACHOWSKI'S RECOMMENDATION

When we first talked with the Coles, they had just paid off most of their debts and set up a retirement fund. They had approximately $100,000 in personal assets invested primarily in money market funds. Because the Coles are young (Gene is 45 and Mary Jo is 40) and have a very long investment timeline, we recommended investing all of their retirement assets in stock mutual funds. We also suggested that they keep 5 years' of anticipated medical expenses in money market funds and intermediate-term bond mutual funds. (This is in addition to the normal "rainy day" money anyone should keep as a liquid reserve. All remaining personal assets should be invested in a portfolio of stock mutual funds.)

The portfolio we recommended for their retirement account is:

Artisan International Fund	15%
Harbor Capital Appreciation Fund	15%
Harbor International Fund II	15%
Oakmark Fund	20%
Selected American Shares	20%
Vanguard/Primecap Fund	15%

As you read this chapter, you know things that we did not know when we wrote it. Time has moved on since we scribbled down these words, and many events have come to pass. Perhaps there has been a horrendous stock market crash such as occurred in that difficult 18-month stretch in 1973–1974, when the S&P 500 fell approximately 40% and some mutual funds plummeted by 60% or more. As we look back on that era, we can see that it was a magnificent buying opportunity. It was a time when Warren Buffett said he felt like a sex maniac in a harem. Yet most investors did not buy, they sold. Most investors did not load up on mutual fund shares that were going begging at 40%, 50%, 60%, or even 70% off.

Or, you may be facing a stock market that seems ridiculously overpriced, just as investors did when the Dow Jones Industrial Average hit 2000, 3000, 5000, or 8000. Earlier, we mentioned an acquaintance who had several million dollars in 1982, at the beginning of the bull market. When the Dow began moving up from its low point, we suggested he buy stocks. At that time, the Dow was at 1000 so he said, "I'll wait until it gets back down to 900." We said buy some now, and buy more if it goes down. When the Dow hit 2000, he said he would buy in when it fell back to 1500. And so the story went. Year after year. Milestone after milestone. 2000. 4000. 7000. Last time we talked to him, he was still waiting.

You Have to Know When to Pull the Trigger

When we were talking with Michael Price (see the interview following Chapter 3) about what it takes to be a good portfolio manager, he said, "They are smart. They work hard and analyze things very intelligently. The final intangible is that they know when to pull the trigger and when to pull back. Pull the trigger—that is a big part."

Many investors cannot pull the trigger because they are afraid that as soon as they do, the stock market will fall. It may seem otherwise, but we can assure you that the stock market does not know what you are doing. Nor does it know at what level you bought in. Maybe those paralyzed investors do not want to look stupid. Maybe they just fear loss so much, it paralyzes them. Maybe they have no faith in the American economy. Whatever the reason, they fail to act.

As an investor, you need to analyze investment opportunities to find those that match your objectives. You also need to analyze yourself in order to set your objectives. But no matter how much and how well you do your analysis, there comes a time to act, a time to "pull the trigger," as Mike Price puts it.

Mistakes Are the Tuition You Pay for Experience

It is inevitable that you will make mistakes. You will buy a fund that does poorly. You will put a percentage in small company stock funds and they will lag the S&P 500. Or, you will buy a bond fund and interest rates will rise. If you are investing with a long-term plan and the bond fund fits that plan, then don't fret. Do not react to short-term market movements and lose sight of your goal.

In January 1987, the S&P 500 soared 13.5%. After that, stocks slowed down, but they still climbed throughout the summer. A large investment firm we know was very cautious going into the year, so they missed out on the big January move. Late that summer, they were feeling anxious to participate in the rally, so they moved very aggressively into small company stocks—just in time to go down in flames when the market crashed on October 19. For the year, small company stocks lost 8.8% when the S&P 500 rose 5.2%.

Had they stuck to their conservative stance for the year, they would have done fine. Had they been aggressive going into the year and remained that way all year long, they would have done fine. But they waffled, flip-flopped, and got whacked. Create a plan that makes sense for you and stick to it.

Here is a plan that will work for any type of goal, financial or otherwise. If you want to reach a goal, no matter how large or small, follow these 7 steps and you will maximize your chance of success.

Seven Steps to Investment Success

1. **Dream.** In the beginning, it was just a dream. Sounds a bit grandiose, but it's true. Before anything else, you must have a dream. What each of us chooses to call *reality* is a dream of our own making. If you wake up in the morning excited about the things you will do that day, you are likely to have an exciting and successful day. If you are bummed out when you start, chances are good you will be bummed out at the end. "We become, by and large, what we think about . . . ." These words, attributed to the great American philosopher and psychologist, William James, say it best.

   In fairness, we must point out that you cannot force the issue. Just because you say, "I am a great investor" or "I am a great mother" or "I am a great physician," that statement alone does not make it so. You have to deliver the goods, too.

2. **Define your dream.** You have to dream and to fantasize what your innermost desire is when you let yourself go. Then you have to analyze what achieving that dream entails. If you want to be a great investor, you have to work at it purposefully. You have to figure out the skills and tools you'll need, and then acquire them. To be a great mother or a great physician, you need to understand the elements of that dream and to take the steps required to attain it.

3. **Set goals to reach the elements of your dream.** Each step along the way is a goal. If you want to have $5 million in net assets by age 50, that is certainly attainable. But if you are 25 and you only have $43 to your name, you need to set a number of goals that take into account your current situation and that lead, with regular steps, to that $5 million goal.

4. **Improve your mind.** The first place to start is inside your head. Not only do you need to believe with all your being that you will reach your goal, but you also have to learn the required skills, to develop the right mindset, to create a positive frame of mind in the face of adversity, to focus on the outcome, not on being "right." No matter what your goal, you have to have one before you can reach it. You have to envision the idea before it can become reality. Your mind is both a resource for dreaming and a tool for achieving.

5. **Visualize your progress.** The mind is the final frontier, and each person's mind is unique. The process of visualizing or imagining the stepping stones to your dream is yours and yours alone. If your dream is to create financial security for your family, then you must define that dream in your own way. Whatever the dream, we believe that your mind will respond to direct sensations more than to mere numbers on a mutual fund account statement. Come up with a picture or a sound or a smell or a feeling for each goal you need to reach. It is easier to remember a person's name when you attach an image and a wordplay to it. A red-haired man named Robert becomes much more memorable when designated mentally as Robert the Red. When you attach an image to a name, your mind stores and retrieves it more easily. Use the language of your mind to create powerful milestones, benchmarks, and pictures of your progress.

6. **Focus your energy.** You cannot do everything. To achieve great success, you must focus your energy, your efforts, and your enthusiasm. To earn material success, you have to put energy and time and money into the process. That means your violin playing or your gardening or your golf game may suffer a bit. There are tradeoffs, and you must make them if you want to reach your dream.

7. **Reward your efforts.** Whether it is a pat on the back, a picture, or a party, you need to give yourself undeniable proof of your progress. Few of us enjoy going down to the vaults and

running coins through our fingers while we think miserly thoughts. Instead, create rewards that are meaningful to you. If a certain amount of money in your account—say, $100,000 (or $10,000, or $1 million, or whatever)—is meaningful, then throw a party for your family and friends when you achieve it. Call it the $100,000 Party. If that seems too boastful or materialistic, then promise yourself you will give a gift to a favorite charity when you reach that amount. When the day comes and you can write that check, you will then have tangible evidence of your success. Revel in it, because you made it happen. Enjoy the moment, enjoy your mastery of money, and enjoy your success.

Once you have taken these steps for investment success, you will be on a path that very few people ever find. Most people long for a certain goal, but they do not take these necessary steps toward realizing it. We guarantee that you will enjoy the process. There are no guaranteed outcomes in life, but you will improve your chances to obtain your dream. If you hold on to your dream and take purposeful steps to attain it, you are more likely to achieve much of what you want. Dream big, pursue the dream steadily, and enjoy whatever results you can make happen.

PART TWO

The
Toolbox

The Top 10 No-Load
Mutual Fund Families

We have based this ranking on information provided to us by The Investment Company Institute (ICI). The ICI does not break out load versus no-load fund families, so we did that research ourselves.

SEI Financial Services would have been fifth on this list, but the funds are not available to investors for direct purchase, so we left SEI out. PIMCO Advisors merged with Oppenheimer Funds, and that might have moved PIMCO up several notches. But because Oppenheimer is a load group, we did not change PIMCO's position as tenth on the list.

1. Fidelity Investments

As the largest mutual fund family, Fidelity has an extensive and varied selection of mutual funds, but the firm is best known for its equity funds, which have been the envy of the industry for years. For example, Magellan alone has more assets under management than most mutual fund families do. Fidelity has had many other top-performing equity funds as well. Fidelity is not a pure no-load fund family; it has both load and no-load mutual funds.

Fidelity Investments
82 Devonshire Street
Boston, MA 02109
800-544-8888

2. Vanguard

The Vanguard Group is unique among major mutual fund companies because it is owned not by its founders or a large bank, but by its mutual fund shareholders. (See our interview with Vanguard founder, Jack Bogle, following Chapter 2.) Vanguard mutual funds have the lowest expense ratios in the industry. And, Vanguard's leadership in the area of index mutual funds dates back to its creation of the first S&P 500

Index fund in 1976. It is generally considered the dominant mutual fund group in the areas of index funds, bond funds, and money market funds.

The Vanguard Group
Vanguard Financial Center
P. O. Box 2600
Valley Forge, PA 19482-2600
800-662-7447

3. Federated Investors

Federated is another quiet mutual fund family. The group has had particular success in bond funds and money market funds. Some of its equity funds have been top performers, but not very many. And because most of the excitement has been in stock funds over the past 5 years, Federated does not receive a lot of publicity. Nonetheless, this is a very solid fund family, particularly for income-oriented investors.

Federated Securities Corporation
1001 Liberty Avenue
Pittsburgh, PA 15222-3779
800-245-0242

4. Premier Mutual Funds (Dreyfus Funds)

The venerable Dreyfus Group is now owned by Mellon Bank and has been renamed Premier Mutual Funds. Dreyfus (Premier) occupies an important historical place in the industry because the firm created the first money market mutual fund, an innovation that has had enormous long-term implications both for the mutual fund industry and for smaller investors. Money market funds brought small investors up to par with returns that had been reserved, until then, for large investors. Premier, with new management in place, is working hard to re-establish with the firm as one of the industry's leaders.

Premier Mutual Funds
200 Park Avenue
New York, NY 10166
800-645-6561

5. T. Rowe Price Funds

T. Rowe Price, the founder of this group, was one of the first advocates of what we now know as "growth" investing. He was an original thinker in an era when most investors shunned stocks, particularly those of small, rapidly growing companies. For that alone, he deserves an important place in investment history. He founded the mutual fund family that bears his name. As a mutual fund family, T. Rowe Price has also done well. For the past 5 years, any list of top mutual funds would have representation from this group.

    T. Rowe Price Funds
    100 East Pratt Street
    Baltimore, MD 21202
    800-638-5660

6. American Century Funds (Formerly Twentieth Century Funds)

What's in a name? Under the stewardship of James Stowers, Jr., the Twentieth Century Fund group built an impressive record in growth-oriented stock funds. But time moves on and so has the group, now renamed American Century Funds. The firm recently acquired the Benham Group, which is known mainly for its bond funds and money market funds.

    American Century Funds
    4500 Main Street
    Kansas City, MO 64141
    800-345-2021

7. SchwabFunds

Charles Schwab & Co. has quietly put together a sizable fund family. The first funds in the group were money market funds, and they remain the dominant component. With the non-money-market funds, the emphasis is on a quantitative approach to selecting securities. For example, the flagship fund is the Schwab 1000, an index fund designed to match the Schwab 1000 Index, which tracks the 1000 largest, publicly traded U.S. companies.

Charles Schwab & Co.
SchwabFunds
101 Montgomery Street
San Francisco, CA 94104
800-435-4000

8. Scudder

Scudder started the first no-load mutual fund in 1928 and also was the first to start an international mutual fund, in 1953. This formerly low-keyed fund family has a number of excellent mutual funds, and it has been a strong influence on the growth of the no-load mutual fund industry. Scudder was recently acquired by a Swiss Company, Zurich Insurance.

Scudder Investor Services, Inc.
2 International Place
Boston, MA 02110
800-225-2470

9. Janus Funds

Denver-based Janus is known primarily for its stock mutual funds. The firm's flagship fund, Janus Fund, has been a solid growth fund for many years. Janus Funds rightly enjoys a reputation for good, long-term track records.

Janus Funds
100 Fillmore Street, Suite 300
Denver, CO 80206
800-525-8983

10. PIMCO Advisors

PIMCO Advisors has been growing very rapidly over the past few years. By virtue of its assets, the firm should be higher on the list, particularly since the recent acquisition of the Oppenheimer Fund Group boosted the assets significantly. PIMCO is a bit hard to place on a list of no-load fund families because most of its mutual funds are load funds. But it also has the very successful no-load PIMCO Total Return

Fund and PIMCO Low Duration Fund. We have used these funds for years, and they are very good. We just wish they would lower their minimum investment and make the rest of the family no-load.

PIMCO Advisors
2187 Atlantic Street
Stamford, CT 06902
800-426-0107

Mutual Funds, Income Taxes, and You

Even though you may think of your investment in a mutual fund as ownership of some amorphous investment vehicle with a catchy name, in essence you are a part owner of all the stocks, bonds, or other securities in the mutual fund portfolio. This portfolio is based on real companies that sell real products or services. If the fund owns stocks, for example, the older established stocks may pay out earnings in the form of dividends, but the younger, faster-growing stocks may decide not to pay dividends because they are plowing earnings back into the growth of the company. In either case, an investor hopes to be rewarded by some combination of dividend income and/or capital appreciation based on the growth of stocks in the portfolio. As an owner of a mutual fund, you are entitled to all the returns—and responsible for the tax liability—that the underlying stocks and bonds generate.

Mutual funds pay out their earnings to shareholders in two ways:

- **Income dividends.** All interest and dividend income earned from the underlying securities in the portfolio—after deducting the mutual fund's operating expenses—is paid out. Bond mutual funds normally pay dividends on a monthly or quarterly basis, and most stock funds pay their income dividends semiannually or annually.

- **Capital gain distributions.** Whenever the mutual fund manager sells a stock, a bond or another security in the portfolio, the sale generates a capital gain (if the fund made money on the transaction) or a capital loss (if the fund lost money). Normally, all capital gains and losses are netted out at the end of the calendar year. If there is a net gain, it is handled as a capital gain distribution.

Dividends and capital gain distributions are paid in cash, but you can reinvest them in more shares of the fund. From a tax standpoint, reinvested shares are treated as additional purchases. Whether you take the cash and run, or invest in additional shares, the IRS and other interested parties (state and local governments) want a cut of all interest, dividends, and distributions. The one exception is dividends from municipal bond funds and municipal money market funds. These are usually exempt from federal income taxes and, in some cases, state income taxes.

As with interest, dividends, and distributions, you generate taxes each time you sell shares in a fund. If you sell shares for more than you paid, then you are taxed on that profit, called *capital gain.* Conversely, if you realize a *capital loss* by selling shares for less than the amount you paid for them, you can use the loss to offset any gains you realized during the year.

Good Tax Records— The Buck Stops with You

There is nothing glamorous about keeping good records, but it's an absolute must if you want to maintain your sanity at tax time. We agree that it is tedious, but it's better to get started keeping good records now than to have to scrounge around in a panic trying to pull together shreds of paper the following April.

We recommend setting up a new, large file each year for each type of account you have (e.g., IRA, pension plan, personal portfolio, custodial account). Even though you won't file annual income tax reports for your tax-exempt accounts—IRAs, pension plans, and so on—it is a good idea to keep records for these accounts also. If you run into a problem later, such as resolving a trade error with the brokerage firm or mutual fund company that has your account, you'll want to have all the backup information. You can throw out all marketing materials from the mutual fund family or brokerage firm, but save all the following "official" statements.

Confirmation Statements

The mutual fund company or brokerage firm will send you a confirmation statement for each purchase or sale you make. The statement will record the date of the transaction, the fund name, the number of shares, the price per share, and applicable fees, if any.

Periodic Account Statements

The fund company or brokerage firm will send you a periodic statement, usually monthly or quarterly, summarizing all of the transactions for the period. You can discard the individual confirmation statements if you have verified that the periodic account statements show the same information. Some mutual fund companies and brokerage firms will send a year-end statement that shows all of the year's transactions, including dividends and capital gain distributions. After you confirm that the year-end statement is correct, save it for your records and throw away the monthly or quarterly statements.

Tax Reporting Forms

Each year, mutual fund companies and brokerage firms are required to report to the IRS certain information about your mutual fund holdings. In January, you will receive the following forms showing what was reported to the IRS:

- **Form 1099-B.** This form reports the proceeds from your sale transactions executed during the year. Use it to help determine your capital gain or loss.

- **Form 1099-DIV.** This form reports the total amount of income dividends or capital gain distributions paid to you. Remember, distributions reinvested in new shares are considered taxable, so they will be included on this form.

If you have better things to do with your time than making cost basis calculations during the wee hours of the morning, there are several tools you can use to simplify your life:

- **The skills of your accountant or tax adviser.** Your accountant or tax adviser might be willing to keep track of these details for you—for a price. Do you feel it is worth it to have someone else sweat the details for you?

- **Software programs.** There are many software programs designed to track tax information for you. They require minimal input from you but will perform all of the calculations. Among the programs that offer these features are Intuit's Quicken and Microsoft Money. Online programs offered by the fund company or brokerage firm where you have your account may offer tracking features.

- **Special account statements.** Some brokerage firms will send you an annual Mutual Fund Average Cost Basis Report, which shows your annualized realized gains and losses and the average cost basis of your mutual fund redemptions for all of your taxable accounts.

---

1. Don't buy a stock fund late in the year unless it's in an IRA or other tax-deferred account. One trap that investors fall into each year is the purchase of mutual fund shares just before the funds pay their year-end capital gains distribution. This can be a costly tax error. If you buy shares just before a distribution is paid, you have to pay taxes on the capital gain even though you haven't earned a nickel yet.

2. Pick solid funds and stick with them. One of the big advantages of owning stocks or stock mutual funds is that you can compound your growth on a tax-deferred basis. As long as you don't sell a security, you don't pay taxes on the appreciation. It pays to keep buys and sells to a minimum. Also, if you're seeking maximum growth, buy funds that seek growth rather than income. (Income will create lots of annual taxable income rather than the compounding tax-deferred buildup.)

Morningstar, Inc.—
The Best Resource for
Mutual Fund Information

Morningstar, Inc. is the premier provider of information about mutual funds for individual investors and for professional money managers. We have been using Morningstar's Principia Plus for Mutual Funds (and OnDisc, Principia's predecessor) product for many years in conducting our mutual fund research. Principia Plus is one of the tools we use to construct mutual fund portfolios for our clients.

Morningstar has a broad range of publications, software programs, and online services that support its open-end mutual funds.

Publications

Morningstar Investor—Monthly Newsletter

Best for: The investor who wants just the basic information about what Morningstar considers to be the top-rated funds.

This newsletter provides articles to help you choose funds for your mutual fund portfolio. You will not get "hot" buy or sell lists. Instead, half of its 50 or so pages are devoted to updated performance and statistical information about the open- and closed-end mutual funds that Morningstar considers noteworthy. If you already have a portfolio of funds, this is a good way to keep an eye on them without spending a lot of time or money.

Morningstar OnDemand

Best for: Those who want information on just one or a few funds right now.

For fast mutual fund information, call Morningstar at 800-735-0700, give the service representative your credit card number and the names of the funds you are interested in, and Morningstar will fax or mail you a one-page report for each fund.

Morningstar No-Load Funds—Monthly Updates

Best for: Those who are interested only in no-load mutual funds and want information presented in the Morningstar format.

A subscription to this publication gets you a hardcase binder with the most recent five issues and future monthly updates. *No-load Funds* covers only 690 no-load funds (including some mutual funds with loads of less than 3%). Each update covers about 50 funds in full-page format. Over 450 statistics are provided for each fund. You also get an instructional video, *Evaluating Mutual Funds with Morningstar.*

Morningstar Mutual Funds—Bimonthly Updates

Best for: The investor who wants all the nitty-gritty statistics on the 1,500 funds Morningstar covers, and who reviews mutual funds frequently.

This is the highest level of mutual fund information Morningstar provides in printed form. Out of the over 7,000 mutual funds available, Morningstar selects a group of 1,500 funds and provides full-page reports on each. The funds are broken out by fund category and you get a new section for your hardcase binder every two weeks. The video, *Evaluating Mutual Funds with Morningstar,* is included in the subscription.

Many of these Morningstar publications can be found at your local library.

Morningstar has developed several software programs to help investors evaluate and screen funds.

Software Tools

Morningstar Ascent

Best for: The do-it-yourself investor who wants software tools to screen mutual funds.

A comprehensive Windows-based software program that allows you to select funds by using various screening criteria. You can put in multiple fund variables (such as performance, risk level, manager tenure), and the software will produce a list of fund candidates that meet your criteria. You can also measure a fund's performance or statistics against other funds within its category. Ascent covers more than 7,300 mutual funds, and you can view them in virtually any way you want. Historical data going back 15 years are included. The software helps you produce graphs so you can see how a fund stacks up. You get your monthly or quarterly updates by floppy disk or CD-ROM.

Principia for Mutual Funds

Best for: The professional investor.

An enriched version of Ascent, Principia is designed for professional investors who need a sophisticated tool for developing portfolios of mutual funds. Principia also includes tools for professional investors to use in presenting material to clients and prospective clients. Updates by floppy disk or CD-ROM.

Principia Plus for Mutual Funds

Best for: The professional investor who needs extensive tools for conducting in-depth mutual fund research.

A more powerful version of Principia, this software combines the basic database and tools of Principia with even more capabilities for in-depth fund research. Principia Plus includes the same 1,500 full-page reports found in Morningstar Mutual Funds. The Portfolio Developer feature allows you to play "what-if" games with hypothetical fund portfiolios. Advanced Analytics adds historical information for performance, portfolio holdings, and analyst reviews. Updates are provided by floppy disk or CD-ROM.

Morningstar, Inc.
225 West Wacker Drive, Suite 400
Chicago, Illinois 60606
800-735-0700
312-696-6000 (from outside United States)
312-696-6001 (fax)

Hours: (Central Time)
Monday–Thursday   7:30 A.M.–7:00 P.M.
Friday   7:30 A.M.–6:00 P.M.
Saturday   9:00 A.M.–4:00 P.M.

Morningstar on the Web: www.morningstar.net

OnLine Tools

Best for: Investors who have access to the Internet and want online access to Morningstar mutual fund information.

For investors who have access to the Internet, Morningstar offers an elegant Web site with commentary on the markets and on mutual fund trends, as well as solid, detailed information about mutual funds. You enter the funds in your existing investment portfolio and track price movements on an ongoing basis, but you can also track a portfolio of funds on your watchlist—an innovation not offered by other price-tracking services. You get information not only on mutual funds but on most stocks as well. Like other Morningstar products, the site is well designed, and finding your way around is pretty simple. At this time, Morningstar is not charging for access to information through their Web site.

Morningstar on America OnLine

Best for: Current America OnLine subscribers. A good, easy way to access Morningstar's extensive database of mutual fund information. Available 24 hours.

For subscribers to America OnLine (AOL), Morningstar's information about 7,300 mutual funds is available through this service (keyword: Morningstar). You can screen funds by investment objective or by Morningstar rating. You can also search by fund name. Morningstar has ranked the top 25 mutual funds in each of its fund groups. From any of these searches, you can get detailed information about each fund. The normal performance and fund statistics are available to you, as are the past month's top ten portfolio holdings. However, because there are no screening tools, you'll have to review the funds using Morningstar's preestablished groups.

Commentary articles from past issues of *Mutual Fund Investor* can be reviewed. Some date as far back as 5 years. Morningstar also hosts Chat Rooms, where members can conduct online conversations about various investment topics.

There are also Message Boards (AOL's term for bulletin board), where you can post messages or queries for other AOL members. The Message Boards are categorized by topics such as Newsletters, Mutual Funds, and so on, as well as by specific mutual funds. You can browse all of the past messages posted in a board or call up all messages posted after a specific date.

Morningstar also maintains, through AOL, a company store where you can get information about all of its products. If you decide to subscribe to or purchase one of their products, you can make arrangements here. Charges are posted to your America OnLine account.

Normal AOL connect time charges apply during your visit to this area, but access to all of the Morningstar services and information is otherwise included in your monthly membership fee.

America OnLine: Call AOL at 800-827-6364 for pricing, program disks, and information.

Internet Investors Network: http://www.networth .galt.com

Best for: Investors who have access to the Internet. Morningstar information is available at no charge.

If you have access to the Internet, you can access Morningstar's mutual fund information through the Internet Investors Network. This site includes general information about personal finance, including a link to Intuit for information you maintain using Intuit's Quicken software. The Morningstar information covers over 5,000 mutual funds. To access the Morningstar information, you need to sign up (online) with them, but there's no charge for unlimited access to the information.

Mutual Fund
Information Resources

With so much being written about mutual funds these days, there are many more resources to assist the individual investor with the selection and maintenance of any mutual fund portfolio. Many investors get information from their local newspapers. Coverage of investment topics and mutual funds has expanded tremendously in these publications. For this book, however, we are only covering national publications. Here are some of our favorite resources that are national in scope. We suggest you go to your public library and take a look at these publications once. Pick out one (at most two) that you like and stick to it. Reading too many investment publications is counterproductive.

NATIONAL NEWSPAPERS:

- *The New York Times* Daily, 800-631-2580 (www.nytimes.com)
- *The Wall Street Journal* Daily, 800-568-7625 (www.wsj.com)
- *USA Today* Daily, 800-827-0001 (www.usatoday.com)
- *Investor's Business Daily* Daily, 800-831-2525 (www.investors.com)

MAGAZINES:

- *Barron's,* Weekly, 800-544-0422 (www.barrons.com)
- *Bloomberg Personal,* Bimonthly, 888-432-5820 (www.bloomberg.com)
- *BusinessWeek,* Weekly, 800-635-1200 (www.businessweek.com)
- *Consumer Reports,* Monthly, 800-234-1645
- *Forbes,* Biweekly, 800-888-9896 (www.forbes.com)
- *Fortune,* Biweekly, 800-621-8000 (www.pathfinder.com/fortune/)
- *Individual Investor,* Monthly, 800-383-5901 (www.iionline.com)

- *Kiplinger's Personal Finance,* Monthly, 800-544-0155 (www.kiplinger.com)

- *Money,* Monthly, 800-633-9970 (www.pathfinder.com/money)

- *Mutual Funds Magazine,* Monthly, 800-442-9000 (www.mfmag.com)

- *Newsweek,* Weekly, 800-631-1040

- *Smart Money,* Monthly, 800-444-4204 (www.dowjones.com/smart/)

- *U.S. News & World Report,* 800-234-2450 (www.usnews.com)

- *Worth,* Monthly, 800-777-1851 (www.worth.com)

ONLINE SERVICES:

- America OnLine, 800-827-6364

- CompuServe, 800-848-8990

- Web Sites: There are many mutual fund Internet Web sites, and more are popping up everyday. Use an Internet search engine to locate the term *mutual fund* or the name of the fund you are interested in. Many mutual fund Web sites offer links to other sites. Some good search engines are:

Alta Vista	www.altavista.digital.com
cNet	www.search.com
Excite	www.excite.com
Infoseek	www.infoseek.com
Lycos	www.lycos.com
Web Crawler	www.webcrawler.com
Yahoo	www.yahoo.com

SUBSCRIPTION SERVICES:

- The No-Load Fund Analyst, 800-776-9555

- The Handbook for No-Load Fund Investors, 800-252-2042

- Hulbert Financial Digest, Monthly, 888-HULBERT (888-485-2378)

- Morningstar Mutual Funds, Monthly or quarterly, 800-735-0700

- Value Line Mutual Funds, Monthly, 800-634-3583

- Vanguard Advisor, Monthly, 800-435-3372

There are many other mutual fund newsletters that we have not listed. Those listed are the ones we are familiar with. There are many good mutual fund newsletters, but we can only recommend those we know. If you are interested in a particular newsletter, you might want to review it in the Hulbert Financial Digest. Or, you can write or call and ask for a trial subscription, to see whether it lives up to your expectations.

BOOKS:

- *Beating the Street*, Peter Lynch, 1994, Fireside

- *Bogle on Mutual Funds*, Jack Bogle, 1993, Irwin

- *Hulbert Guide to Financial Newsletters*, James Hulbert

- *The Intelligent Investor*, Benjamin Graham, 1986, Harper-Collins

- *Learn to Earn*, Peter Lynch, 1996, Simon & Shuster

- *Making the Most of Your Money*, Jane Bryant Quinn, 1991, Simon & Shuster

- *One Up on Wall Street*, Peter Lynch, 1990, Penguin

- *The Handbook for No-Load Investors*, Sheldon Jacobs, 1996, Irwin

- *The Only Personal Finance Book You Will Ever Need*, Andrew Tobias, 1996, Harcourt Brace

---

The American Association of Individual Investors
625 N. Michigan Avenue
Suite 1900
Chicago, IL 60611
312-280-0170
800-428-2244

Resources For Mutual Fund Information

The American Association of Individual Investors (AAII) is an independent, not-for-profit organization that assists individuals in becoming effective managers of their own investments. AAII seeks to achieve this through publications, nationwide seminars, home study texts, educational videos, and local chapters that focus on investing and investment techniques. Current membership is 175,000.

The *AAII Journal* is published for members 10 times a year. Members also receive an annual mutual fund guide and other publications. AAII sponsors 60 local chapters around the country. These groups meet regularly to hear speakers on various investment topics. AAII also has a forum on America Online (to access it, type in the keyword: AAII). The World Wide Web address is http://www.aaii.org

---

The Investment Company Institute
1401 H Street, N.W.
Suite 1200
Washington, DC 20005-2148
Telephone: 202-326-5800

The Investment Company Institute (ICI) is a trade association that represents its member mutual funds and their shareholders in a variety of legislative, tax, and regulatory matters. It also acts as a clearinghouse for industry information in many areas affecting mutual funds, mutual fund shareholders, and the investing public. The following are two examples of publications available from ICI.

Directory of Mutual Funds

In addition to fund names, addresses, and telephone numbers (many toll-free), the directory lists each fund's assets, initial and subsequent investment requirements, fees charged, where to buy shares, and other pertinent details. Content serves as a short course in mutual fund investing.

An Investor's Guide to Reading the Mutual Fund Prospectus

This brochure offers a guided tour of 18 important items in prospectuses. In sample language from actual prospectuses, it describes how each item affects the investors, what to look for, and why.

For more information, call Michelle Worthy, at 202-326-5872, or write to her at the address above, and ask for a complete list of the publications available from ICI.

New Ways to Invest in Mutual Funds

As a mutual fund investor, you have many new services to help you invest more efficiently. Discount stock brokerage firms such as Charles Schwab & Co., Fidelity Investments (a separate company from Fidelity's mutual fund group), and Jack F. White & Co. have led the way in developing new services for mutual fund investors. Full-service brokerage firms are also beginning to innovate in this area. Following is a description of the services available at Schwab. Similar services may be available at Fidelity Investments and Jack F. White, but we have little or no experience with either of these firms. Because most of our clients hold their accounts at Schwab, we have years of experience and lots of confidence in the Schwab offerings. We recommend you look at discount brokerage firms as a first step in planning your investment portfolio.

The Mutual Fund Marketplace allows Schwab customers to easily buy and sell mutual funds from many fund families. Customers receive account statements showing their mutual fund positions, notices of dividends and capital gain distributions, prospectuses, shareholder proxies, and other shareholder materials directly from Schwab.

Charles Schwab & Co.'s Mutual Fund Marketplace

OneSource

Building on the success of the Mutual Fund Marketplace, Schwab has added a service known as OneSource, which allows its customers to buy and sell mutual funds without paying commissions. It does this by charging the mutual funds that want to be represented on OneSource.

Besides the Mutual Fund Marketplace and OneSource, Schwab offers:

♦ **Toll-Free Mutual Fund Trading.** The contact number, 1-800-2NO-LOAD (1-800-266-5623). Available 24 hours a day, 7 days a week.

- **Mutual Funds Performance Guide®.** This guide includes comparative data on all of the mutual funds available through Schwab. Grouped by fund investment objective, the data include 1-, 5-, and 10-year returns, expense ratios, risk ratings, and total assets.

- **Mutual Fund Select List™.** Published in association with Morningstar, Inc., this quarterly guide summarizes high-performing (based on 5-year performance) no-load funds available through Schwab.

- **Morningstar Mutual Fund Reports.** You can request a Morningstar Mutual Fund Report for any individual fund offered by Schwab. Each report provides all of the information found on a typical Morningstar page. Call Schwab at 1-800-752-9295 for this service.

- **Charles Schwab Mutual Fund Selection Planner™.** This questionnaire guides you through the process of asset allocation and fund selection.

- **Automatic Investment Plan.** Using this service, you can make automatic monthly, semimonthly, or quarterly investments in any of the no-load funds offered through OneSource.

- **Buy Funds on Margin.** For nonretirement accounts, Schwab offers investors the opportunity to buy most mutual funds on margin. Investors can also borrow against the mutual fund positions in their accounts.

Charles Schwab & Co.
101 Montgomery Street
San Francisco, CA 94104
800-435-4000

Fidelity Investments
82 Devonshire Street
Boston, MA 02109
800-544-8888

Jack F. White & Co.
9191 Town Center Drive, Suite 220
San Diego, CA 92122
800-216-2333

We have said everything we came to say. Now, it's time for us to stop talking and for you to start investing. Please write and give us any comments you have about our book. We would particularly like to hear how you are using this material as you move down the road to Mutual Fund Mastery.

> Kurt Brouwer and Steve Janachowski
> Brouwer & Janachowski, Inc.
> 1831 Tiburon Blvd.
> Tiburon, CA 94920

As the Spanish say, we wish you *Salud, Amor y Pesetas* (Health, Love, and Wealth).

GLOSSARY

12b-1 fee   An annual fee charged to shareholders by a mutual fund, to pay for marketing, advertising, and certain other expenses.

401(k) plan   A qualified retirement plan that allows employees of a company to contribute pretax earnings to a tax-deferred retirement plan. Generally, 401(k) plans offer participants investment choices for their contributions. Earnings on the contributions are tax-deferred until withdrawal, which is subject to some restrictions. The Department of Labor establishes maximum contribution limits each year.

Annuity   A contract, sold by insurance companies, that provides a fixed or variable periodic payment to the annuitant. Earnings are generally tax-deferred until withdrawals are made.

asset allocation   A descriptive term for the percentages of an investor's holdings in different asset classes—stocks, bonds, money market funds, real estate, and so on.

Bear market   A market in a prolonged downward price trend.

beta   A mathematical measure that compares the relative volatility of a stock or stock mutual fund with the stock market as a whole. Assuming the S&P 500 is used as the benchmark for the stock market, it is assigned a beta of 1. By comparison, a stock fund that is more volatile than the S&P 500 would have a beta greater than 1. A less volatile fund would have a beta less than 1.

bond   An IOU issued by a governmental entity or a corporation, often to gain long-term funding. The issuer/borrower agrees to repay the principal and to pay interest at a given rate over a period of time. At maturity, the issuer repays the principal amount, plus any unpaid interest, to the bondholder. Because most bonds carry fixed rates of interest, bond prices tend to fluctuate considerably, due to changes in the level of interest rates in the economy. Bonds issued by corporations trade on the major exchanges; government bonds do not.

bull market   A market in a prolonged upward price trend.

Capital gain   The amount realized from a sale of an asset where the proceeds exceed the purchase price or cost. The current federal income tax rate for long-term capital gains (those held more than six months) is 28%. There is strong support for a reduction in this rate, to stimulate investment.

capital gains distribution   Payment to mutual fund shareholders based on profits from sales of stocks and/or bonds in the portfolio.

capital loss   The amount realized from a sale of an asset where the purchase price or cost exceeds the proceeds.

certificate of deposit (CD)   A time deposit made into a bank or savings and loan. At maturity, the depositor receives interest plus the original amount of the deposit. Maturities may range from one week to several years. Certificates of deposit are generally insured by an agency of the United States up to a maximum of $100,000.

closed-end mutual fund   A mutual fund that issues a fixed number of shares and does not redeem those that are outstanding. Shares of a closed-end mutual fund trade on a stock exchange or over the counter (OTC), and their value is based on demand, not on the value of the underlying assets.

commercial paper   A short-term unsecured promissory note, generally issued by a corporation, with a minimum face amount of $25,000. The notes are usually sold at a discount from face value, with maturities ranging from 2 to 270 days.

Consumer Price Index (CPI)   A measure of the relative cost of living at a given time, compared to a base year (currently, 1982). The CPI is maintained by the Department of Labor's Bureau of Labor Statistics, which collects price information from thousands of businesses throughout the country. The prices are then averaged and compared to the base year. The CPI, commonly known as the rate of *inflation,* has come under fire recently because many believe it significantly overstates actual inflation. The Department of Labor is reviewing possible changes to make it more accurate.

correction   A sharp, relatively short price decline that temporarily interrupts a persistent upward trend in the market or the price of a stock.

CPI   See *Consumer Price Index.*

crash   An extended steep drop in prices in the securities markets.

custodian   An organization, typically a commercial bank or trust company, that is responsible for custody and safekeeping of a mutual fund's assets, such as cash, stock, and so on.

Default risk   The possibility that a borrower will be unable to meet interest and/or principal repayment obligations on a loan agreement when due. Default risk has a significant effect on the value of securities issued by a corporation or a government. If a borrower's ability to repay debt is impaired, the default risk is higher and the value of the entity's securities will decline.

deficit   The amount by which expenditures exceed income.

deflation   A persistent decline in the price of goods and services; the opposite of inflation. Deflation is rare, but it can occur during a recession or depression.

depression   An economic downturn marked by falling prices, high and rising unemployment, an excess of supply over demand, deflation, reduced purchasing power, contraction of general business activity, and public anxiety over the future.

derivative   A security that derives its value from another security. For example, a Treasury bond option is a derivative instrument whose value fluctuates in line with changes in the pricing of the underlying Treasury bond market.

discount brokerage firm   A brokerage firm that executes buy and sell orders at lower commission rates than those charged by a full-service broker.

dividend (mutual fund)   A distribution of a mutual fund's net income to shareholders. The dividend is generally paid in a fixed amount for each share. Mutual fund dividends are declared and approved by the fund's trustees and may be either taken in cash or reinvested in additional shares of the fund. (See *capital gains distribution*.)

DJIA   See *Dow Jones Industrial Average*.

Dow Jones Industrial Average (DJIA)   An index that represents the price-weighted average share price of thirty large, seasoned U.S. companies. Although the index is comprised mainly of industrial companies, other market segments, such as financial services, are also included.

duration   The number of years required to receive the current value of future payments, both principal and interest, from a bond. Duration is significant because it is used to relate the sensitivity of bond price changes to changes in interest rates. For example, the principal value of a bond fund with a duration of 5 years would normally go down by 5% if interest rates suddenly rose 1%.

EAFE   See *MSCI Europe, Australasia and Far East Index*.

emerging growth   A phrase that generally refers to small, rapidly growing companies that have very good growth prospects. This kind of stock offers the potential of large returns coupled with high risk.

emerging market   Countries whose economies and financial markets are less developed than industrialized countries such as the United States, Great Britain, or Germany. Some emerging market countries are Brazil, India, Korea, Malaysia, Mexico, Peru, Portugal, and Turkey.

equity   Another name for stock, both common and preferred.

exchange   A facility for the organized trading of securities.

ex-dividend   The time between the declaration and the payment of a dividend. When a

mutual fund declares a dividend, the fund's net asset value is decreased by the amount of the dividend. A mutual fund investor who buys shares during this time is not entitled to receive the dividend.

expense ratio   The annual operating expenses and management fees of a mutual fund, expressed as a percentage. The expense ratio is independent of any sales fee.

Federal Reserve   The Federal Reserve Board (FRB, or the Fed) sets U.S. monetary policy. Among other activities, the Fed regulates the national money supply, controls the printing of currency, regulates the banking system, sets bank reserve requirements, and acts as a clearing agency for transferring funds throughout the banking system.

fixed-income security   Another term for bonds or other securities that pay a fixed rate of return.

futures   A contract to buy or sell a financial instrument or commodity at a specific price at a future specified date.

Government obligations   A term covering U.S. government debt instruments, including Treasury bills, bonds, and notes. Obligations of the U.S. government are considered to have little or no risk of default because they are backed by the full faith and credit of the federal government.

Great Depression   A period of time that began with the stock market crash in 1929 and extended through the decade of the 1930s. The economic situation was characterized by falling prices of goods and services, high and rising unemployment, an excess of supply over demand, reduced purchasing power, contraction of general business activity, and public anxiety over the future. There was widespread unrest and dislocation around the country and in much of the entire world. Economic activity did not pick up until the onset of World War II.

gross domestic product (GDP)   A measure of the value of all goods and services produced by workers and capital within U.S. borders over a particular period o time. Real GDP is the inflation-adjusted version of GDP.

Hedging   A strategy used to neutralize investment risk.

Index mutual fund   A mutual fund that invests in a portfolio of securities designed to match the performance of a given index, such as the Standard & Poor's 500 or the Lehman Brothers Aggregate Bond Index.

Individual Retirement Account (IRA)   A retirement account, established by an employed person, that allows the funds within the account to grow on a tax-deferred basis. Contributions sheltered from income tax are limited to $2,000 per year ($4,000 for a working couple). Most brokerage firms, mutual funds, banks, and insurance companies have IRA accounts. Discount brokerage firms offer the greatest investment flexibility because they allow IRA investors a choice among mutual funds, stocks, bonds, Treasury bills, certificates of deposit, and other investment opportunities.

inflation   A continuing upward trend in prices, caused by demand outstripping the supply of goods and services. Moderate inflation is normally associated with periods of expansion and high employment.

interest   Payment for the use of borrowed money. The interest rate is usually expressed as a percentage of the amount borrowed.

intermediate-term bond   A bond with a maturity of 5 to 10 years.

international mutual fund   A mutual fund that invests in non-U.S. stocks.

investment adviser   A person who offers professional investment advice. Investment advisers are required to register with the Securities and Exchange Commission.

investment advisory firm   An individual or organization that provides investment advice for a fee. In most cases, investment advisers with more than $25 million in assets under management must register with the Securities and Exchange Commission and must abide by the Investment Advisers Act of 1940.

investment grade bond   A bond that is rated Baa or higher by Moody's Investors Service, or BBB or higher by Standard & Poor's.

IRA   See *Individual Retirement Account.*

Junk bond   A high-risk, high-yield debt security that, if rated by bond rating agencies such as Standard & Poor's or Moody's, is generally less than BBB.

Keogh plan   A retirement program that permits unincorporated self-employed individuals to set aside savings for retirement. Contributions and income earned by the assets in the account are tax-deferred until withdrawals are made during retirement.

Large cap   A descriptive term for stocks of large companies—in general, companies that have market capitalizations of $5 billion or more.

large company   See *large cap.*

Lehman Brothers Aggregate Bond Index   Covers the U.S. investment grade fixed rate bond market, including government and corporate securities, mortgage pass-through securities and asset-backed securities. The average duration is approximately 5 years and the average maturity is approximately 9 years.

leverage   A use of borrowing that attempts to increase the rate of return from an investment. Although leverage can operate to increase rates of return, it also increases the amount of risk inherent in an investment.

load   Sales charge paid by investors when purchasing shares of a load mutual fund or units of an annuity—sometimes called "front-end load." This contrasts with a back-end load, which charges a fee when investors redeem their investment. A mutual fund that does not charge a fee is called a no-load fund.

long-term bond   A bond with a maturity of more than 10 years.

Market capitalization   The total value of all of a company's outstanding shares. The value is calculated by multiplying the market price per share times the total number of shares outstanding.

maturity   The date on which payment of a financial obligation is due.

mid cap   Generally, companies that have market capitalizations of $1 billion to $5 billion.

money market fund   A mutual fund that invests in short-term, high-quality securities such as Treasury bills, negotiable certificates of deposit, and commercial paper. Shares of a money market mutual fund are usually priced at $1.00 per share. This type of mutual fund generally pays a return that reflects short-term interest rates. It is very liquid and safe, but yields and risk levels may vary slightly.

MSCI Europe, Australasia and Far East Index (EAFE)   An index developed and maintained by Morgan Stanley Capital International. Over 900 selected international stocks, trading on 18 exchanges in Europe, Australia, and the Far East, are listed.

mutual fund   An open-end investment company that offers the investor the benefits of portfolio diversification (providing greater safety and reduced volatility), and professional management. The shares are redeemable on demand at their net asset value. The fund invests the pooled assets into various investment vehicles, including stocks, bonds, options, commodities, and money market securities. How the fund invests is determined by the fund's objectives. The mutual fund's prospectus details this type of information, along with a statement of fees, a description of the management company, and other relevant data. A mutual fund that continually offers new shares and redeems existing shares is an open-end mutual fund.

NAV   See *net asset value.*

net asset value (NAV)   An open-end mutual fund's per-share market value. Most funds compute the NAV after the close of the exchanges each day. It is calculated by taking the sum of the closing market value of all securities within the fund plus all other assets (i.e., cash), subtracting all liabilities, and then dividing the result (total net assets) by the total number of outstanding shares. The total number of outstanding shares usually varies daily because of redemptions and purchases.

New York Stock Exchange (NYSE)   The largest and oldest organized securities exchange in the United States. Founded in 1792, it trades about 85% of the nation's listed securities. The Exchange lists over 1,600 securities.

no-load mutual fund   A mutual fund that allows shares to be purchased or sold without a sales charge.

Option   A contract that permits the owner, depending on the type of option, to purchase or sell an asset at a fixed price until a specific date. An option to purchase an asset is a *call*, and an option to sell an asset is a *put*.

Recession   An extended decline in general business activity; usually defined as three consecutive quarters in which gross domestic product falls.

record date   The date on which a shareholder must own shares of a mutual fund in order to receive a fund's dividend or to vote on a fund's proxy issues.

Russell 2000 Stock Index   An index of approximately 2,000 small companies in the United States.

Sales charge   A fee paid to a broker in connection with the purchase of a load mutual fund. The sales charge, or load, generally decreases as the size of the investment increases.

short-term bond   A bond with a maturity of 3 years or less.

small cap   The stock of relatively small companies—those with market capitalizations of less than $1 billion.

small company   See *small cap*.

S&P 500   See *Standard & Poor's 500 Stock Index*.

Standard & Poor's   A provider of a wide variety of investment-related services, including rating bonds, stocks, and commercial paper; publishing statistical information and reports; and compiling indexes.

Standard & Poor's 500 Stock Index   A composite index that tracks 500 industrial, transportation, public utility, and financial stocks. The selection of stocks to be included in the index is determined by Standard & Poor's Corporation, which also publishes the index. The index includes 400 industrials, 40 utilities, 20 transportation, and 40 financial companies, a group that represents about 75% of the New York Stock Exchange market capitalization or 30% of the NYSE issues.

stock brokerage firm   A company that executes trades of stock and other securities.

Total return   Dividend or interest income plus any capital gain. Total return is considered a better measure of an investment's return than dividends or interest alone. Total return is generally expressed as a percentage.

transfer agent   A company, usually a bank or trust company, appointed by a mutual fund company to transfer the fund's securities into the name of new shareholders.

Treasuries   Bonds backed by the United States Department of Treasury. The safety of Treasuries is the benchmark against which all other debt securities are measured.

Treasury bill   A short-term debt security of the United States Government. A T-bill is sold in a minimum amount of $10,000 and in multiples of $5,000. T-bills with 13-week and 26-week maturities are auctioned each Monday, and 52-week T-bills are sold every four weeks.

Treasury note   An intermediate-term (1 to 10 years) interest-bearing debt of the U.S. Treasury.

Yield   The annual interest return from an investment. Yield is not particularly useful as a way to evaluate the potential of any investment other than an insured bank account and a money market fund. For bond funds and stock funds, it is better to analyze the total return of the investment. See *total return*.

INDEX

F

fad funds, 39
fads, impact of, 152–53
Fear:
   of loss, 154–55, 157, 175,
      186
   risk-taking and, 9, 94
Federal Communications
   Commission (FCC), 29
Federal Deposit Insurance
   Corporation (FDIC), 29
Federal Reserve, 5, 24, 116, 217
Federated Investors, 194
Federated Securities Corporation,
   194
fees:
   load mutual funds, 30, 32
   redemption, 56
   Vanguard Group, 58
Fidelity, 18
Fidelity Asset Manager Fund, 55
Fidelity Growth Company Fund,
   66
Fidelity Institutional Short-
   Intermediate Government
   Portfolio, 102
Fidelity Investments, 193
Fidelity Magellan Fund, 65–66
Fidelity Management & Research,
   32
Fidelity Trend Fund, analysis of,
   81–83
financial management, saving habits,
   21–22, 162
financial markets, power of, 6–7
financial planners, compensation of,
   30–31
financial planning, 4–5, 149
First Boston High Yield Index,
   103
First Eagle Fund of America, 98
fixed-income:
   investments, 93, 106
   security, 217

Fleming, Robert, 28
Fleming's Scottish American Trust,
   28
Forbes, 51, 207
foreign stock funds, 101
Form 1099-B, 200
Form 1099-DIV, 200
Fortune, 4, 51, 177, 207
Founders Growth Fund, 98, 137
Founders Worldwide Growth Fund,
   101
401(k) plans, 11, 18, 39, 41, 52–53,
   105, 146, 178, 215
403(b) plans, 53
Franklin Templeton Group, 73
Fremont Bond Fund, 88–90, 94
Friedman, Rob, 74
Friess, Foster, 62
fund of funds, 47
Fund performance, 61–62,
   178–79
Fuss, Dan, 93, 172
Futures, 217

G

Gabelli, Mario, 4, 69–70, 73,
   173
Gabelli Asset Fund, 69–70
Garea, Ray, 74
Gingrich, Newt, 5
Ginnie Mae, *see* GNMA (Ginnie
   Mae bonds)
Gipson, Jim, 171, 173
Glass-Steagal Act of 1933, 29
global bond funds, domestic bond
   funds *vs.,* 45
global investments, 133–34
global stock funds, 42–43
GNMA (Ginnie Mae bonds), 90
goal-setting, importance of, 3, 125,
   127, 181–82, 188
gold funds, 45–47
Goleman, Daniel, 155

value mutual funds, 16, 73, 98,
    133
value stocks, 73
Vanguard Group:
    advisor, 209
    Balanced Index Fund, 55
    Bond Index Fund Total Bond
        Market Portfolio, 140
    expense ratio, 90
    generally, 18, 32–33, 193–94
    Horizon Fund, 56–57
    Index Trust Extended Market
        Portfolio, 140
    Index Trust 500 Portfolio, 54, 140,
        147
    Index Trust Small Capitalization
        Stock Portfolio, 140
    International Equity Index Fund
        Emerging Markets Portfolio,
        137, 140
    International Equity Index Fund
        European Portfolio, 140
    International Equity Index Fund
        Pacific Portfolio, 140
    interview with John C. "Jack"
        Bogle, 52–58
    Municipal Bond Fund High-Yield
        Portfolio, 103
    Municipal Bond Fund
        Intermediate-Term Portfolio,
        103, 139–40
    Municipal Bond Fund Limited-
        Term Portfolio, 139
    Municipal Bond Fund Long-Term
        Portfolio, 103
    Primecap Fund, 98
    Tax-Managed Fund-Balanced
        Portfolio, 54
    U.S. Growth, 180
    Wellington Fund, 38, 53–54, 56,
        100
    Windsor Fund, 53–54, 56
Vinik, Jeff, 65–66, 176
volatility, growth funds and, 39, 42,
    59–60, 64, 168

W

Wall Street Journal, The, 51, 109,
    207
Wal-Mart, 171
Wanger, Ralph, 173–74
Warburg Pincus:
    Emerging Markets Fund, 160
    Emerging Markets Fund-Common
        Shares, 101
    Fixed-Income-Common Shares,
        102, 138–39
    funds, 121
    International Equity Fund,
        123–24, 160
wealth-generating stocks, 106
Web Crawler, 208
Weiss, Dick, 173
Western Asset Trust Core Portfolio,
    102
Westwood Balanced Fund-Retail
    Class, 100
World Stock Funds, 101
World Wide Web, as information
    resource, 14, 205
Worth, 51, 208
Worthy, Michelle, 210

X

Xerox, 24

Y

Yacktman, Don, 173
Yahoo, 208
yield:
    bond funds, 36–37, 89, 139
    defined, 220
    money market fund, 35–36

Z

zero coupon bond funds, 36

ABOUT THE
AUTHORS

Kurt Brouwer and Steve Janachowski have specialized in no-load mutual fund investing since 1985. They are the founders of Brouwer & Janachowski, Inc., a Tiburon, California, firm that manages over $500 million for corporations, charitable groups, and private investors. Because they believe that patience and prosperity go hand-in-hand, their investment strategy is to invest in great mutual funds that take a long-term approach to building wealth.

Kurt Brouwer is the author of *Kurt Brouwer's Guide to Mutual Funds* (Wiley) and he has written articles for *Forbes, Barron's, The San Francisco Chronicle, California Business, The San Francisco Examiner,* and *Pension World.* He attended Calvin College and is a graduate of The University of San Francisco. He lives in Belvedere, California, and spends his free time in his kayak, looking for harbor seals and exchanging witticisms with sea lions.

Steve Janachowski is a coauthor of articles for *Barron's* and *The San Francisco Chronicle.* He graduated from The University of Chicago. He lives in Mill Valley, California, with his wife and daughter, and spends his free time cycling in the hills of Marin County and conducting research on the perfect espresso.